THE ELEVEN DAYS OF CHRISTMAS

THE ELEVEN DAYS OF CHRISTMAS

America's Last Vietnam Battle

MARSHALL L. MICHEL III

ENCOUNTER BOOKS
SAN FRANCISCO, CALIFORNIA

First edition published in 2002 by Encounter Books, an activity of Encounter for Culture and Education, Inc., a nonprofit tax exempt corporation.

Encounter Books website address: www.encounterbooks.com

Manufactured in the United States and printed on acid-free paper.

The paper used in this publication meets the minimum requirements of ANSI/NISO Z39.48-1992 (R 1997)*(Permanence of Paper)*.

FIRST EDITION

Library of Congress Cataloging-in-Publication Data

Michel, Marshall L., III, 1942–
    The eleven days of Christmas : America's last Vietnam battle / Marshall Michel.
        p.   cm.
    Includes bibliographical references and index.
    ISBN 1-893554-24-4 (cloth)   ISBN 1-893554-27-9 (pbk.)
        1. Vietnamese Conflict, 1961–1975—Aerial operations, American. 2. Hanoi (Vietnam)—History—Bombardment, 1972.   3. Haiphong (Vietnam)—History—Bombardment, 1972.   4. United States. Air Force—History—Vietnamese Conflict, 1961–1975.   I. Title: 11 days of Christmas.   II Title.
    DS558.8.M532   2001
    959.704'348—dc21

                                                                2001042114

10   9   8   7   6   5   4   3   2   1

Table of Contents

Foreword

On August 3, 1964, I was a young college student invited to the White House for a state dinner in honor of U Thant, the secretary general of the United Nations. It was going to be an extravaganza, with the folk-singing trio of Peter, Paul and Mary as the entertainment. When I arrived, one of the White House guards told me that the dinner might be cancelled because "the North Vietnamese just attacked one of our ships."

But the dinner went on. Peter, Paul and Mary made an emotional appeal for peace and than sang "Blowing in the Wind." I have a vivid memory of President Lyndon Johnson—famous for staying at White House parties to dance into the early morning hours—leaving almost immediately after the performance. What he did then is now well known. The next day, U.S. Navy carrier aircraft attacked North Vietnamese PT boat bases, and the first American aviator was shot down over North Vietnam and taken prisoner.

Over three thousand days later, on December 18, 1972, I was an F-4 pilot with some 280 combat missions behind me, standing at the scheduling desk of the Fourth Tactical Fighter Squadron at Udorn RTAFB in Thailand. The squadron had "stood down" all day and had been told to come in at three o'clock that afternoon, but it was nearly four when Jon Baker arrived from wing headquarters with the flying schedule for that night. When I saw it, I— and I suspect many others—realized "this is it. We're going to end it." It was history, and we knew it, and when it ended and the POWs came home, few of us were surprised.

Still, many of the accounts of the ensuing battle written over the next decade were unsettling. The crews who flew the missions were all aware of the mistakes that had been made, yet these accounts made it seem as though the confrontation had unfolded exactly according to plan. Additionally, there seemed to be a number of questions about how important Linebacker II had been in forcing the peace agreement. When I was writing my first book, *Clashes: Air Combat over North Vietnam, 1965–1972,* I originally intended for the story of Linebacker II to be part of it; but because the book was becoming overlong, I removed that portion and planned to turn it into a long article or perhaps another book.

It was pure, serendipitous luck. As I began my research, I found a large amount of previously unpublished material, and I saw that the story of Linebacker II was much more complex and nuanced that I had initially thought. I found that, like most battles, this was a story of mistakes, misfortunes and heroism, but I also learned that the American side was beset by turf wars. Many of the decisions were made not in the combat zone but far away, in Omaha, Nebraska, by men who had never seen a missile in flight and who were so focused on internal politics that the outcome was nearly a disaster. Like Waterloo, it was "a damned close-run thing." I also learned that the North Vietnamese have their own history of the battle, a history that is very different from the American one.

This, then, is the story of the men who fought through those eleven nights, jammed into the crew compartments of B-52s or in the command vans of the SA-2 missiles, never seeing each other except as electronic indications on flat screens, yet embroiled in as deadly a conflict as if they had been twenty yards apart with rifles. It is also the story of how one man risked his career to change the way the battle was being fought; of how his actions would in fact cost him his career afterward; and of how the real history of the battle has been hidden until today.

Peace Is
Our Profession

D uring World War II the American public was captivated by newsreels and magazine articles that showed stately formations of B-17s and B-24s pounding targets in Germany and huge silver B-29s fire-bombing Japanese cities. The high tech bombers became, in many ways, the American way of war, and by the end of the war the need for an independent Air Force to use this new weapon was a forgone conclusion. Additionally, the rapidly disarming United States was faced with the vast land armies of the Soviet Union, and until the advent of the ballistic missile the main deterrent—indeed, the only deterrent—to Soviet expansion was bomber-delivered nuclear bombs. Bombers also had the advantage of being relatively cheap, both in terms of manpower and dollars, when compared to large land forces. In 1947 the United States consolidated its nuclear bomber force into the Strategic Air Command, SAC, and soon thereafter approved an independent Air Force. SAC's mission, nuclear deterrence, became the lynchpin of U.S. postwar nuclear policy and this mission gave SAC a strong, coherent vision and a motto—"Peace Is Our Profession."

SAC received a significant boost when the charismatic General Curtis LeMay became commander in late 1948. LeMay had been a distinguished B-17 commander in Europe and later the leader of the B-29 assault on Japan, and within a few years after taking over SAC he had captured the American imagination. LeMay was short, stocky, cigar smoking, stubborn, and unsmiling, an iron willed, blunt speaking commander who was willing—indeed anxious—to use nuclear weapons to devastate an enemy to protect or advance what he perceived as U.S. national interests. He soon came to personify, in the best and worst sense, the caricature of the military man.

LeMay believed that the defense of the United States should be almost entirely entrusted to his strategic bomber force, and he convinced the leadership of the newly independent Air Force to fight to acquire most of America's defense budget for SAC. It was not a difficult sell. Most of the new Air Force's generals had been World War II Air Corps bomber pilots who had fought for strategic bombing and an independent Air Force separate from the U.S. Army for years even before World War II, and they were quite willing to follow LeMay's lead. In a series of bruising bureaucratic and budgetary battles, the Air Force, SAC and LeMay—it soon became hard to tell them apart—routed the Army and Navy, and national defense policy began to reflect SAC's strategic vision. But SAC's efforts were not limited to battles with the other services. LeMay set about having the Air Force drastically cut its tactical forces, especially its fighter forces, to provide more money for SAC. One senior Air Force officer noted that "bomber generals had an inflexible orthodoxy . . . and were . . . ruthless and unforgiving in squelching opposition within the Air Force." In the process LeMay ignored an agreement made with General Dwight Eisenhower, Chief of Staff of the Army, to keep strong tactical air forces in return for Eisenhower's and the Army's support of the Air Force becoming a separate service.

SAC's domination of the defense budget became a problem when the Korean War began in 1951. The U.S. Air Force had few modern tactical weapons systems and fought most of that war with weapons of World War II vintage, but that did not bother LeMay. What did bother him was that this "little war" cut into the defense budget and absorbed money that might have been sent to SAC. Even worse, the United Nations commander, U.S. Army General Douglas MacArthur, asked for some of SAC's B-29s to be sent to Korea to conduct bombing operations in support of the force under his command. Notwithstanding the involvement of U.S. forces in the "police action," SAC strongly objected to turning their bombers over to MacArthur. LeMay believed that only he and his staff knew how to use strategic bombers properly, and the last thing he wanted to do was to send some of his precious B-29 force to fight a "little war" under the command of an army general. When LeMay was finally forced to yield, he spitefully sent his worst B-29 units to Korea.

As a result, LeMay (and thus SAC) became inalterably opposed to such small-scale conflicts. In such wars SAC's nuclear force was useless, SAC aircraft might be asked to operate outside of SAC's direct control, and such wars would have to be fought primarily by the other services and tactical air forces, with the concomitant diminishment of SAC's share of the defense budget. SAC and LeMay preferred to focus on nuclear war, which was all theory and where such soft terms as "experience" and "expertise" could be used to make decisions. If pressed, LeMay would advocate ending "limited wars" by the use of strategic air power (though it was unclear what types of targets the bombers would strike in a third-world country), and he constantly made the point that even the smallest war could be controlled by the intimidation of SAC's bomber forces.

The Korean War showed some serious shortcomings in the U.S. tactical air forces and highlighted their need for more funding, but domestic politics continued to work in SAC's favor. The new Eisenhower administration wanted to reduce the defense budget and SAC's bomber force continued to offer a relatively inexpensive but highly visible deterrent, so consequently SAC got an average of 46 percent of the *total* defense budget during the Eisenhower years from 1952 through 1960. This was almost ten times as much money as the tactical air forces, and the Air Force's tactical shortcomings that showed up in Korea—lack of a modern, durable ground attack airplane, poor weapons, and a very limited night capability—were ignored. One of LeMay's deputies commented that he "became more and more insistent on SAC being 'it.' [The other Air Force commands] were purely secondary." In 1957 LeMay put forth a proposal that would have cut the budget of the Tactical Air Command (TAC, the fighter equivalent of SAC) so severely the command would have been virtually wiped out. When the Air Force Chief of Staff, General Nathaniel Twining, refused to make the cuts, LeMay was reported to have said, "Well, what is TAC's mission?" Twining, a former bomber pilot himself, replied, "Hell, I don't know, but an Air Force has to have fighters."

But what was going on inside the U.S. Air Force was lost on the American people and the Congress. A significant component of SAC's power was generated by a powerful public relations machine, and through the 1950s and early 1960s LeMay and SAC were viewed—in many ways, correctly—as America's bastion against the worldwide spread of communism. SAC became the darling of the Congress and the public, glorified in hundreds of adoring magazine articles and in such movies as *Strategic Air Command*, *Bombers B-52* and *A Gathering of Eagles*. SAC was the vanguard, the cavalry, and Fortress America rolled into one.

BECAUSE SAC'S BOMBERS had to be prepared to launch quickly in the event of a surprise nuclear attack, SAC developed a unique command and control system where the bomber crews' routes and targets were planned long before they took off, and all integrated into a nuclear attack plan involving all the U.S. nuclear forces. This meant every facet of SAC's wartime missions had to be planned ahead of time, and this required a centralization of all mission planning at SAC Headquarters in Omaha, Nebraska. Soon SAC Headquarters contained all of SAC's expertise and became the center of gravity for all decisions about the planning for using SAC's forces. (The irony of this was apparently lost on LeMay, who during World War II had made his most important decisions in the field without consulting his headquarters. Now that he became a headquarters commander he deprived the field commanders of the flexibility of action that he had enjoyed.)

The requirement to be ready at a moment's notice to fight a nuclear war drove SAC to create a disciplined, highly standardized crew force whose role was simply to execute SAC's plans. SAC crews had manuals that told them exactly how to perform every task and strict adherence to checklists developed from these manuals was demanded. Special crews—called Standardization and Evaluation (STANEVAL) crews—at each SAC base insured strict compliance with these materials, with an emphasis on "zero defects"—no mistakes. The necessary structure of central control from SAC Headquarters soon expanded to every area of the command, and the more powerful the headquarters became the more displays of initiative at lower levels were discouraged. A classic example was an aircraft commander whose plane developed a problem. In SAC, he was not expected—indeed, not allowed—to solve it himself. He had to call his Wing Command Post, who phone-patched him through to the SAC Headquarters Command Post where a senior officer—or officers—would tell him what to do. The end result was a highly centralized, disciplined organization where the smallest decisions were micromanaged by SAC Headquarters—which was exactly what the SAC leadership wanted.

LeMay also believed in keeping the crews and their commanders in a constant state of crisis with the fear of a surprise "no-notice" checks and inspections, especially the Operational Readiness Inspection (ORI), a test of a whole SAC wing. Failure was not tolerated, and it was not uncommon for a wing commander who failed an ORI to be told to "be off the base by sundown." This high level of stress flowed down to the crews who, not surprisingly, did not care for it.

LeMay made no attempt to be empathetic with his subordinates—in fact, just the opposite. He considered it important to be a "son of a bitch," and cultivated a reputation for being humorless, blunt and tough. One officer remembered, "you could tell he liked something by the way he grunted," and later a reporter described him as "cold as a terra-cotta statue . . . he could sit through a meal with fellow fliers and never utter a syllable."

As the years progressed, loyalty became the coin of the realm in SAC, and there was no distinction between loyalty to LeMay and loyalty to SAC. Many SAC officers felt that imitation was the sincerest form of flattery, and those who wanted to rise in the ranks often tried to imitate LeMay and his successor at SAC, the sadistic General Thomas "Tommy" Powers.

These characteristics—the massing of all expertise at SAC Headquarters, highly disciplined crews unquestioningly following top-down guidance, blind loyalty to LeMay and the SAC leadership, and the belief that "limited wars" were unimportant—became what was known as the "SAC Way."

WHILE SAC CONTINUED to be the most powerful military force in the world and the major deterrent to Soviet expansion, its internal policies caused morale problems with many of the lower-ranking officers. The discouragement of initiative has been mentioned, and adding to that was nuclear alert, where SAC kept a significant percentage of its crews in a fenced-off "alert facility" ready for immediate launch with their fully fuelled and loaded aircraft. Alert kept the crews away from their families for as long as a week at a time and was stiflingly boring but very stressful at the same time, since they were always liable to be scrambled at any hour of the day or night to take off for an exercise or to go fight a nuclear war. Standing alert also meant that SAC crews flew very little, compared to their counterparts in other Air Force units.

Many young officers chafed under the combination of the lack of initiative, limited flying, and the family separation and boredom of alert. Adding to their discontent was the fact that many of SAC's bases were on the "northern tier" in such bleak outposts as Minot AFB, North Dakota; K. I. Sawyer AFB, Sault Saint Marie, Michigan; and Ellsworth AFB, South Dakota. It was not surprising that a large percentage of SAC's crewmembers separated from the Air Force as soon as their commitment was completed, and by the mid-1960s SAC was considered the most undesirable assignment by new pilot training graduates.

But these warning signs had little effect on SAC's leadership. The United States had an abundance of young men available to the military from America's universal draft, and the Air Force flying program offered an attractive alternative to other forms of service. SAC, as the preeminent command in the Air Force, was able to fill its ranks with a steady stream of crewmembers to replace those who departed, while SAC's dominance of the higher ranks meant that its loyalists could expect to be promoted faster and advance further than their contemporaries.

BY 1960 SAC APPEARED to be at the height of its power, but international events were to test it—and the country—in ways that no one could have anticipated. Ironically, SAC's massive deterrent capability had been at least partially responsible for the Communists' realization that they could not expect to win a nuclear conflict. In early 1961 the Soviet leader, Nikita Khrushchev, announced that the Soviets would begin to challenge the United States in small-scale "people's wars of liberation" in the Third World where the SAC force would be neutralized.

As the Kennedy administration moved into Washington in 1961 with its "can do" mentality, there was the beginning of an understanding that "little wars" could become important. Even so, there was no indication that there would be problems with LeMay, now Air Force Vice Chief of Staff. In fact, LeMay quickly proved to be a help. Soon after Kennedy took office came the Bay of Pigs fiasco, and the administration realized it could use LeMay's formidable reputation to rehabilitate their damaged military credibility. The new Secretary of the Air Force, Eugene M. Zuckhart, also considered LeMay the most capable officer in the service, and Kennedy appointed him as Air Force Chief of Staff in July 1961.

As soon as LeMay moved into his new position, he set about molding the entire Air Force in SAC's image, and the fighter forces were his main target. He quickly appointed a SAC general, Walter C. Sweeny, to command the Tactical Air Command and had SAC set up liaison offices at TAC as well as in the headquarters of the United States Air Forces, Europe (USAFE, a mainly fighter force) to help the benighted fighter commands to become like SAC— "SAC'emcised," as the popular saying went. As a sop to the fighter forces, LeMay appointed a fighter general as Vice Chief of Staff of the Air Force but then, after finding that his Vice Chief was actually interested in promoting fighter operations, LeMay quickly fired him.

LeMay was already anathema to the fighter forces, and these actions generated even greater hostility. Sweeny proved to be a total disaster for TAC. He fired several of the highly regarded fighter generals and instituted an almost complete change in TAC operations modeled on SAC, ignoring that the way SAC operated—central planning focused on a single preplanned nuclear mission—was the polar opposite of tactical operations. The fighter units also felt SAC's maintenance and management philosophy was inefficient and uniquely unsuited to tactical operations, and they felt that SAC's reporting procedures were unrealistic and would force them to falsify reports. Most importantly, SAC's overall approach to flying— highly regimented and dominated by rules and safety considerations—was onerous to the individualistic members of the fighter community and resulted in a precipitous drop-off in flying skills, especially in air-to-air combat. LeMay's heavy-handed actions joined small amounts of money spent on tactical forces and SAC's rapid promotions on the long list of grievances the fighter forces already had against SAC.

BY THE TIME LeMAY TOOK command of the Air Force, he had been a high-ranking commander for fifteen years. During that period virtually no one questioned his methods or his decisions, and this fed his obsession with control and his unwillingness to tolerate dissent. It is not surprising that LeMay never considered that there might be other ways to do things besides his way—the "SAC way." Since many, if not most, of the senior officers in the Air Force had served under LeMay at SAC, his views permeated the upper echelons of the Air Force.

But LeMay's position as Chief of Staff soon proved to be a two-edged sword. While it allowed him an unprecedented opportunity to dominate the Air Force, it also brought him into direct, regular contact with the new Secretary of Defense, Robert McNamara. It soon became clear that LeMay and the new administration were completely out of sync. President Kennedy walked out in the middle of his first SAC briefing, a shallow "doomsday scenario," and at another point McNamara told Secretary of the Air Force Zuckhart that Air Force position papers were "lousy" and didn't support the Air Force positions. In the Air Force, many had scant regard for the Kennedy administration. At least one Air Force general officer felt that the "liberal ideals" of the new administration made them "nervous" with military power, and one of LeMay's deputies was later to say, "McNamara was not fond of the Strategic Air Command or its capabilities." Social issues were also a problem. LeMay and his Inspector General, General John Ryan (who was later to become Chief of Staff of the Air Force), were unwilling to fight rampant segregation outside of southern Air Force bases, to the dismay of Attorney General Robert Kennedy.

Once settled in, the administration quickly showed it was more than rhetoric. When Secretary Zuckhart received the list of colonels that the Air Force had selected for promotion to brigadier general and saw that half the list was SAC officers, he sent the list back and told the Air Force to do it again with more balance. LeMay—who had personally given the promotion board its instructions—was furious, and a SAC general later remembered, "we [in SAC] had a new ball game and knew it but we didn't *really* know how new it was."

The situation worsened as McNamara and his highly educated Defense Department staff, known to the military as the "Whiz Kids," began to ask the senior Air Force leadership for detailed rationales for their decisions. LeMay's unwavering answer was "this is our judgment, based on our lifetime of expertise and our combat experience," a response that did not impress McNamara or Kennedy. LeMay's fifteen-year-old World War II combat experience, his nuclear-only force, and his absolutist approach seemed hopelessly out of date. What the new administration wanted was flexible conventional forces to do battle with the charismatic revolutionaries of the Third World on their own terms, and LeMay quickly began to decline in the administration's eyes, to the delight of the Army and Navy leadership. Both resented SAC's dominance of the defense budget and its heavy-handed insistence that it be the single focus of U.S. defense policy, and now these services were able to offer the flexible conventional forces that McNamara wanted. The Air Force tactical forces also viewed the new administration with hope.

It did not help LeMay's relations with the "Whiz Kids" that the leading Air Force generals, especially those from SAC, were often poorly educated (LeMay's successor at SAC, General Powers, was only a high school graduate). LeMay had always adamantly refused to allow SAC's most qualified officers to go to assignments outside of SAC, including civilian universities, the Air Force Institute of Technology (AFIT) and the Air War College, because LeMay said that "everything [my officers] need to know they can learn in SAC." Since LeMay and his cohorts believed that there was only one way of doing things, the SAC way, any exposure to other thinking was not only unnecessary, but also dangerous for one's career.

THESE TENSIONS BETWEEN the Air Force and the administration were very much in play when the Cuban missile crisis arose in October 1962. LeMay recommend an immediate air strike to knock out the missiles, followed by an invasion, and expressed the strong belief that the Soviets would be cowed by SAC's bombers and do nothing. President Kennedy and his staff were appalled by how cavalierly LeMay treated the possibility of a nuclear war and were stunned when LeMay, asked how many of his bombers could carry conventional weapons, replied proudly, "none of them."

The disconnect widened after the crisis when LeMay and the civilians in the administration took away entirely different lessons. While the members of the administration thought that negotiation and the quick deployment of tactical forces to Florida resolved the crisis, LeMay believed that the overwhelming strength of SAC's bomber force, aimed at the USSR, had forced the Soviets to back down.

The Cuban missile crisis accelerated LeMay's fall from grace, and as LeMay went, so went the Air Force. When the time came for LeMay's term to be renewed as Air Force Chief of Staff, Kennedy only renewed for one year, instead of the normal two. Meanwhile, McNamara had taken charge of the Air Force budget priorities and tactical fighters and airlift moved to the top of the list, while LeMay's top priority—a new manned bomber—was almost ignored. It was clear that Kennedy and McNamara wanted more flexible forces to fight the "limited wars" LeMay despised, and this was to have a profound effect not only on U.S. military policy but also on U.S. history.

ONE

War Is Our Hobby

By 1964 LeMay had temporarily returned to grace because of his friendship with Lyndon Johnson, now the president. Johnson asked him to stay on as Air Force Chief of Staff for an extra seven months, until January 1965, in part to help Johnson with Vietnam, which was rapidly becoming the central military issue of the administration. LeMay agreed, but was certain he would not be retained beyond that time. As the situation in Vietnam continued to deteriorate, both Johnson and McNamara pressed LeMay and the rest of the Joint Chiefs of Staff for solutions to the problem. LeMay offered a variation of the same solution he had for the blockade of Berlin, the Korean War, aiding the French at Dien Bien Phu, and the Cuban missile crisis—a massive strategic bombing attack, this time on ninety-four North Vietnamese "vital centers," military and industrial targets that the Air Force had selected.

When both Johnson and McNamara expressed their concern about a Korean War scenario where the possibility of a North Vietnamese defeat would bring China into the war, LeMay made it clear he was not concerned about a war with China. In fact, he looked forward to a Chinese intervention in Vietnam as an opportunity to knock out the fledgling Chinese nuclear weapons program. Johnson rejected his recommendations, and the frustrated LeMay retired soon after and became a virulent critic of what he saw as a "weak-kneed" leadership.

AS THE WAR IN VIETNAM expanded and U.S. ground forces were introduced in greater numbers, the Commander of U.S. Forces in Vietnam, General William Westmoreland, saw a need for saturation bombing of Viet Cong jungle strongholds in South Vietnam.

11

But after trying an attack with tactical fighter-bombers that took 12 hours and 230 aircraft flying 433 sorties, he knew that something more efficient was required. The B-52s seemed ideal, and Westmoreland began to press to have them sent to the theater to support his forces.

Even though the Air Force leadership continued to push for a massive strike against North Vietnam, SAC itself dug in its heels to avoid to getting involved in the conflict. The SAC leadership still believed that SAC's sole mission was nuclear deterrence, and fighting a war in Southeast Asia (SEA) had nothing to do with that. It was Korea all over again, and SAC protested that its bombers were needed on nuclear alert, that it would take too much time to reconfigure the nuclear bombers to carry conventional bombs, and that if any B-52s were lost their systems would be captured and ultimately exploited by the Soviets.The commander of SAC, General Thomas Power, said, "[Vietnam] is not our [SAC's] business. We don't want to get into the business of dropping conventional bombs." Another SAC general later remembered, "There was a lot of opposition in SAC and in the Air [Force] Staff to B-52s being used for conventional bombing. Some say SAC was dragged kicking and screaming into SEA."

But SAC's position was soon overtaken by events and, like it or not, the B-52s were going to Vietnam. In December 1964, SAC's new commander, General John Ryan, indicated that he was willing to send the B-52s to operate in the combat theater, with one stipulation—this time, unlike the Korean War, SAC would retain operational control over the bombers.

The idea of divided control of the B-52s was directly contrary to both Air Force doctrine and common sense, and SAC's argument that the command needed to be able to use the bombers in the event of a nuclear war was disingenuous. Instead, it reflected a new chapter in the battle between the Air Force's bomber commanders and its newly revitalized fighter commanders. Air Force operations in Vietnam were controlled by Westmoreland's Air Force deputy, always someone with a fighter background, and it was intolerable to SAC that its forces would come under the command of a fighter pilot.

But there were obvious problems in having B-52s bombing in Vietnam commanded from SAC Headquarters in Omaha, Nebraska, halfway around the world from Saigon. Initially SAC arranged for the B-52s to be under the command of a SAC general at Andersen Air Force Base on the island of Guam, just a few hours from Vietnam, and eventually SAC offered to set up a SAC unit, the SAC ADVON, in Westmoreland's headquarters in Saigon. Westmoreland accepted the solution. For the rest of the war this awkward arrangement bothered Westmoreland's Air Force deputies and they constantly complained about it, but politics generally trumped priorities in the war and the entire command structure of U.S. air forces in Southeast Asia was so convoluted this one piece seemed of little importance.

IN FEBRUARY 1965 THIRTY B-52Fs specially modified to carry conventional bombs were sent to Guam. The B-52Fs had added wing racks to carry 24 bombs in addition to the 27 bombs they could carry internally, increasing their conventional bomb load from ten tons to almost twenty tons. After many delays, on June 18, 1965, thirty B-52s took off with great fanfare from Andersen on their first combat mission, called Arc Light One.

The mission was a disaster. The B-52s flew to their airborne tanker refueling rendezvous in groups, called "cells," of three aircraft, each cell twenty miles behind the other. The first cell arrived early for the rendezvous and then inexplicably did a circling turn to burn up time, a turn that brought their planes head on into the cell behind them. Two of the B-52s collided, killing eight of the twelve crewmembers, including the brigadier general who was in overall command of the mission. To add to the problems, fewer than half the B-52s' bombs hit in the target area, and those caused no Viet Cong casualties and no damage. The mission was later charitably described as "ineffective."

Nevertheless, Secretary of Defense McNamara ordered more B-52s modified for conventional operations and the Arc Light missions continued, and it was soon clear that a bombing attack by a three-ship cell of B-52s was an awesome spectacle that impressed both the U.S. Army and the Vietnamese. Even when the raids had no visible results, the B-52s were considered to be effective in denying the Viet Cong jungle sanctuaries, and soon Arc Light operations had become a permanent part of the Vietnam War.

Faced with this reality, SAC decided to modify all the oldest B-52s in its inventory, the B-52Ds, to improve their conventional bomb loads. The modification, known as the "Big Belly mod," increased the internal bomb load from 27 to 84 bombs, which, combined with the bombs on the wing racks, gave the "Big Belly" Ds the capability of carrying up to 108 bombs totaling 60,000 pounds. By April 1967 the newly modified B-52Ds were arriving at Andersen.

At about the same time, the United States made an agreement with the government of Thailand that allowed the B-52s to use the U-Tapao Royal Thai Navy Base on the Gulf of Siam. SAC's KC-135 tankers were already using the base, and the first B-52 missions from U-Tapao—"UT," as it was quickly dubbed—were flown on April 1, 1967. U-Tapao missions lasted about four hours and were a significant improvement over the twelve-hour missions from Guam, which were wearing on the crews and aircraft. As an added benefit, the base itself was next to a port, Sattahip, which made it easy to bring in bombs and other bulky supplies. U-Tapao soon became an extraordinarily efficient base, essentially one that was tailor-made for the dual mission of flying B-52 and KC-135 missions.

Off-duty life at U-Tapao was also more enjoyable than at Andersen, despite occasional political turbulence and tension. Living in Thailand was inexpensive, public transportation was readily available, and the Thai people were very pleasant. U-Tapao was close to Pattaya beach, soon to become the "Riviera of Southeast Asia" and a popular spot for European vacationers. The base also had what one official Air Force history called a "definitely sleazy quality" in the immediate vicinity of the base, with numerous local bars with "hostesses." Still, one man's sleaze is another man's diversion, and few at U-Tapao complained; those whose interests lay in different directions simply avoided the bars. One crewmember recalled, "It was totally different from Andersen. There we flew a couple of times a week and all officers in the crew had to stay in one big room with one bathroom, and we had to take the bus everywhere. At UT we each had half a trailer to ourselves with a bathroom in the middle and a maid that cleaned up, shined our shoes, etc. We flew every day for a week, then had three days off to go to Bangkok or Pattaya. The base was small and the club was an easy walk (or crawl) . . . it wasn't at all what Sherman had in mind."

AS THE B-52 MISSIONS continued, there was increasing debate about the effectiveness of the strikes, which were based on intelligence reports or designed simply to harass the enemy. Time and again reconnaissance into areas where B-52s had struck showed nothing but craters and wrecked trees, and one wag said a B-52 raid "made toothpick manufacturers curse their outmoded methods." Even some ground troops were not impressed, and a former Special Forces sergeant told a Senate committee that B-52 raids "mostly killed a few monkeys and some birds and tore up a lot of vegetation."

But inefficient is not the same as ineffective, and when there was a worthwhile target the B-52s were very effective. Flying at very high altitudes where they could not be heard or seen, they were greatly feared by the North Vietnamese and Viet Cong; often the only warning a Communist unit received of a B-52 attack was when bombs started to explode around them. A three-ship cell of B-52s laid their 324 bombs, 500 or 750 pounds each, over a rectangular area a mile long and a half-mile wide, and those close to such an attack agreed it was a terrifying experience, much like an earthquake or other force of nature.

As the war progressed, the B-52s become the stuff of fearsome legends among the North Vietnamese, who viewed them with a complex combination of awe, fear and hate. A North Vietnamese officer famously remembered, "[When] I experienced a B-52 attack ... it seemed ... that I had been caught in the Apocalypse. The terror was complete. [I] lost control of bodily functions and the mind screamed incomprehensible orders to get out." Soon stories of the B-52s' raids permeated North Vietnam as soldiers returning home from the battlefields in the south described the awesome power of a B-52 strike to mesmerized family and friends. The B-52 legend was enhanced by the almost overall black camouflage scheme that gave the bomber an especially sinister appearance.

Most U.S. forces were no less impressed with the B-52 operations. After the battle of Khe Sanh, a Marine commander said that a B-52 strike looked as if "a little part of the world blew up from no apparent cause," and General Westmoreland commented, "The thing that broke their back ... was the fire of the B-52s. Khe Sanh was a battle that was won by [the B-52s]."

BEGINNING IN 1966 B-52S began occasionally striking in areas of Laos and the Demilitarized Zone (DMZ), and the North Vietnamese began to move Soviet-supplied SA-2 Guideline surface-to-air (SAM) missiles to areas where they could fire at the giant bombers. The North Vietnamese missile men and their Soviet advisers had used the SA-2 successfully against U.S. fighters around Hanoi, and they had high hopes as they moved the missiles and their support equipment south. The SA-2 system was transported on truck and vans, each about the size of a tractor-trailer, and a firing battalion had missiles, launchers, and a variety of support equipment as well as two radars, one for long-range target acquisition, called the Spoon Rest, and a shorter-range radar, called the Fan Song, for actually guiding the missiles. The Fan Song radar had two trough-shaped antennas, one of which scanned a fan-shaped horizontal pattern while the other scanned a fan-shaped vertical pattern (thus the *Fan* part of the name). The radar gave off a peculiar noise that could be detected on American warning equipment (resulting in the *Song* part of the name).

When a target came into range it was centered in intersection of the two radar beams of the trough antennas. When the missile was fired it followed the beam of the radar, guided by three radar controllers in a control van. The entire system was movable and under good conditions could be taken down, moved by road on truck-transporters to a new position, and reassembled in a few hours, but the SA-2 was really not designed for fast-moving operations. By the end of 1966 the unit in the North Vietnamese panhandle that was assigned to attack the B-52s, the 238th Missile Regiment, had fired several SA-2s at the bombers but missed by a wide margin, much to the frustration of the Vietnamese and their Soviet advisers.

The failures should not have been surprising. Even though the SA-2 system was designed to be "soldier proof, durable ... with large knobs and switches and required little training when compared to similar western systems," it was relatively primitive. Most of the SA-2s' problems were unavoidable, and many were specific to operations in Southeast Asia. The system was designed for use in the cold, relatively dry climate of Europe, and Vietnam's heat and humidity caused great problems with the missile and radar electronics (as it did with much U.S. equipment). To make things worse, when the missiles arrived from the Soviet Union they were painted white to reflect heat, but the white color was very conspicuous in the jungle and American air attacks forced the North Vietnamese to paint the missiles dark green for camouflage, increasing the overheating problems. The problems were bad enough in the relatively fixed sites around Hanoi, but when the system had to be moved across hundreds of kilometers of bad road and set up in unsurveyed sites, the problems increased exponentially. Additionally, the simplest forms of electronic jamming rendered the system almost useless.

These shortcomings were exacerbated by intercultural problems. The North Vietnamese were paranoid and xenophobic, and most had no technical training; dealing with them was at times quite frustrating for their Soviet advisers, despite their dedication. Time and again the Soviets watched as the North Vietnamese missile crews made mistakes in the launch sequence or in the complex missile operating and guidance sequence, mistakes that gave the missiles no chance of a hit.

But even though the first SA-2s fired at the B-52s missed, they had a traumatic effect on SAC, which was determined not to lose one of its precious B-52s in combat. The command took immediate action, decreeing that as soon as a Fan Song radar's emissions were detected the B-52s would break off their attacks and go to a secondary target far from the SAMs.

To the U.S. fighter crews who had suffered heavily from the dense North Vietnamese defenses around Hanoi—where the B-52s never ventured—seeing the bombers break off a mission rather than face a single missile caused both derision and real resentment. These fighter crews and their leadership—who had been young fighter pilots in the 50s and early 60s when SAC was making its most strenuous efforts to gut the tactical air forces—freely mocked the B-52s, called them BUFFs (Big Ugly Fat Fuckers) and impugned the manhood and courage of the B-52 crews.

The tensions were exacerbated in 1969 with the publication of *Thud Ridge,* an extraordinary account of F-105s flying over North Vietnam written by a retired Air Force Colonel, Jack Broughton. In *Thud Ridge* the highly decorated Broughton pulled no punches, and one of his many targets was the B-52 crews. At one point he wrote, "I guess even our B-52 crews faced some problems [in combat], like stepping on each others' fingers reaching for the coffee pot and things like that." Broughton's book was wildly popular among the fighter community and further inflamed the fighter pilot/ bomber pilot conflict.

Broughton was not only caustic about the B-52 crews (and any others who did not meet his standard of courage) but he also had a keen eye for larger combat operations. He made a penetrating observation about General John Ryan, the former commander of SAC, who was Commander of Pacific Air Forces (PACAF) and in charge of all Air Force operations in Southeast Asia during Broughton's tour: "the World War II, bomber oriented viewpoint of General Ryan and his staff [was] the flawed routine of approaching Hanoi at the same time, the same altitude, the same heading and airspeed every day. They had no appreciation for the principle of surprise...."

As fate would have it, General Ryan was Chief of Staff of the Air Force in December 1972, when the last great air battle of Vietnam began, and Broughton's observation was to be startlingly prophetic.

AS THE WAR PROGRESSED, the Air Force's tactical forces, especially the fighter forces, had become the most significant Air Force units both in terms of activity and publicity, and SAC's preeminent position in the Air Force began slipping away. Its percentage of promotions decreased, especially in the area of "below the zone" promotions, where young officers were selected for early promotion because of exceptional promise. To an Air Force promotion board, a SAC B-52 pilot sitting nuclear alert in North Dakota was little competition for a fighter pilot of equal rank with a combat tour and a chest full of combat ribbons. Even more disconcerting were the statistics for general officers. Because of the war, combat wing commanders in Southeast Asia, mostly tactical fighter pilots, were getting promoted in greater numbers than SAC commanders. By 1970 there were two "fighter generals" for every "bomber general" (though most of the "fighter generals" were younger and in the lower ranks).

The war also rapidly expanded the size of the tactical forces while SAC stayed the same size, and the internal Air Force policy for combat tours in Vietnam—"no non-voluntary second tours until everyone has their first tour"—further increased the number of pilots the tactical forces needed. Since a combat tour lasted from six months to one year there was virtually a 100 percent turnover in the combat zone every twelve months, causing a steady demand for new tactical pilots.

When aircrews returning from combat tours in Southeast Asia were assigned (or reassigned) to SAC, they brought with them more than a chest full of ribbons and a repertoire of war stories. In Vietnam, their flying missions had given them a great deal of freedom and autonomy, and not surprisingly the lessons they drew were that flexibility and decision making by those closest to the battle were the keys to success in combat. Their combat experience and "lessons learned" directly clashed with some of SAC's core cultural beliefs, notably the doctrine of strict adherence to published procedures and one-way, top-down decision making from SAC Headquarters.

SAC also faced internal personnel problems with the six-month B-52 Arc Light tours, which were mainly flown by only a part of the B-52 force, the D model wings. Many of these D model crews were in a cycle of six months of Arc Light, six months at home sitting nuclear alert, then another six-month Arc Light tour. These crews faced a further problem because the Arc Light tours were not considered a "combat tour," so junior B-52 crewmembers were regularly taken from bombers and sent to fly a one-year combat tour in Southeast Asia in another aircraft, then sent back to SAC, and where further problems arose. SAC was still very unpopular with young officers and a SAC general said later "most [former SAC] crew members went to Vietnam or Thailand for their [combat] tour ... hoping for an assignment out of SAC on their return ... [when they came back to SAC] for some this was a morale problem."

It soon became the norm for many young SAC B-52 crewmembers to be away from their families 24 months out of 30—two 6-month Arc Light tours in an 18-month period, then a full one-year combat tour in Vietnam—then return to B-52s where they began the Arc Light cycle again. This caused great difficulties, especially for those who had new families, and the problems were compounded by SAC's policy of protecting its more senior crewmembers from both Arc Light tours and full combat tours.

As these patterns continued SAC crewmembers' morale plummeted and along with it SAC's reputation inside the Air Force. But SAC refused to adjust its internal policies, and instead blamed the war for SAC's decline. When he became Air Force Chief of Staff, General John Ryan complained that "the Vietnam War was ruining SAC" much as a Russian prince had complained during World War I that "wars were terrible because they ruined armies."

TWO

Getting Serious

When Richard Nixon took office in January 1969, one of his top priorities was to end the Vietnam War, while at the same time fulfilling America's ultimate aims in Southeast Asia—keeping South Vietnam from being overrun, preserving American credibility in Asia, and securing the release of American POWs. Nixon realized that additional American casualties were the biggest immediate problem he faced in pursuing these objectives, and he knew that his biggest danger was that Congress would cut funds to continue the war. To help with that problem, Nixon appointed Melvin Laird, a congressman from Wisconsin who was well connected in the Republican Party as well as in Congress, as his Secretary of Defense. But the politically savvy, strong-willed Laird soon showed he was his own man and was determined to get the United States out of Vietnam as quickly as possible. His opposition to virtually all forms of military escalation would prove a constant thorn in Nixon's side for the rest of the war.

To reduce casualties Nixon began to withdraw American troops and turn the ground combat mission over to the South Vietnamese Army, a program called "Vietnamization" (a term attributed to Laird), while continuing to support them with massive air power. On the diplomatic front, Nixon's National Security Adviser, Dr. Henry Kissinger, carried on secret negotiations with the North Vietnamese while at the same time pursuing another track, the thickening of relations with the Soviets and Chinese. This was expected to have many benefits, and Nixon and Kissinger especially hoped that one would be convincing the Soviets and Chinese that the advantages of a closer relationship with the United States were worth reducing their support of the North Vietnamese. But progress was slow. Nixon often felt frustrated that he could not threaten the North Vietnamese militarily and considered increasing military action to try to end the war, but the lack of realistic military options, Laird's opposition and escalating anti-war popular sentiment held these inclinations in check.

Still, by late 1971 the policies began to bear fruit and Nixon and Kissinger felt they had the Vietnam problem somewhat under control. There were on-going peace talks in Paris with the North Vietnamese, U.S. troops were coming out, casualties were down, the Soviet Union and China were not increasing their aid to Hanoi, and the South Vietnamese were gradually beginning to take hold of their country.

While the North Vietnamese realized that their position in the South was seriously deteriorating, they also saw an opportunity now that the United States was no longer fighting with ground troops. From the beginning of the war, their revered leader Ho Chi Minh (who had died in 1969) had said that the Americans had to be driven out before the country could be united, and the new leadership felt the time was ripe to escalate. The North Vietnamese Chief of Staff, General Vo Nguyen Giap—one of Ho Chi Minh's "Marxist mandarins," whose first wife had died in a French prison—proposed a full-scale invasion of South Vietnam aimed at defeating the South Vietnamese army and capturing and holding key cities and provincial capitals. This would also demonstrate to the United States that the South Vietnamese Army couldn't—or wouldn't—fight, even with massive U.S. air support.

In late 1971, Giap began a buildup of forces close to the South Vietnamese border in the demilitarized zone (DMZ), which put Nixon in an awkward position. He wished to preserve the negotiations in Paris between Kissinger and the Hanoi regime, but as the U.S. military leaders detected the buildup they began to press for permission to attack the North Vietnamese forces. Nixon waffled, hoping that he could bluff the North Vietnamese with a show of strength. He authorized more aggressive "protective reaction" strikes when U.S. reconnaissance flights were attacked and allowed a few heavy fighter-bomber strikes into southern North Vietnam. When these strikes had no apparent effect, in early February Nixon ordered twenty-nine more B-52Ds to Andersen (Operation Bullet Shot) to augment the B-52s already at U-Tapao and also ordered an increase in B-52 bombing raids. Still, Nixon did not launch the all out bombing campaign against the North Vietnamese buildup that the military wanted, gambling that Kissinger's negotiations would succeed before action became necessary.

The gamble failed. On March 30, 1972, under cover of bad weather, 120,000 North Vietnamese troops backed by six hundred tanks and artillery pieces launched Operation Nguyen Hue, a massive invasion of South Vietnam. The attacks were initially successful, capturing the provincial capital of Quang Tri and moving towards several more key capitals, as well as almost wiping out three South Vietnamese divisions.

As the situation on the ground became desperate, Nixon ordered more B-52s to Guam and, to ease the pressure on the beleaguered South Vietnamese, the United States began an aggressive bombing campaign against North Vietnamese targets up to the 20-degree north parallel line. But bad weather grounded virtually all of America's air power in the region, and on April 6 a frustrated, "wild-eyed" Nixon met with the new commander of Seventh Air Force, General John S. Vogt, to tell him how unhappy he was with the air campaign.

Vogt had been a fighter ace in Europe in World War II, but he did not look or act the part. Short, bald and somewhat rotund, he was intellectually the antithesis of most Air Force generals of the SAC generation. Vogt had grown up in New York City and had a BA from Yale, an MA from Columbia, and had also spent a year at Harvard. He had avoided assignments to SAC and instead had spent a great deal of time at the Pentagon, but he had gained significant Vietnam experience while he was Deputy Director of Plans and Operations at the headquarters of Pacific Air Forces (PACAF) during the first major air campaigns against North Vietnam from August 1965 through June 1968. While his enthusiasm for some of his pet programs occasionally clouded his judgment and led him to fits of hyperbole, overall he was to prove to be an excellent commander of Air Force tactical operations against North Vietnam in 1972.

In Washington, the Joint Chiefs of Staff were not enthusiastic about Nixon's expansion of the war, and Secretary of Defense Laird called the president's reactions to the situation "wild." But Nixon was in charge. He hectored the Joint Chiefs to use B-52s to "send a message" to the North Vietnamese that this air war would be different from the 1965–1968 Rolling Thunder campaign against North Vietnam. The Chiefs responded by ordering, for the first time, several B-52 "special missions" flown from U-Tapao deep into North Vietnam. On the night of April 9, twelve B-52s made their deepest strike into North Vietnam, hitting the Vinh petroleum storage area and railroad yards in the central panhandle, and on April 12 eighteen B-52s attacked the Bai Thuong airfield in the same area.

There was an even greater escalation on the early morning of April 16 when seventeen B-52s bombed the North Vietnamese port city of Haiphong, the first time the big bombers had hit a target in the heavily defended Red River delta, an area known as Route Package VI. On April 21 B-52s bombed deep in North Vietnam again.

The escalations concerned some of Nixon's staff because they felt they put him in a potentially difficult position with the Soviets. Nixon had a summit meeting scheduled with the Soviet president, Leonid Brezhnev, in late May, and it was hoped the two would sign a new strategic arms limitation treaty. Many of his advisers feared the bombings would jeopardize the summit. Nixon disagreed, adding that even if the summit were canceled, it was worth it. He then sent Kissinger to Moscow to discuss the situation with the Soviets and to see how successful their plan to split the North Vietnamese and their allies had been.

Kissinger was pleased with what he found in the Soviet capital. The atmosphere was "extremely cordial, almost effusive," and he realized that Brezhnev was very unhappy with the North Vietnamese. Kissinger noted to Nixon that "the bombing of Haiphong was an absolute necessity. We certainly got their attention." He played on Brezhnev's unhappiness, pointing out to the Soviet premier that supplying material to the North Vietnamese was a drain on Soviet resources and put Hanoi "in a position to use military means ... for purposes over which you have no control." Brezhnev appeared to agree.

Kissinger's reports confirmed for Nixon that the administration's policy of co-opting the North Vietnamese allies had worked; the president wrote back with satisfaction: "the effect on Hanoi of

Moscow receiving you [Kissinger] three days after we bombed Haiphong . . . accomplished a tremendous amount indirectly by the message it sends to Hanoi . . . [and] may open the door for future progress on Vietnam where the Soviets may play a more helpful role."

THE "SPECIAL MISSIONS" deep into North Vietnam were the B-52s' first encounter with the main part of the North Vietnamese air defense system, and the attacks were watched carefully to see how the big bombers would fare, especially on the Haiphong raid. Prior to the mission there had been a great deal of discussion between the Eighth Air Force staff at Andersen and the SAC staff about the B-52s' tactics, much of it focused on a steep, 45-degree banked turn—the "post-target turn," or PTT—that SAC directed the B-52s to make immediately after they released their bombs.

This post-target turn was an anachronism from the 1940s designed to get a high altitude bomber away from a nuclear blast. It was used when the B-29 *Enola Gay* dropped the first nuclear bomb on Hiroshima, and SAC had continued to use it unquestioningly since then, even though there was no reason to use the maneuver with conventional bombs. Like the other B-52 conventional tactics, the seemingly innocuous 45-degree post-target turn had never been tested against the captured Fan Song SAM radars available in the United States, an oversight that was to have tragic consequences later. A SAC general who was to become one of the post-target turn's greatest critics said later, "It was one of those 'we've always done it that way, so let's do it that way' things that we did with conventional weapons."

For the mission to heavily defended Haiphong, the staff at Eighth Air Force wanted to do two shallow turns of fifteen degrees of bank instead of the steep banked turn, because the jamming antennas on the B-52s were on the bottom of the aircraft and the steep, 45-degree banked turn would blank out the antennas, making the B-52s more visible to the Fan Song guidance radars. SAC agreed that the steeper banked turn would blank the jammers, but still insisted that the B-52s use it.

In the event, no B-52s were hit over Haiphong and, though an SA-2 badly damaged a B-52 on one of the other "special missions," there were no losses. The result was that the Americans developed a false sense of security about the B-52s' ability to survive North Vietnamese defenses, perhaps because of a sense that America's ultimate air weapon would not be vulnerable to a third-world defense force. A SAC post-mission report said: "[B-52] penetration tactics and ECM [electronic countermeasures] support proved highly effective as evidenced from the fact that only one B-52 sustained battle damage during the five special [North Vietnam] strikes."

Despite their impact, on April 21 the "special missions" ended temporarily because General Abrams, the commander of U.S. forces in Vietnam, worried that the war would be lost in South Vietnam and demanded that the B-52s be diverted to attack North Vietnamese forces there. The end of the "special missions" also ended the discussions about the B-52s' tactics in a heavy SA-2 environment.

THE B-52 RAIDS DEEP into the north, especially the one on Haiphong, had a major impact on the North Vietnamese populace. One North Vietnamese remembers: "the people were frightened and in a panic about the B-52s because word got around about how good they were and the number of bombs they could carry. The people were much more afraid of them than any other aircraft. People were feeling pessimistic about the chances of being able to shoot any of them down and the government had to work really hard to keep the people's spirits up. The government promised everyone that they would be able to shoot one down, but no one really believed them."

AFTER HIS VISIT TO MOSCOW Kissinger went to Paris where, on May 2, he met Le Duc Tho, another of Ho's "Marxist mandarins" and the chief North Vietnamese negotiator. Tho was emboldened by the North Vietnamese military successes and arrogantly told Kissinger the North Vietnamese had no intention of stopping their offensive when they were so close to victory. When Nixon heard about Tho's response he ordered another major escalation and began the mining of the North Vietnamese ports, something the military had been pressing for since the beginning of the war but which President Johnson had adamantly refused to do. Nixon also expanded the tactical air campaign by resuming the bombing of Hanoi, an operation known as Linebacker, telling Kissinger: "I am absolutely determined to end the war and will take whatever steps are necessary to accomplish this goal. . . . I cannot emphasize too strongly that I have determined that we should go for broke. . . ." Soon large formations of Air Force fighter-bombers armed with the deadly new laser-guided bombs were making daily raids over Hanoi and the rest of North Vietnam, destroying bridges and generally wreaking havoc, while Navy aircraft continued attacking other targets mainly using normal bombs.

When the B-52s in the theater stopped bombing North Vietnam to turn their attention to supporting the South Vietnamese forces, Nixon demanded that more B-52s be sent to increase the effects of the air attacks. SAC, following the lead of Secretary of Defense Laird and the Joint Chiefs, balked. All of the B-52D models were already in the theater, and any more B-52s sent from the U.S. would cut down on the number of B-52s on nuclear alert. Additionally, the only B-52s available—the B-52G—carried only twenty-seven bombs, about a quarter of what a D model carried. Nixon was furious at the hesitation, and told Kissinger and the Deputy National Security Advisor, Army General Alexander Haig, "I want more B-52s sent to Vietnam. I want this order carried out, regardless of how many heads have to roll in carrying it out. Even though the bomb load [of the G model] is smaller . . . the psychological effect of having 100 more B-52s on the line would be enormous. I either expect this order to be carried out or I want the resignation of the man who failed to carry out the order when it was given."

Soon more B-52Gs—dubbed by their crews as "the herd shot round the world"—were on their way to Guam. By the end of May, over 200 B-52s and almost 300 crews, capable of flying about 105 sorties a day and more for short periods, were in Southeast Asia.

Nixon and Kissinger had gotten their way, but the delay in sending more B-52Gs further solidified their perception that the military—especially the Air Force—was either incompetent or unwilling to execute the president's orders, or perhaps both. Nixon told Kissinger in mid-May: "The crowning insult is the military whine . . . that they were not getting enough support from [me] in giving them targets they could hit in North Vietnam. . . . I want you to convey directly to the Air Force that I am disgusted with their performance. . . . I do not blame the fine Air Force pilots who do a fantastic job in so many other areas. I do blame the commanders who, because they have been playing 'how not to lose' for so long, now can't bring themselves to start playing 'how to win.' ... If there is one more instance of whining about target restrictions we will simply blow the whistle on this whole sorry performance of our Air Force in failing for day after day after day in North Vietnam this past week to hit enormously important targets when they had an opportunity to do so and were ordered to do so and then wouldn't carry out the order.... I want you to convey my utter disgust to Moorer which he can in turn pass on to [the Joint Chiefs of Staff and the senior commanders in Vietnam]. It is time for these people either to shape up or get out...."

This *leitmotif* would continue to play for the rest of U.S. operations against North Vietnam, sometimes swelling, sometimes muffled in the background. Actually, most of the problem was with Secretary of Defense Laird, who was pushing hard to get the U.S. out of the war and used his position to try to keep the bombing campaigns as limited as possible.

Ironically, what Nixon and Kissinger seemed to want was someone like General Curtis LeMay, a smart, savvy and aggressive combat leader who would have enthusiastically and expertly followed his instructions for a massive bombing campaign—exactly what Lyndon Johnson and Robert McNamara did not want.

BY THIS TIME, Nixon decided that increasing the bombing and reducing the role of Hanoi's Communist allies were not enough to end the war—he had to make some concessions on the ground. On May 8 he announced the United States would no longer demand removal of North Vietnamese forces in South Vietnam if they stopped their attacks. While this position had been part of U.S. proposals since 1970, when it was originally conceived there were a far smaller number of North Vietnamese troops in the South, and this public announcement infuriated the South Vietnamese government, who viewed it as a betrayal.

When Nixon met with Leonid Brezhnev in Moscow late in May to sign the strategic arms limitation treaty, Vietnam was also on the agenda, and Nixon used this statement to show the Soviets how reasonable he was. The Soviet leader noted the concessions and told Nixon that he was not particularly concerned about the new bombing campaign, even though four Soviet ships had been hit in Haiphong during the initial American attacks. Brezhnev also made a decision that would have a long-term impact on Nixon's future plans, though the U.S. appears to have been unaware of it at the time. The Soviets were training North Vietnamese missile crews on a new surface-to-air missile system, the SA-3 Goa, which had been very effective against Israeli F-4s over the Suez Canal in the 1969–70 War of Attrition. The SA-3 would give the North Vietnamese a quantum leap in their defenses, but while Brezhnev allowed the North Vietnamese crews to continue training he also ordered that the missiles and their equipment not be sent to North Vietnam yet. The status quo remained.

As the weather improved, the U.S. bombing campaign began to bear fruit. In past campaigns the North Vietnamese army simply vanished in the face of American air attacks, but now it was heavily committed to full-scale battles and holding territory. These large, fixed-piece battles required a steady stream of supplies that were exceptionally vulnerable to American air attacks. Gradually, with the help of tactical air strikes and heavy B-52 bombing, the South Vietnamese resistance stiffened, and by July the North Vietnamese offensive ground to a halt.

The North Vietnamese had brought a number of SA-2 battalions with their forces to try to engage the B-52s, but they were ineffective. The missile sites were hectored by U.S. fighter-bombers and frustrated by the B-52s' heavy jamming support, and the North Vietnamese history noted: "No B-52 was shot down . . . because the missile battalions were not yet refined enough to meet the new jamming conditions."

WHILE NIXON CONTINUED to be frustrated at what he perceived as the Air Force's lack of aggressiveness, in fact many in SAC had had a change of heart and now wanted a "piece of the action." SAC had discussed bombing Hanoi with B-52s in general terms since 1965, but beginning in May 1972 the command began to seriously consider the possibility. Part of SAC's attitude can be traced to its new commander, General John "J. C." Meyer, a fighter ace in World War II. When bad weather hampered tactical strikes at the beginning of

Linebacker, General Meyer suggested that B-52s be used as an all-weather alternative to fighter-bomber strikes against Hanoi, especially the Kinh No rail yard just north of the capital, but the U.S. ground commanders in Saigon squelched the idea because they wanted the B-52s to continue supporting the southern battle-fields. Meyer's aggressive attitude was also endorsed by the new Air Force Chief of Staff, General John Ryan. While Ryan had been thoroughly despised by many fighter pilots earlier while he was controlling the air war over North Vietnam as commander of the Pacific Air Forces, he was amenable to sending the B-52s deep into North Vietnam and thought losses would be acceptably low.

Admiral John S. McCain Jr., the commander of U.S. forces in the Pacific (CINCPAC), sided with the ground commanders but did tell his air deputy, General Lucas Clay (CINCPACAF), to work with General Meyer and SAC on a plan for hitting North Vietnamese air fields. But the U.S. ground commanders were not the only obstacle. The Joint Chiefs of Staff, reflecting Secretary of Defense Laird's reluctance, refused to send B-52s deep into North Vietnam for fear of being seen as escalating the war.

WHILE MUCH OF THE credit for stopping the North Vietnamese advance must go to the Andersen's Bullet Shot B-52s, morale problems with these same crews were beginning to become a major concern. All the Bullet Shot aircraft and crews went to Andersen, which had been designed for 4,000 personnel but which now housed over 12,000. There were long lines everywhere, and many of the B-52 crews were jammed in barracks with all five crewmembers living in two connecting rooms with a single bathroom in between. Putting five different personalities in such close quarters was quite stressful on some crews and there were occasional problems. Additionally, the B-52 crews on Guam flew relatively rarely, generally only twice a week, which gave them a great deal of spare time that the wing staffs tried to fill with "busy work," which further irritated the crews. They were also harassed by a number of Andersen-based senior staff officers the crewmembers mockingly called the "shoe shine colonel," the "haircut colonel," and the "mustache colonel," who seemed to enjoy haranguing crewmembers about their appearance.

Even in the middle of combat operations one of the Guam staff had time to send Craig Mizner, an aircraft commander from Carswell Air Force base, a formal "Letter of Admonition" saying, "a member of your crew ... was found to be wearing a style of mustache which is in violation of AFR 30-1 standards. ... You will be closely observed in the future to insure that you properly enforce Air Force standards ... failure to do so will seriously reflect on your effectiveness as a supervisor. You will reply [in writing] herein indicating receipt and understanding of this letter."

The crews were not safe from such harassment even when flying. Steve Brown, a G model copilot from Beale AFB in California, remembers that during the height of Linebacker II, "we started getting notes from some maintenance officer saying we were leaving the airplanes a mess after the missions. He said if we didn't start cleaning them up he was going to take the matter to General Johnson, the Commander of Eighth Air Force."

Adding to the stress was family separation. Many Bullet Shot crews had just flown Arc Light tours or had just returned to their families from full one-year tours in Southeast Asia, and family problems arose with a vengeance, fueled by the growing unpopularity of the now seemingly endless Vietnam War. A feeling of futility and helplessness was in some cases exacerbated by the fact that the B-52s were in no danger from North Vietnamese defenses, which actually seemed to *hurt* morale. Flying far beyond the reach of enemy defenses and never seeing the results of their strikes gave some of the B-52s crewmembers a "sense of detachment" that made them further question why they were there.

There was also little to do off base on Guam. While the island was a popular vacation spot for Japanese honeymooners, most of the entertainment was concentrated in tourist hotels that tended to be very expensive. There were some beaches on the base and other recreational activities, but most entertainment was located well away from Andersen and there was little public transportation. Another important factor was that, at this time, the military was virtually all male, with all the difficulties that implies.

Adding to the difficulties for the B-52 crews was the situation at the Andersen Officers' Club. Before Bullet Shot the Club had been quiet and sedate, and some of officers and their wives looked askance when the crews descended on the Club. The Bullet Shot crews expected the Andersen Club to be like every other club in the combat zone: open twenty-four hours, flight suits allowed everywhere, and a large, freewheeling bar with few rules. As the club got rowdier and rowdier some of the wives pressured the commanders to have certain songs banned, among them "Detroit City (I Wanna Go Home)" and "Yellow River," which the wives felt "made the crews too wild." The crews responded by becoming even more obnoxious, and eventually senior officers had to be assigned to "baby sit" the crews at the Club and keep them under control.

The morale problems worsened as Bullet Shot continued with no end in sight. The official Eighth Air Force history noted that the tours "had the effect opposite of enhancing the appeal of a career in the Air Force." In October 1972 Eighth Air Force said in a message to SAC Headquarters: "We may be approaching the limits of our ability to sustain this operation without severe morale and welfare problems ... experienced B-52 crew members are tired of TDY [temporary duty] in Southeast Asia without tour credit and worried about the impact on family life of constant TDY ... there is deep concern regarding family separation over this holiday season."

MEANWHILE, THE G MODELS at Andersen were proving a mixed blessing. The G had a lighter structure and a "wet" wing, where the fuel was in the wing itself instead of in fuel tanks. This gave the G much greater range than the D model, and Gs could usually fly from Guam to Vietnam more quickly because they did not require in-flight refueling, allowing more missions to be flown. The gunner in the G also sat in the forward compartment where he had an ejection seat, unlike the D model where he sat in the extreme tail and had to bail out manually.

But by other combat criteria the Gs were much less effective than the older D models. The Gs were visibly distinguishable from the Ds in the tail area, where the G had a squared-off vertical stabilizer that was eight feet shorter than the D models' "shark fin." The shorter tail and a new control system made the G less stable, prone to rolling and harder to keep on a straight flight path during a bomb run. The small, twenty-seven-bomb load was also a problem because it took four cells (twelve aircraft) of Gs to drop the same number of bombs a single cell of B-52Ds could drop. Additionally, the Gs' bomb-release mechanism was prone to a malfunction that prevented the bombs from dropping. Some thought the lighter structure and "wet" wing might make the G more vulnerable to battle damage, but this seemed a moot point since the only B-52s that had gone into SAM areas were the Ds from U-Tapao.

But the G models' most serious problems were in its electronic countermeasures and jamming equipment, known as ECM, especially when compared to the D model. The B-52s had a number of jammers to fill enemy radar screens with what can best be described as electronic "visual static," and the more power the jammers put out the more electronic static appeared on the enemy radar screens. Only about half of the Bullet Shot G models—57 out of 98—had the most modern jammers for the SA-2, the ALT-22, while the others carried the ALT-6B, only about half as powerful. SAC claimed that the ALT-6B was just as effective as the ALT-22, but General Gerald W. Johnson, the Eighth Air Force Commander, was unconvinced. He tried to have the Guam-based Gs' jammers upgraded, but SAC refused to fund the upgrade.

The B-52D models at this time were considered "the most sophisticated ECM airplane in the Air Force inventory," not just by the Americans but by the North Vietnamese, who saw them almost every day. They said the B-52 was an "electronic battle center" and that "its jamming was equal to an EB-66 [a twin jet light bomber full of electronic equipment that had been completely converted for electronic warfare]" and that "the electronic warfare officer was the most respected member of the B-52's crew."

But these electronic warfare officers—EWs—on the B-52Ds did not share the North Vietnamese assessment of their jamming equipment or of their status on the crew. Bud Hughes, an EW flying on Craig Mizner's B-52D crew from Carswell Air Force Base, had flown a combat tour over North Vietnam in EB-66s. "I found myself in an aging B-52D with a seriously small set of equipment. Some of the jammers and receivers were the same as the ones in the EB-66, but there just weren't enough of them ... [and] over Hanoi they were woefully inadequate." As for being the "most respected member of the crew," Hughes remembered, "my job was to primarily keep logs for the aircrew. I easily memorized everyone's social security number and could put all the correct entries in the maintenance log. I considered myself a glorified secretary, and felt that the crew regarded me as such."

In the summer of 1972 normal yearly rotations began, and new faces appeared at U-Tapao. On June 5, Colonel Glenn Ray Sullivan arrived to take over command of the 17th Air Division, the umbrella organization responsible for the three U-Tapao wings—one of B-52s, one of KC-135s, and their maintenance wing. Sullivan arrived on his birthday and when he took command he also put on the single star of a Brigadier General. It was, he remembered, "a pretty good birthday present."

The commander of Sullivan's B-52D wing, the 307th, was Colonel Don Davis, known as a real expert on the B-52 and its operations, and in August Sullivan and Davis were joined by Colonel Bill V. Brown, who became Davis's Vice Wing Commander. Bill Brown was a B-52 pilot and former commander but had also flown F-105s in 1967 during Rolling Thunder and had over 100 missions over North Vietnam, including many to Hanoi.

Sullivan, Davis and Brown proved to be a perfect team. Sullivan, a friendly, avuncular Southerner with a quick, impish grin, had long been associated with B-52Ds and quickly set up a true "open door" policy where crewmembers were welcome to come into his office at any time, plop down on his couch and talk. He was also easily accessible after hours at the Officers' Club. Brown remembered: "He didn't carry his rank around with him, and he had a great rapport with the crews. He had been the Wing Commander at March Air Force base and there were a lot of March crews at U-Tapao, and he knew all of those crews by name and knew their families."

Davis and Brown were also highly regarded, and one crewmember recalled: "Both were blue ribbon, Class A, *numero uno* leaders and gentlemen. Colonel Davis was really cool under the pressure. During Linebacker II he was in command of SAC combat forces being lost in action for the first time and this should have been enough to overload any commander's central nervous system, but if it bothered Colonel Davis he never showed it. Colonel Brown was a Thud (F-105) Driver and he flew with my crew once on a mission in the north around Vinh. We had a few SAMs in the area, none real close to us but certainly close enough to see. Colonel

Brown was just sitting there in behind us with no ejection seat, enjoying the view and nonchalantly commenting on the activity out the windscreen. What a cool guy, role model, and super leader. I really, really admired him. Yep—two really great officers. We were really lucky to have them at that time...."

IN AUGUST THERE WAS a sharp change in atmosphere at Eighth Air Force. SAC sent Eighth a list of targets around Hanoi and the staff began to work long days to select what were known as "radar off-set aiming points." These radar offset aiming points were critical because B-52s aimed their bombs using their bombing radar rather than visually, giving them the capability to bomb in any weather. While it was possible—indeed, more accurate—to bomb "direct" if a target showed up on radar, many of the targets the B-52s were expected to bomb did not give a radar return. To bomb such targets, prominent points near the target that did show up on radar were used as aim points. Because these radar points were "offset" from the target, the range and bearing to these radar-visible aim points from the target were calculated and inserted into the B-52's bombing computer, and the computer corrected and used them to steer the bomber to the target. Each target had several "offset aim points" so the bombardier—now called the "radar navigator," or RN—could move back and forth between them to check and make sure he was bombing the right target.

The location and selection of the radar reflective offset aim points in the vicinity of targets were the most critical, challenging and time-consuming tasks for the mission planners, but once calculated, most of the offsets could be used indefinitely. Many of the offsets used around Hanoi and Haiphong had been calculated years before, and in many cases it was simply a matter of pulling maps and photography—both radar and visual—out of the files, checking the points against current photography to make sure nothing had changed, and using them again.

After the offsets were selected, the planners briefed them to the Eighth Air Force Commander, General Johnson, then sent them on to SAC. This was to prove fortunate. When Linebacker II began, almost all the radar offset aiming points for the targets had been selected and briefed at least once and had been forwarded to SAC for approval.

If Seventh Air Force commander Vogt in Saigon was the visual antithesis of a fighter ace, General Gerald W. Johnson at Eighth was typecast for the part—tall, lean, handsome, and darkly tanned. Johnson had been the second American fighter ace in Europe and had eighteen air-to-air victories before he was shot down and captured by the Germans in 1944. By the early 1950s he had joined SAC and spent the rest of his career in the bomber command. Prior to his assignment to command Eighth Air Force, he had been SAC's Deputy Chief of Staff for Operations, and had been responsible for SAC's plans for B-52s to raid Hanoi. Johnson was a strong advocate of sending the B-52s deep into North Vietnam, and he had the opportunity to describe in detail the B-52s' capabilities to both Kissinger and Nixon on separate occasions when they stopped at Andersen. Johnson had been a flying-school classmate of General Vogt at Seventh Air Force, and ironically the three generals who were to be most involved in the B-52 attacks were all ex-fighter aces.

Johnson's wife Anne had died just before he arrived on Guam in September 1971, but he soon remarried. His second wife, Mardi, was much younger, a striking brunette who was also tall, slender and tanned. She and the general made a fine couple, and she often joined him when he visited the bases around the Pacific, shopping while he visited the units.

AT THE SAME TIME Eighth was preparing a Hanoi target list, the B-52s were wreaking more and more havoc with the North Vietnamese troops and supply lines in southern North Vietnam, and so far the defenses had been helpless to stop them. The North Vietnamese General Staff ordered the formation of special headquarters group, Division H61, to solve the problem of shooting a B-52 down. The H61 group immediately ordered a number of radar operators from Hanoi to go to the center of the country, known as Military Region Four, and to have the missile crews there carefully document the B-52s' jamming patterns and to take photos of the jamming on their radarscopes for further study. While the radar operators were there they observed first hand B-52 raids with full jamming support, and they returned with a great deal of new information.

The North Vietnamese task was made easier because SAC had completely standardized the B-52 formations and electronic jamming techniques. The B-52s always flew in the same offset V-shaped, three-ship "cells" with precise spacing and altitude divisions both within the cell and between the cells, and they always flew at the same altitudes and airspeed. Additionally, SAC instructed the B-52 electronic warfare officers precisely when to turn on their jammers and the number and type of jammers to allocate to the various North Vietnamese radars. Analysis of the stereotyped formations and jamming patterns gave the North Vietnamese a complete picture of the B-52s' electronic warfare tactics, which allowed them to learn how to overpower or avoid the jamming.

At about the same time in September, the North Vietnamese General Staff ordered its Air Defense Command to develop a plan for defending Hanoi and Haiphong against B-52 attack, projecting five to seven days of B-52 night attacks with a large number of escorts including F-4s that dropped "chaff," thin, small strips of metal, foil, or metal-laced glass fiber that looked very much like aluminum foil. Chaff had been used since World War II and was cut into different lengths to reflect radar energy on different frequencies, and when used in large amounts it could flood the radarscopes by reflecting the radar beams back. It had proven very effective in protecting tactical strikes over Hanoi, so effective no U.S. strike aircraft had been lost in a chaff corridor in all of Linebacker I.

The North Vietnamese also expected the United States to use jamming aircraft and Wild Weasel fighter-bombers, which specialized in locating missile sites and attacking them with anti-radiation missiles (ARMs) that homed in on North Vietnamese radars. The attacks were expected to come from

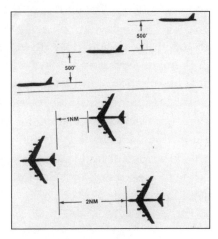

B-52 cell formation. The three-ship "cell" was the standard formation used by the B-52s throughout the war, including Linebacker II.

all quadrants and the jamming was expected to force the missile crews to use the least effective method of guiding the SA-2.

There were essentially two methods of guiding the SA-2 missile, "three-point" and the more accurate "half-angle elevation." The three-point method involved having the missile follow the beam of the Fan Song radar that was aimed directly at the aircraft, much like following a flashlight beam. This was believed to be the only practical method to use when the target was jamming and the radar return could not be picked up out of the static, but as the missile got closer to the target it often had to make sharper and sharper corrections, which gave the large, heavy SA-2 significant problems. The "half-angle" method let the missile lead the target and thus have less of a turn at the end, but the radar required a clean, jam-free return to calculate the "half-angle" flight path. In either mode the missile could be guided manually or automatically in a mode called "auto-track," but automatic guidance also required a "clean" radar return.

The Air Defense Command drew up a battle plan, called the "September Plan," which called for an increase in the number of SAM battalions around Hanoi and for two SAM regiments (three battalions each) to form a "ready reserve" to reinforce the city's defenses if there was an attack. The General Staff agreed to the plan and began to implement it.

On October 6 the H61 group convened a meeting of the North Vietnamese radar operators from the southern part of the country in Hanoi to review what they had learned, and H61 combined the new observations with a loose collection of informal documents on B-52 jamming which the missile units had been collecting since 1969. Using this information, the Air Defense Command produced a new document called "How to Fight the B-52," complete with several meters of film taken of radarscopes full of B-52 jamming. "How to Fight the B-52" was quickly distributed to all the SAM battalions in the country.

BY THE BEGINNING OF OCTOBER the South Vietnamese army had recaptured most of the territory it had lost, including all of the provincial capitals. In Paris, Kissinger found that the more the North Vietnamese Army suffered, the more willing the North Vietnamese chief negotiator, Le Duc Tho, was to talk seriously, and he and Nixon sensed an opportunity. Nixon wanted a peace agreement before the presidential election, and to put added pressure on the North Vietnamese early in October he told Soviet Foreign Minister Andrei Gromyko that the United States would make "final proposals" on October 8 in Paris. If the proposals failed, Nixon said, the United States would use "other methods" to get results. The seed quickly sprouted and at the October 8 meeting the North Vietnamese made several proposals that were more forthcoming. Kissinger remembered "the event that moved me most deeply [in public service] has to be that cool autumn Sunday when the shadows were falling over the serene French landscape ... [and] we stood on the threshold of what we had long sought, a peace compatible with our honor and our international responsibilities."

Nevertheless, Kissinger and Nixon fully understood the link between military results and North Vietnamese willingness to negotiate, and with the military successes in the South Nixon now felt free to order U.S. commanders to move B-52 operations to more lucrative targets deeper in North Vietnam. But despite Nixon's orders and even though SAC commanders admitted that the B-52 strikes were "vital to the [United States'] military and political goals at this time," SAC's ambivalence about the war remained. SAC gave its B-52 crews orders that "no combat mission was important enough for a crew to ... risk the loss of the [B-52]" and that the mission commanders were authorized to "break off or divert a mission if the anticipated or encountered threat became severe." Some—but not all—B-52 mission commanders began to break off and divert to a safer target if they received electronic indications from Fan Song SAM guidance radar on their electronic gear or saw a missile fired.

The North Vietnamese soon realized this and when a B-52 raid approached, a Fan Song radar would come up briefly, just long enough to be detected on the electronic warfare officers' scope, and this was sometimes enough to have the B-52s break off the mission. If the B-52s continued the site would fire a singe missile and often that would send the B-52s scurrying away.

Whenever the bombers raided areas where they might encounter SA-2s, the Seventh Air Force provided them with large escort forces, called "Tiny Tim" packages, for protection. The new generation of fighter crews escorting the B-52s were veterans of Linebacker operations to Hanoi and had faced SAMs and MiGs every day (with concomitant heavy losses). Like the fighter crews in 1967, they were appalled at the sight of a force of heavily escorted B-52s turning back because of a single SAM radar indication. Such behavior confirmed the fighter crews' stereotype that B-52 crews and SAC didn't have the stomach for combat, and they mockingly called the B-52 rules for breaking off the missions the "no sweat" criteria. The scorn rankled SAC crewmembers who had flown combat tours in other aircraft and disliked breaking off the missions. One commented, "SAC fliers were widely regarded by TAC flyers as having no guts, and being only concerned with haircuts and shoe shines."

General Vogt, whose Seventh Air Force fighters had to provide the escort force for the B-52s, was also very upset when the bombers turned back at the hint of enemy defenses because he could have used the escort force for attacking other North Vietnamese targets. He discussed the situation several times with General Meyer but Meyer, at the urging of the SAC staff, refused to reconsider.

While some of the missions turned back, others did not, and the B-52 crews were becoming concerned about the North Vietnamese defenses. On October 13 Craig Mizner and his crew were flying out of U-Tapao attacking a target near Vinh in the central panhandle of North Vietnam when they were fired on by two SA-2s. Mizner's navigator, Bill Beavers, remembered: "It was our first visual sighting of SAMs aimed at us. The pucker factor went up exponentially but they detonated a few thousand feet below us."

By late October, Mizner and his crew were flying half their missions into North Vietnam and Beavers noted: "The stakes were getting higher for us and some rumblings among crewmembers at U-Tapao were stealthily heard, 'I'm not sure I want to do this any more. How can I get PCS'd [transferred] out of here?'"

THREE

"Attacks must be brutal . . ."

Suffering from military setbacks and with their allies wavering, the North Vietnamese in mid-October made more concessions to Kissinger in Paris. By October 21, 1972, both sides had agreed to a draft peace agreement to be signed ten days later. Kissinger felt the agreement met U.S. aims—the South Vietnamese government was left intact, all the fighting in Indochina would end, there would be no more infiltration of South Vietnam, North Vietnamese troops would leave Laos and Cambodia, and all U.S. prisoners of war would be returned and Americans missing in action would be accounted for. He was confident enough with the agreement to advise Nixon to stop the bombing of the Hanoi area: "I know the President's objection to ending the bombing but ... ending the bombing would support the public impression that an agreement is near."

Nixon reluctantly ordered a bombing halt for the Hanoi area and the rest of the northern third of North Vietnam, but fearing a ruse leading to a Tet-type offensive, he increased the number of B-52s strikes into the southern part of the country. The bombing was intended to keep the pressure on the North Vietnamese and prevent troop movements, but it had another, equally important aim—to demonstrate to the South Vietnamese president, Nguyen Van Thieu, that the United States was not backing down. This was especially important because Kissinger had to take the new agreement to Saigon to persuade a skeptical Thieu to accept it. Unlike Nixon and Kissinger, Thieu did not believe that a Korea-style arrangement was possible, especially with a substantial number of North Vietnamese soldiers but no American troops in his country. It was doubtful he would accept an "in place" cease-fire, and

Kissinger lamented: "We face the paradoxical situation that the North, which has effectively lost, is acting as if they had won, while the South, which has effectively won, is acting as if it has lost.

Kissinger was met rudely in the South Vietnamese capital. At their first meeting, in a "tense and highly emotional state," Thieu completely rejected the new agreement, saying: "The issue is the life and death of South Vietnam and its 17 million people. . . . We have been very faithful to the Americans and now feel we are being sacrificed. . . . If we accept the document as it stands we will commit suicide—and I will be committing suicide."

Kissinger was unsettled. He had an agreement in hand that was far better that anyone expected, and now Thieu was rejecting it! His cable to Nixon revealed his frustration: "[Thieu's] demands verge on insanity. . . . He is totally oblivious to the scope of the North Vietnamese concessions [and] the ramifications [of his refusal]."

Meanwhile, the North Vietnamese were becoming concerned with the delays and, on October 26, they published the full text of the agreement, apparently to put pressure on the U.S. Still, Kissinger remained hopeful and made his famous "peace is at hand" statement, while adding the agreement needed "clarifications."

In fact, the agreement was dead. Nixon decided not to risk an argument with the South Vietnamese just before the U.S. election, so he let the October 31 deadline pass without forcing Thieu to accept the agreement. Instead, Nixon tried to reassure Thieu by ordering an increase in weapons shipments to South Vietnam, while calling for a resumption of the peace talks in Paris to try to pressure Hanoi for a few—mainly cosmetic—changes. The final nail in the coffin of the agreement came on November 2 when Nixon ordered B-52 strikes to be moved slowly north from a line established when the agreement had been settled.

The North Vietnamese—with some justification—felt betrayed. Not only had the United States not signed the agreement on the agreed date, but it was also increasing its bombing, sending more equipment to South Vietnam, and demanding the negotiations be reopened to revise the agreement Kissinger negotiated in October. Adding to the North Vietnamese chagrin was the fact that Viet Cong units had come out of hiding in many places in South Vietnam at the end of October to try to lay claims to territory in anticipation of the October 31 cease-fire signing. When there was no cease-fire the South Vietnamese forces decimated them.

IN EARLY NOVEMBER Major Andy Borden, part of SAC's Intelligence Directorate and the officer in charge of all conventional weapons planning at SAC Headquarters, was sent to Hickam AFB, Hawaii, to meet with the Pacific Command and Pacific Air Forces staff. Borden would be a key player in any attacks on Hanoi, and suddenly his trip was interrupted by calls from SAC Headquarters telling him that "unspecified people at the highest levels of the Pentagon" were asking questions about targets around Hanoi, mainly "political targets more than logistically important targets." Many of the questions were about the Hanoi International Radio station. Borden, who was very familiar with Hanoi area targets, pointed out that the radio station was a poor target for B-52s because it was so small and well protected by blast walls, but said that the barracks next door could be considered an acceptable target.

But while Eighth Air Force and the SAC Directorate of Intelligence targeting staff were considering targets for raids on Hanoi, the SAC Directorate of Operations staff, led by General Peter Sianis, was not. Even though General Meyer had been pushing such missions since May, Sianis and his staff, who were responsible for actually planning the raids, seemed to ignore the possibility, and there is no evidence that they attempted to prepare a realistic plan for an attack on Hanoi.

There were reasons for this. SAC did not know critical things about how the B-52 would fare against the SA-2, and if the Operations staff had begun to plan the missions they would have had to look at the standard B-52 tactics, most of which had never been tested against the SA-2 and its radars. Among the questions that would have had to be answered were:

- What was the effect of a steep post-target turn on the B-52s' jamming capability?
- How effective was mutual, overlapping cell jamming? How far apart could the B-52s in a cell be—spread laterally, horizontally and vertically—before the distance started to impact on their mutual jamming?

- How did SAC's standard anti-SAM maneuver, a series of gentle turns, climbs and descents known as the "TTR maneuver," affect the Fan Song's ability to track a jamming B-52?
- Did opening the bomb doors increase the B-52s radar return? If so, by how much?

Answering these questions would involve scheduling B-52s to fly over simulated SA-2 radar sites in the United States, either at the highly classified Area 51 at Nellis Air Force Base in Nevada (known as "Dreamland"), or at the test range at Eglin Air Force Base in Florida. These projects would have to be paid for out of the SAC budget, and there was always the possibility that someone—specifically General Meyer—might ask the Operations staff, "Why are we just getting around to testing these tactics after using them for seven years?"

It was far easier to ignore the possibility of raids on Hanoi. Air Force generals had been coming up with plans to "win the war" for years and were still doing it, and yet nothing had changed. The Operations staff thought these new requests were just another "Target List of the Month Club" that was going nowhere, and that planning for raids on Hanoi and the tactics changes they might require would just be a waste of time.

ON NOVEMBER 7 NIXON won a huge victory, 61 percent to 38 percent, over Senator George McGovern, but the Republicans suffered major losses in the congressional elections. The anti-war members of the Senate had increased to the degree it was certain that Congress would demand an end to the war when it returned in January.

To make matters worse, Kissinger was having more difficulties in Paris with the North Vietnamese, and he felt there was a possibility that the negotiations might have to be broken off. Thieu still remained as much of an obstacle as the North Vietnamese, and suddenly there seemed to be a possibility that the United States might have to negotiate a separate agreement with Hanoi. Kissinger told the President: "If the negotiations break down ... we will have to resume massive bombing and take the position that our only objective henceforth will be U.S. military disengagement in return for the release of our prisoners ... we have proven it is impossible to negotiate a more comprehensive settlement because of the implacability of the two Vietnamese sides." Time was running out for Nixon and his team. Somehow a peace agreement had to be completed and Thieu convinced to sign it before the new Congress returned in early January.

THE HEAVY NEW B-52 STRIKES in November increased the pressure on the North Vietnamese, and using the techniques from the new "How to Fight the B-52" manual the Air Defense Command began to strike back against the big bombers. The manual also offered suggestions on how to avoid the much feared anti-radiation missiles (ARMs) that homed in on the SA-2's Fan Song guidance radar. To avoid the ARMs, the North Vietnamese began to follow the B-52s' jamming strobes with long-range search radars (too numerous to be jammed or effectively attacked by American aircraft) and pass the information by phone or radio to the SA-2 battalions. The SA-2 battalions could then follow their course on a plotting board and wait until the bombers were close, then turn on the Fan Song radar, point the antennas at the B-52s, track briefly, and fire. This technique minimized or entirely avoided exposure to anti-radiation missiles because of the short time the Fan Song was on the air. For the SAM crews, transmitting for such a brief period was not optimum, but it least it gave them a chance to fire and guide their missiles without being attacked.

Using these techniques, the North Vietnamese heavily damaged a B-52 with an SA-2 on November 5. Not surprisingly, this had a further chilling effect on SAC, and the B-52s began to divert more regularly. During the next ten days over 30 percent of the B-52 sorties into North Vietnam diverted because of a perceived SAM threat. In Saigon General Vogt had finally had enough of sending heavy escort forces to watch the B-52s break off their attacks. He sent a sharply worded message to General Meyer at SAC Headquarters spelling this out and saying that it was "very frustrating when B-52s cut and run with just a SAM indication."

The large number of aborted B-52 missions was also attracting attention in Washington, reaffirming the perception that the Air Force was unwilling to carry out the president's orders. SAC finally realized they had to accept the risks of combat, and General Meyer agreed to designate most missions into North Vietnam as "press on" missions where the B-52 crews were to continue in spite of aircraft malfunctions and/or threats from MiGs and SAMs. This did not sit well with some of the B-52s crews. One copilot remembered, "We were not happy about these 'press on' missions. The target significance never seemed enough for us to be hanging our asses out. I didn't want to die over a suspected truck park."

On the night of November 22, eighteen B-52s with a heavy support package were sent on a "press on" mission against a storage area in the center of the North Vietnamese panhandle. All B-52 cells used colors as call signs, and Olive cell was the first to attack. Just after Olive 01 dropped its bombs, two North Vietnamese SA-2s broke out of the overcast, accelerated, and then exploded beneath the B-52.

The missiles caused severe damage, riddling the aircraft with shrapnel, setting an engine on fire and starting a massive fuel leak. All aircraft power was knocked out, and the pilots had to read their instruments with a flashlight as the fire ate down through both wings. As the stricken bomber turned towards Thailand, an American fighter pulled along side, but he was not able to contact the crew until the tail gunner took his battery-operated emergency radio from his survival vest and began to talk.

The B-52 continued to fly straight and level in a slight descent, but the fire was eating into the wing and now the ribs and stringers could be clearly seen. Finally the B-52 crossed the Mekong River into Thailand, and then the front of the aircraft erupted in five small jets of flame as five ejection seats fired. The tail gunner dumped his turret and manually rolled out of the gaping hole, and the B-52 turned into a fireball as, with its wings folded like a huge dragonfly, it plunged to earth. This was the first combat loss of a B-52 after more than seven years and 112,000 missions, and it jolted the crews with the reality of war.

It also spurred the Eighth Air Force staff to look carefully at what happened, and U.S. intelligence quickly realized that the North Vietnamese were using their search radars to pass information to the SAM sites' Fan Song radar. Not only did this technique neutralize the Wild Weasels, specially modified two-seat F-105Gs armed with a variety of anti-radiation missiles, but it also gave the electronic warfare officers on the B-52s little time to detect the Fan Song radar and jam it. The staff also found that B-52s had been scheduled to fly in a chaff "corridor" laid by F-4s, but the chaff corridor had been blown off the B-52s' track by high-altitude winds and Olive 01 was outside of it. It appeared that, even with its ECM systems, a B-52 outside of a chaff corridor was vulnerable to SA-2s. Eighth Air Force reported these findings to SAC, also noting that the B-52s had been using the same tactics—airspeeds, altitudes, jamming patterns, formations—since 1967. Eighth apparently hoped that SAC Headquarters would reexamine the B-52 tactics for missions flown into a heavy missile environment, but SAC was still not prepared to reevaluate their standard procedures, and still did not test the B-52s' jamming and tactics against captured SA-2 radars available in the United States.

EVEN THOUGH THE NORTH VIETNAMESE missile crews had downed a B-52, they remained frustrated because it had crashed in Thailand and not "on the spot," where they could actually see the wreckage. After examining this and other missile firings, they concluded there were two problems: the SA-2 battalions were firing while the B-52s were too far away, and the batteries could not operate out of fixed positions with overlapping coverage because of American attacks. A SAM battalion was only able to fire one time from a site, and then it had to move quickly to another location before it was attacked. These moves, while frustrating to the Americans, were hard on the equipment because it had to be recalibrated after each move. The North Vietnamese concluded that "fighting in the north, especially in Hanoi and Haiphong, would offer a much greater chance of success than fighting in Military Region Four [the center of the country]. The overlapping sites [in Hanoi] would increase the number of missiles that could be brought to bear and also reduce the impact of the enemy's electronic warfare."

THE UNITED STATES HAD BEEN CONCERNED for some time that the North Vietnamese were getting advance information about the B-52 raids into central North Vietnam and that they might use this information to attack the bombers with MiG-21 fighters. Secretary of Defense Laird—who opposed the B-52 attacks—used this possibility to try to slow the B-52 raids down, and in November a study group made up of representatives from Pacific Command, SAC, and the National Security Agency looked at the situation. By the end of the month they concluded that the North Vietnamese were not getting advance information of the raids, but the group did note that B-52 raids into North Vietnam were characterized by highly stereotyped operations, including the use of specific electronic countermeasures tactics and the standdown of the B-52s prior to any large operation.

At about the same time these conclusions were being reached, Colonel Ted Hanna, chief of the SAC ADVON in Saigon, sent a message to SAC about the B-52 tactics. "There is no doubt that the North Vietnamese have studied the tactics of the B-52 force and have made every effort to take advantage of the way we have repeatedly used long streams of bombers flying the same route. This tactic has enabled the North Vietnamese SAM operators to predict with some accuracy where each cell should be in relation to the preceding cell and the North Vietnamese have used this to their advantage in firing [SAMs]."

All of these cautions went unheeded at SAC Headquarters.

IN LATE NOVEMBER NIXON received some disconcerting news about congressional support that he passed on to Henry Kissinger in Paris. "The result of this check indicates that [these senators] were not only unanimous but vehement in stating their conclusions that if Saigon is the only roadblock for reaching an agreement . . . they will personally lead the fight when the new Congress reconvenes . . . to cut off all military and economic assistance to Saigon . . . under such circumstances we have no choice but to go it alone and make a separate deal with North Vietnam for the return of our POWs and for our withdrawal. These are [senators] who have loyally supported us. . . ."

At the same time it was becoming clear to Kissinger that the North Vietnamese *politburo* was beginning to have real second thoughts about the agreement they had negotiated in October, and the prospects for a revised agreement were diminishing.

On November 30 Nixon met with Secretary of Defense Laird and Admiral Moorer, the Chairman of the Joint Chiefs of Staff, and told them he wanted to bomb Hanoi with B-52s. Laird and Moorer remained unconvinced that more intense military actions were necessary, repeating the Air Force Staff's fear that B-52s would be lost and that the downed aircraft would allow the Soviets to fully evaluate the bombers' electronic capabilities and vulnerabilities. But the president was adamant, and when Admiral Moorer left the meeting he called General Meyer at SAC and the commanders in the Pacific and told them to be prepared for the breakdown of cease-fire negotiations and to prepare a plan for an integrated and sustained air campaign against North Vietnam "for maximum psychological impact."

WHILE THE UNITED STATES BEGAN to prepare for a major escalation, the North Vietnamese were fully occupied with the B-52 attacks in the south. As their official history noted: "The enemy's air force, especially its B-52s, were bombing very fiercely and our strategic transportation encountered many difficulties." The North Vietnamese had a relatively small number of missile battalions, and the attacks whipsawed the General Staff into making a choice between protecting their southern units against daily raids or keeping battalions around Hanoi—which had not been bombed since October—to protect against potential raids. The General Staff decided to partially dismember the "September Plan," developed just a few months before to protect Hanoi against B-52 attack, in order to redeploy their missile defenses. In mid-November the 267th Missile Regiment, part of the Hanoi reserve force under the "September Plan," was ordered to move south to Military Region Four, and on December 1 one hundred missiles were sent south from Hanoi. This was followed by a far more serious move on December 8 when the General Staff ordered the crack 261st Missile Regiment to move from Hanoi to the center of the country. Additionally, the 285th Missile Regiment, which in the "September Plan" had been another reserve unit for Hanoi, remained in Haiphong. There was a new unit assigned to protect Hanoi, the 268th Missile Regiment, but it had no weapons and existed only on paper. To make matters worse, since August most of the new missile equipment arriving in North Vietnam had been sent straight to the south, and now the Hanoi missile battalions had the oldest missile equipment in the North Vietnamese inventory, some of it with 6000 hours of use. This equipment needed major overhaul and repairs, but as more and more missile equipment was sent south the Hanoi systems could not be taken off the battle line.

The North Vietnamese Air Defense Command and the unit that was responsible for defending Hanoi, the 361st Air Defense Division, vigorously protested that the new orders would strip Hanoi of a significant part of its defenses. They asked not only that the 261st Regiment remain in place but also that another regiment, the 267th, be moved close to the capital to be used as a reserve force. The General Staff took the Air Defense Command's objections under advisement, but meanwhile it ordered the 261st to continue preparations to move.

There was some relief for the Hanoi defenses when some units of the 274th Missile Regiment arrived in Hanoi from the south to replace the 261st, but the 274th's weapons were still being shipped, so the battalion was temporarily useless.

ON NOVEMBER 28 CRAIG MIZNER'S crew had eight SAMs fired at them on a mission over Vinh. On December 2, they deployed back to Guam for what Mizner's navigator, Bill Beavers, expected to be "a respite and a breath of fresh Pacific Ocean air, leaving the 'press on' missions behind. Guam had not flown ANY 'press on' missions to North Vietnam. They were still bombing in South Vietnam. But as soon as we got there three out of our six missions were into North Vietnam—more missiles, more often. . . ."

At about the same time, Bob Morris's crew from Kinchloe AFB in Michigan had arrived in Guam to begin an Arc Light tour. Morris's copilot, Bob Hudson, had just graduated from pilot training and persuaded the crew to come because he was afraid the war would be over before he could "do his duty." Hudson remembered his first "press on" mission to North Vietnam: "We were really nervous coasting in, in absolute radio silence, when over the UHF radio came this voice, 'Men, I want you to remember that no bastard ever won a war by dying for his country. He won it by making the other poor dumb bastard die for his country. . . . The stuff you heard about America not wanting to fight, wanting to stay out of the war, is a lot of horseshit. Americans traditionally love to fight. . . .'

"It was George C. Scott's speech from the movie *Patton!* It was great, all the tension melted away. I would give my right arm to know who played that tape."

At Griffis Air Force Base, a B-52 base in New York State, Deputy Commander Colonel Bill Maxson got what he thought was bad news. He was to report to U-Tapao immediately to take over as commander of the maintenance wing. "The only response I could find was something like 'that's fine ... I used to be a maintenance officer.' But I dreaded telling my family that I was leaving a few days before Christmas, being shuffled out of the way for a 'nothing' job. Little did I realize ..."

NIXON TOOK A FURTHER STEP on December 6 when he ordered the Joint Chiefs of Staff to form a special working group to begin planning for B-52 strikes against Hanoi. "The strike plan ... must be so configured as to create the most massive shock effect in a psychological context," he ordered. "There is to be no dissipation of effort ... but rather a clear concentration of effort against essential national assets designed to achieve psychological as well as physical results. ... B-52s should be employed in the Hanoi area as close as can reasonably be risked.... [Do not] allow military considerations such as long term interdiction, etc. to dominate the targeting philosophy. Attacks ... must be massive and brutal in character. No other criteria is acceptable and no other conceptual approach will be countenanced.... Air Force assets, due to their more sophisticated technological capabilities, are best suited for many of the high priority targets."

Nixon also addressed the problems of SAC's control of the B-52s: "Be aware that we visualize a revised command and control system which will place responsibility for the air war in the North ... under MACV." This would place SAC's B-52s under the command of Seventh Air Force in Saigon.

THE PARIS TALKS DRAGGED ON until December 12. On that day Tho withdrew from some previously agreed positions and told Kissinger that North Vietnam was willing to continue the war rather than yield on Nixon's new points. It was clear the two sides had reached an impasse and Kissinger realized the North Vietnamese were giving just enough to keep the talks going until Congress intervened. Chillingly, the North Vietnamese also hinted that they might not even agree to the release of the American POWs. On December 13 both Kissinger and Tho left Paris, leaving their deputies behind.

One of things the North Vietnamese felt was in their favor as the negotiations broke off was the weather. North Vietnam was in the heart of the northeast monsoon, which was dominated by long periods of heavy overcast and had historically meant a pause in the serious bombing of North Vietnam. Except for a small number of Navy A-6s and Air Force F-111s, the United States' tactical aircraft had little all-weather bombing capability and the deadly laser-guided bombs needed relatively clear weather to operate. It seemed unlikely the U.S. would opt for bombing raids at this time.

This was Hanoi's first serious mistake. Despite the mining of Haiphong and the extremely aggressive Linebacker bombing campaign, the North Vietnamese still did not understand how aggressive Nixon could be. The second mistake was not looking at the calendar. They chose to be intransigent at a time when the U.S. Congress, their biggest ally, was out of Washington on Christmas recess. Hanoi's third mistake was to ignore the fact that the United States did have one aircraft with complete all-weather capability—the B-52.

FOUR

"Maximum effort, repeat, maximum effort . . ."

Kissinger returned to Washington on December 14 and briefed Nixon on the failure of the peace talks. Nixon immediately sent Hanoi an ultimatum, telling them to resume serious negotiations in seventy-two hours. In the discussions that followed, Kissinger recommended resuming the bombing using tactical fighters, but Nixon had already made up his mind that this time he was not going to peck away with a few Phantoms. It was time for America's big stick, the B-52s. Nixon felt the criticism would be the same whether he used B-52s or fighters, and the B-52s would be a quantum leap in force much more likely to lead to a quick resolution. The Deputy National Security Advisor, General Alexander Haig, agreed with the President. Haig had been the first Army battalion commander in South Vietnam to use the B-52s for close support of his troops, and his experience with the destructive power of the giant bombers made him think they would be just the thing to move the intransigent North Vietnamese. He also made a critical point—time was running out and the United States could not afford to wait for good weather. Unlike the tactical aircraft, the B-52s could strike in the bad weather of the northeast monsoon.

Kissinger remained hesitant. He felt that using B-52s was premature, and he was concerned about possible losses, which would give the North Vietnamese more American POWs and thus more leverage in the bargaining ahead. He was also concerned about the possibility of a large number of civilian casualties, further inflaming public opinion, but in the end he accepted the plan.

Secretary of Defense Laird and Secretary of State William Rodgers were opposed to bombing in general and using the B-52s in particular on domestic political grounds. Laird's opposition kept Admiral Thomas Moorer, the Chairman of the Joint Chiefs of Staff, in a difficult position between Laird, his immediate boss and the president. Moorer seems to have been ambivalent about the escalation, but he was able to convince General Haig that he was willing—indeed, anxious—to bomb, though earlier he had told Nixon he was in favor of bombing only if the peace agreement had been signed and then violated. Additionally, in the fall when Kissinger had asked him how many B-52s were available around the world, Moorer, sensing the reason behind the question, was "unenthusiastic" about using B-52s over Hanoi because he was concerned about the compromise of the B-52s' electronic warfare equipment and possible civilian casualties. Once again, Nixon hoped for decisive military leadership in the manner of Curtis LeMay or George Patton, and once again he received ambivalence.

Nixon later said sending in the B-52s to Hanoi was his loneliest decision, but the evidence suggests he was not reluctant to do so and saw few alternatives. Nixon had seen President Dwight Eisenhower end the Korean War by bombing North Korean dikes to flood their rice paddies, then threatening the Chinese with nuclear weapons, and the decision to bomb was probably based on Nixon's hope that he could do the same in Vietnam. He also believed that the North Vietnamese respected nothing but force and were contemptuous of the United States because of its ambivalence and timidity in fighting the war. He may also have felt he was exorcising the frustration of many Americans who had watched the U.S. suffer tens of thousands of casualties while fighting a war "with one hand tied behind its back."

But Nixon knew sending the B-52s involved significant risks. The B-52 production lines had long since closed and, since all B-52s had a nuclear commitment, any losses would diminish America's strategic nuclear force. Additionally, B-52s had a crew of six and losses would, as Kissinger had noted, swell the number of POWs. There was always the chance that some of the B-52 bombs would go astray and cause significant civilian casualties. The raids would also certainly provoke a huge international outcry and possibly large domestic protests like those that had shaken America during the Cambodian invasion.

Still, Nixon felt the risks he would take by not using the big bombers were even greater. He was sure that Congress would cut funds for the war when it returned in January, so he had only three weeks to force the North Vietnamese back to the peace table to sign the modified agreement and also to show Thieu that the U.S. could protect South Vietnam. If there was no peace agreement, the fall of South Vietnam was inevitable and the American POWs would remain in Hanoi, where they were certain to be used as bargaining chips. America's long, humiliating nightmare in Vietnam would continue, with uncertain results throughout Asia and the world. A successful B-52 blitz of Hanoi appeared to be the only hope.

Moreover, the very fact that Nixon was willing to risk a key part of America's nuclear force over Hanoi would add to the B-52s' effect by displaying his determination not only to the North Vietnamese and their Soviet and Chinese allies, but also to Thieu and the South Vietnamese. Nixon was certain if he could get a peace agreement Congress would not overturn it. In the end, the bombing was simply a part of the negotiating process.

On the afternoon of December 14, Nixon told Admiral Moorer to begin the bombing campaign on December 17 with B-52s hitting the targets deep in North Vietnam, especially around Hanoi. As he had stated earlier, Nixon wanted the strikes to have a psychological as well as military effect, and he did not want narrow military considerations to dominate. He wanted the B-52s to pound Hanoi, to have its people hear and feel the bombs, but with a minimum of civilian casualties. As one observer said later, "he wanted the North Vietnamese to feel the heat, then see the light," and to that end he approved an initial three-day campaign but emphasized that the military should be prepared to extend the campaign indefinitely.

But Nixon did not stop there. Concerned that the military might frustrate his aims by using half measures again, he issued Moorer a blunt warning: "In the past ... our political objectives have not been achieved because of too much caution on the military side.... This is your chance to use military power effectively to win this war and if you don't I'll consider you personally responsible." He also emphasized that White House would not interfere with target selection. "I don't want any more of this crap about the fact that [the Air Force] couldn't hit this target or that one."

Still, Nixon was aware that two things could affect his plan—heavy North Vietnamese civilian casualties or heavy B-52 losses. Limiting the B-52s' targets to those on the outskirts of Hanoi could minimize civilian casualties, but B-52 losses also had to be kept at a reasonable level. Nixon knew there was a definite link between U.S. casualties and America's willingness to fight, and he also knew the North Vietnamese knew it. If the North Vietnamese defenses could inflict significant casualties on the B-52 force, they might both demoralize the U.S. and stiffen their countrymen's will to resist until Congress returned.

But the B-52s still had an aura of invincibility about them, and heavy losses seemed unlikely. It was clear that the U.S. aircrews knew how to counter the North Vietnamese defenses. Seventh Air Force's fighter-bombers had bombed the Hanoi area regularly from April 1972 until the end of October and had lost only one aircraft to the SA-2 missiles around the capital, expected to be the biggest threat to the B-52s. The B-52s were designed to penetrate the Soviet Union, and it was believed that their electronic countermeasures would surely overpower the defenses of a third-world country. Nixon and his staff were expecting SAC to conduct the type of hard-hitting, resourceful campaign Curtis LeMay would have executed; they expected losses, but they anticipated that the operation would, from a military point of view, be easy.

AS SOON AS ADMIRAL MOORER returned from his meeting with Nixon he called Admiral Noel Gayler, the new commander of U.S. forces in the Pacific, and told him to begin preparations for B-52 attacks on Hanoi beginning about 7:00 P.M. Hanoi time on Sunday, December 17. Since the bombing campaign earlier in the year had been called Linebacker, this new campaign would be called Linebacker II. Moorer then called General J. C. Meyer at SAC and gave him the same message and told Meyer to send him a proposed list of North Vietnamese targets. The only restrictions were to "minimize the danger to civilian population to the extent feasible without compromising effectiveness" and to "avoid known POW compounds, hospitals, and religious structures." The Chiefs and Laird would approve targets from this SAC list and send them back to

SAC to form an "approved target list" that SAC could choose from. Then Moorer called a meeting of the Joint Chiefs of Staff and told them about Nixon's decision. The Chiefs voted secretly to officially note they were not recommending bombing Hanoi and declared the bombing a political, not a military, decision.

As the afternoon progressed, the Chiefs approved sending all available B-52s to Hanoi the first night, followed by slightly smaller B-52 attacks the second and third nights. Seventh Air Force's tactical forces would support the operations with chaff missions, electronic warfare and escort fighters, and during the day Seventh's fighter-bombers would attack Hanoi with their laser-guided bombs if the weather was good; in case of bad weather, they would attack area targets using an instrument bombing system, LORAN.

Immediately after General Meyer received Admiral Moorer's message, he and his staff made a critical decision. The most important part of these missions, the part into and out of Hanoi, would not be planned in the combat theater but at SAC Headquarters in Omaha. Passing the planning function down to a subordinate unit had never been the "SAC way," and Eighth Air Force on Guam would have little involvement in deciding how to conduct the operation.

The irony of the situation was lost on General Meyer and the members of the SAC staff. For years, the Air Force had been complaining about having its operations micromanaged from Washington instead of in the combat zone. Now a president had given the Air Force almost completely free rein in planning and executing its missions, and the Air Force simply substituted micromanagement from SAC Headquarters for micromanagement from Washington.

MAJOR ANDY BORDEN was about to leave his office at SAC Headquarters the evening of December 14 when his boss, Colonel Richard Peterson, Chief of the Weapons Effects Division, came in and told everyone to "hang around for a while." He then gathered them together and told them about the upcoming missions. Borden remembered: "We were 100 percent ready. ... I didn't have much doubt we could do what was expected of us. We did need to know

the predicted bombing accuracy for the targets, which we measured as CEP [circular area probable]. That would tell us how many
B-52s we would need to assign to each target. A CEP increase of 50
percent—for example, from 800 feet to 1200 feet—would reduce
bombing effectiveness by half, which meant twice as many bombers
would have to be sent to the target. We camped out at the door of
the Bomb/Nav people who figured that out until we got the CEP—
800 feet for all targets.

"Unfortunately, the Bomb/Nav people did not consider
whether the target was to be hit by direct radar return, which was
very accurate, or by using a radar offset, which was of variable accuracy depending on the offset type, what the threat was, etc. They
just gave us 800 feet. This turned out to be important later and really
affected the bombing results because the CEP was actually much
greater, about 1200 feet, and in the end the CEP was not even near
1200 feet for some targets."

The other issue the predicted accuracy affected was the selection of the targets. The 800-foot CEP meant targets closer to civilian neighborhoods could be attacked.

The SAC staff had just begun planning the missions when
they suddenly realized it was impossible to carry out the operation
on December 17 as the president had directed. The problem was
KC-135 tankers—there were simply not enough of them in the Pacific
area to refuel the planned B-52 strikes from Guam on the 17th.
SAC's leadership went into a mild state of panic that was alleviated only when, a few hours after his initial order was issued, Nixon
moved the operation back 24 hours to December 18. He did so
because Le Duc Tho, the chief North Vietnamese negotiator in Paris,
was concluding a visit to China on the 17th and Nixon did not want
to offend the Chinese. The president also apparently wanted to
avoid beginning the bombing on a Sunday. The SAC staff heaved
a huge sigh of relief and rushed 24 KC-135s to the Pacific, where
they arrived in time to support the operations.

As the planning progressed there remained one question that
everyone, including the president, wanted answered: "How many
B-52s might be lost in the operation?"

SAC had conducted a test of several possibilities for high-
altitude attacks against multiple SA-2 sites, and the tests had shown

that the B-52s could expect a 2 percent loss rate. But General Meyer chose to ignore these tests, and Brigadier General Harry Cordes, SAC's Chief of Intelligence, remembered: "General Meyer took ... model estimates, tempered them with his own judgment and that of his staff, and perhaps put some political English on the final estimates he passed out." The "political English" Meyer applied was to *overstate* the expected losses, saying that they would be 3 percent, creating an expectations game similar to those in a political campaign. If the operation was completed and the B-52s' losses were lower than predicted, SAC could take credit for planning and executing it efficiently. As it turned out, General Meyer's predicated 3 percent loss rate was to be far more useful to SAC than they could have possibly imagined.

ON THE AFTERNOON OF DECEMBER 15, General Gerald Johnson, the Eighth Air Force Commander at Andersen, was notified about the raids and told that the main part of the missions would be planned by SAC Headquarters rather than by his staff. Eighth would only be responsible for coordinating SAC's plan with the support forces and for planning the early parts of the mission. Johnson remembered, "By the time this got to me the decision ... had already been made. The [only] part I played was in terms of recommendations." He and his staff were surprised at SAC's decision, because they could clearly see numerous reasons why the missions should not be planned at SAC Headquarters. The most obvious reason was that the headquarters was halfway around the world from the combat zone. This meant *the SAC staff would have to complete their planning forty-two hours in advance of each mission* so Eighth Air Force could fold it into the overall plan and send it on to the other units participating in the operation. Just coding, transmitting and sending the plan from Omaha to Guam would take about ten hours of uninterrupted transmission over the few lines that were able to handle such highly classified information, lines that were never intended for such long, high-density communications. The distance would also exponentially increase coordination problems and mean there would be no feedback from the returning crews about enemy actions and about what changes should be made before the next missions were launched.

Additionally, the Eighth staff had been planning B-52 missions over Vietnam for years and had already developed a plan for attacks on the Hanoi area that they had forwarded to SAC in September. The SAC staff was accustomed to planning only single-ship, low-level and one-time nuclear missions against the Soviet Union and Communist China. They had never planned a complex, high-altitude strike with a large number of B-52s.

SAC Headquarters chose to disregard these potential problems. Many at SAC believed that this was their chance to show the fighter forces of Seventh Air Force who had ridiculed them and the rest of the military, especially the Navy, how to fight and win a war the SAC way.

Back in the White House President Nixon had received his first briefing on the strikes and learned that SAC would control the B-52s from Omaha instead of passing control to the combat theater. He had a sense of foreboding and remembered later, "I was appalled to find that the planes had to be borrowed from different commands, involving complicated logistics and large amounts of red tape."

ON DECEMBER 15, THE JOINT CHIEFS of Staff sent SAC a list of eight targets to be bombed the first night—the Kinh No vehicle repair facility, the Yen Vien railroad yard, the Hanoi railroad repair shop, the Hanoi International Radio station, and the MiG bases at Hoa Loc, Kep, Yen Bai and Phuc Yen. This selection showed a lack of understanding of the B-52s' capabilities and the North Vietnamese defenses. B-52s were a broadsword, not an épée, and were best suited for large "area" targets such as storage areas and railroad yards because the bombing patterns spread a large number of bombs over a fairly large oval-shaped area about a mile long and half a mile wide. Even though the target area might be saturated with bombs, hitting a small, precise target, known as a "point" target, was a matter of luck.

The Hanoi International Radio Station was a perfect example. The station's propaganda broadcasts had been a longtime irritant to both the Americans and South Vietnamese, and the White House insisted that it be on the target list, but the station was a singularly poor target for B-52s. It was housed in a very small building surrounded by thick walls where only a lucky direct hit would take it out, and it was also located in the most heavily defended area of the city. But the White House was adamant, and the radio station went to the head of the target queue instead of more militarily significant targets better suited for B-52 attack.

The MiG airfields were also "point" targets and, more importantly, unnecessary ones. Everyone in the combat theater knew that SA-2 missiles would be the greatest threat to the B-52s at night, but MiG airfields were targeted while the SAM threat was ignored. No SAM sites were on the target list, and more critically neither were the North Vietnamese SAM storage facilities. The SAM battalions kept only twelve missiles at the site; once they were fired, more had to be trucked in from the large warehouse complexes that assembled the missiles from their shipping canisters. These warehouse facilities were the key to the North Vietnamese defenses, and the fragile buildings loaded with highly volatile missile fuel tanks and the production lines where the missiles were assembled were wonderful B-52 targets, but they were left off the target list entirely.

There was also no difference between the targets allotted to the B-52D and G models. The D models, with their heavier bomb loads, should have been sent against the large, important targets on the list, but instead they were often shunted off to bomb airfields and other minor targets while the G models, carrying a quarter of the bombs, were sent against major targets. It took many more G sorties to knock out a target, and the more sorties and the more aircraft that were exposed to the defenses, the greater the chances of a loss.

WHILE THE SAC LEADERSHIP made some crucial errors, so did the North Vietnamese General Staff. As early as December 15 the General Staff had begun to get intelligence clues that there might be something in the wind. The General Staff did cancel the orders sending the 261st SAM Regiment to the south, but that was the only action they took. They again declined to bring the 267th SAM Regiment from the south to reinforce the capital, and also did not cancel the leaves of the 261st's crews, including the regiment's commander, who were visiting their families.

At the same time, the North Vietnamese leaders were actively engaged in their propaganda war. On December 16, four American

anti-war activists—the popular folk singer Joan Baez; Telford Taylor, a retired U.S. Army brigadier general and Columbia University
professor; Michael Allen, assistant dean of Yale Divinity School; and
an ex–U.S. Army lieutenant, Barry Romo, from Vietnam Veterans
Against the War—flew from Vientiane, Laos, to Hanoi's international
airport at Gia Lam, across the river from the capital. The four were
ostensibly there to bring mail and presents to American POWs, but
for the North Vietnamese it was one more propaganda opportunity
to play to the American anti-war movement and to increase pressure
on the administration in the next few critical weeks.

AT TWO O'CLOCK ON THE AFTERNOON of December 16 there was a
briefing for all the Andersen commanders to give them a general
outline of the mission and to tell them to make sure their crews
were available, but not to give any details. All the B-52 aircraft commanders were to meet on the 17th at five o'clock in the afternoon.

Later that day it was announced that all the U.S. air bases in
Southeast Asia would stand down the next day, December 17. When
the Andersen crews heard about the standdown they began to pay
attention to the large number of KC-135s taking off and landing. A
hopeful rumor began to spread that the B-52s were being prepared
for a mass return to the U.S. and that the KC-135s were to refuel
them and take the maintenance personnel home. For a few of the
crewmembers, this raised a pragmatic concern. The Andersen leadership had instituted a program for crewmembers who wanted to
bring their families to the island for Christmas. Those who brought
their families over could fly extra missions before and after the holidays, and take "comp time" in the form of two weeks leave during the holidays while others volunteered to fly in their place. Now
some who had brought—or were bringing—their families were
beginning to wonder it they had wasted their money.

At the same time, all rotations were stopped from both Guam
and U-Tapao. At Andersen, Captain Robert Certain, the navigator
on Lt. Col. Don Rissi's crew from Blytheville AFB, Arkansas, was
scheduled to rotate back to the U.S. on December 18. He remembers the crew took the news "pretty hard" because two earlier
planned departures had already been scrubbed. Certain had been
married for only six weeks when he left on Bullet Shot and was

anxious to return for the holidays, but he hoped the sudden change in schedule meant that the war was almost over and they would be sent back to the States for good.

Captain Steve Brown, a B-52 copilot from Beale AFB in California, had spent the early morning hours of the 16th sitting in the right seat of a B-52 acting as a "manned spare" for any aircraft that aborted for a routine Arc Light mission to South Vietnam. The spare had not been needed, and according to the flying schedule Brown and his crew now had two days off, so he grabbed his snorkeling gear and headed to the remote south end of Guam where he planned on staying on the beach for the next two days.

Brown's next-door neighbor at Beale, aircraft commander Terry Geloneck, and his crew had heard about the stand-down that afternoon. Geloneck's wife, Jane, was pregnant, and he remembered "hoping that the war was finally over, and that we would be spending Christmas with our families.... My crew and I discussed how great it would be to fly a B-52 back home."

Craig Mizner's navigator, Bill Beavers, noted in his diary: "ALL crews are 'restricted to base.' Something BIG is up. Are we going North? North to Bullseye [universal code name for Hanoi]? Has Kissinger succeeded in a 'peace?' Are we going home? Many, many rumors but no word."

Brent Diefenbach, a former forward air controller and now back on Bullet Shot as a B-52D aircraft commander, heard about the aircraft commanders' meeting and thought to himself, "We're going to do something at low level."

Later that afternoon, Bob Certain and the rest of his crew took a crew truck to the Andersen flight line: "What we saw dashed all hope for the end of the war. All aircraft were being refueled and loaded with bombs. Some enormously important and dangerous mission was clearly in the works. We suspected that we were going 'downtown' to Hanoi. When we returned to quarters, I called the scheduling officer and reminded him that we had flown 13 missions in the previous 25 days and that our crew had been scheduled to return home on Monday. I said 'I don't know what's going on Monday, but I would appreciate it if you would make us a spare.' "

At the Andersen Officers' Club that night, the standdown and the aircraft commanders meeting the next day were the central topics of conversation. As rumors flew, most of the crews speculated—wishfully—that a peace agreement would be completed before Christmas, and many continued to fixate on Kissinger's October "peace is at hand" statement. But a few had heard rumors from the commanders' meeting earlier that afternoon and thought that, whatever they were going to be doing, they were not going home.

AT U-TAPAO GENERAL GLENN SULLIVAN was returning from Hong Kong with his wife, Nadine, and Colonel Don Davis was the acting commander. When Davis and his deputy, Colonel Bill Brown, were notified of the operation they immediately tried to contact Sullivan and began to organize the missions. Then, suddenly, they got a call from Colonel Bill Maxson, who had arrived at U-Tapao two days earlier to take command of the 340th Consolidated Maintenance Wing. Maxson told them that something was happening that threatened the entire operation.

"A young black airman was dragged from his dormitory by the Security Police and put in the brig," Maxson recalled. "Whatever his offenses were, the way it was handled by the Security Police set off a racial reaction that culminated in a gathering of hundreds of black airmen at the baseball diamond that evening at dusk. Though I didn't know it at the time, racial tensions had been building among the enlisted ranks, but because everyone was so occupied with launching and recovering aircraft the situation was left to fester."

Most of the airmen on the baseball diamond were bomb loaders, absolutely critical to what was to come, and some were armed with sticks and chains. It was clearly a volatile situation that was about to go out of control. Colonels Brown and Davis were the only two officers at U-Tapao who knew about the upcoming raids, but since Davis, as the acting Wing Commander, had been peripherally involved in the incident the solution was left in the hands of Brown and Maxson. The two of them, alone and in uniform, went to the diamond and waded into the agitated crowd to try to find the leaders and calm the situation.

Maxson continues: "A shouting match followed between several factions, but I was able to identify some voices of reason and I was able to convince those present that as their new Commander

I would form a Human Relations Council immediately to listen to their grievances. Thank heavens, the crowd dispersed and order was restored. If this situation had worsened, there is no telling the adverse impact it could have had on Linebacker II, now only 48 hours away."

BACK IN OMAHA, the SAC Operations staff was paying a price for its failure to take the possibility of raids against Hanoi seriously. Pressed for time, the staff made a critical decision: *mid-air collisions would be more dangerous to the B-52s than the North Vietnamese defenses.* The best way to avoid collisions, they decided, was to send the bombers to Hanoi in a single file, one cell behind the other, all flying basically the same route to the target area.

Ironically, the plan was exactly the opposite of SAC's nuclear attack plans. From 1958 to 1962, SAC had flown large, simulated raids of as many as seventy-five bombers at the same time against the North American Radar Air Defense System [NORAD] to see how it responded to a mass attack like the Soviets might mount. It was also a chance for SAC to test its tactics against a sophisticated national radar system, and one of the most important things SAC learned was the need to vary timing and routes when going against a radar-defended target. After the exercises, SAC developed a very intricate system to increase the survivability of their attacking bombers in case of a nuclear war. The bombers would fly crossing flight paths and come to their targets from different directions, called "Basketweave" flight paths, to disrupt the air defense system. But the SAC Operations staff had never made a plan to attack Hanoi from different headings. (In September 1972, Eighth Air Force had submitted a plan to attack Hanoi using principles very similar to the "Basketweave" techniques, but SAC Operations staff apparently ignored it.)

Additionally, because of the short time before the missions would have to be launched, the Operations staff decided they had to send the B-52s to Hanoi using the same procedures—formations, altitudes, airspeeds and jamming techniques—they had been using since 1967, procedures that the North Vietnamese were very familiar with.

According to the plan, the B-52s would fly through Laos north towards the Chinese border, turn east into North Vietnam, then

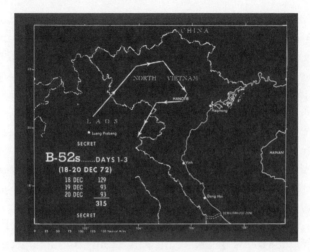

U.S. routes, December 18–21: The stereotyped entry and exit routes used by B-52s on Nights One though Three. The North Vietnamese took advantage of the repetitive routes and post-target turn to devastate the force the night of December 20–21.

southeast down the Tam Dao mountain range, known to U.S. pilots as "Thud Ridge," to Hanoi. The southeast run-in would give the B-52s a 100-knot jet stream tailwind blowing from the northwest and would move them over the heavily defended target area quickly. After dropping their bombs, the B-52s would make their steep-banked post-target turn to the right and exit to the west towards Laos.

There were more than 200 B-52s available for the operation, and about two-thirds of them would be sent on the first night's missions. The 129 bombers would attack Hanoi in three waves, the first raid of 48 arriving just after dark, the second raid of 30 aircraft striking at midnight, and a third raid of 51 attacking at four in the morning. Splitting the force into three parts would, the SAC staff reasoned, keep Hanoi's citizens up all night.

SOON THE FIRST SPECIFIC MESSAGES about the raids began to be sent from Omaha to Eighth Air Force at Andersen, where the staff waited anxiously for the information so they could make up mission folders for the crews, coordinate the raid with the tankers and the Seventh Air Force support package, establish communications procedures, and perform a myriad of other tasks necessary for a large-scale raid against very heavy defenses. From the time the Eighth staff heard that the missions would be planned in Omaha, they had been concerned about getting the planning materials from SAC in time to completely plan the missions. As the SAC's first messages came in, the signs were not good. These first messages were so highly classified that the normal mission-planning staff did not have a high enough security clearance to even see them, and the mission planning was delayed until frantic phone calls made SAC repeat the messages with a lower security classification.

Once they began to read the messages, the Eighth staff quickly saw the SAC plan contained the seeds of disaster. The single file of B-52s would allow the North Vietnamese to easily track one cell after the other and engage them one at a time. The 100-knot jet stream wind would move the B-52s through the target area quickly, but it also would give the radar navigators less time to get lined up on their targets. But the major problem was that, after bomb release, the SAC plan called for the B-52s to make their post-target turn west, back *into* the jet stream wind, a wind that would slow the bombers dramatically over the heaviest part of the NVN defenses.

The Eighth staff also saw a serious problem with the decision to attack in three raids with four hours between each raid. It might minimize the risk of collisions but splitting the bombers into three raids would prevent the B-52s from overwhelming the North Vietnamese defenses. With a four-hour break between each of the raids, the SA-2 crews would have a chance to engage the first raid, resupply their launchers and engage the second raid fully armed, then resupply their missile sites again for the third raid.

Splitting the B-52s into three waves would also dilute the Seventh Air Force tactical support force. Most of the Wild Weasels and other support aircraft could only stay close to the target for a short period—no more than an hour—and three waves of B-52s with four hours between them meant that support aircraft would have to be split into three small groups. Because of this, the support package for each raid would be *smaller* than the support force the B-52s had received going to much less heavily defended areas the month before.

The reduced support force would have the greatest impact on the chaff corridor. There were only about 24 chaff-dropping F-4s available, so splitting them into three groups meant that each of the three B-52 raids would get only about 8 chaffers. The result would be that the B-52s would get only two thin corridors of chaff, one into and one out of the area, and the corridors would probably be so narrow that the U.S. bombers' best countermeasure against the North Vietnamese missiles would not be effective.

But the Eighth Air Force staff had little time to reflect on this as it focused on the task at hand, taking the information provided by SAC and converting it into a useful plan to send to the combat wings. The information from SAC was coming in slowly, and adding to the problem was that as soon as a part of the plan arrived SAC would follow with changes. Most were minor ones such as changes of a few minutes in a time over target (TOT), a slight change in the number of aircraft assigned to a target, or the change of a few degrees in a heading. But even minor changes had to be checked and inserted into the plan, tracking changes made, and the entire plan checked again. Additionally, there were mistakes in the details that Eighth could not correct—every mistake had to be sent back and corrected in Omaha and the Eighth planners had to wait for new information so they could start again. To compound the difficulties, the communications links were becoming more and more congested as the beginning of the operation approached, and each message was taking longer to send and each answer taking longer to receive. The planning process was slipping further and further behind.

Major Andy Borden at SAC Headquarters tried to speed things along, but found that this often ran into bureaucratic turf wars at SAC and Andersen. As Borden remembered, "I worked for the Director of Intelligence at SAC and when we got a target change my boss told me to send our Intelligence counterparts on Guam a FLASH message with the changes so they could take it to the target planners on the Eighth Air Force Operations staff to get started on the mission planning. The problem was there was a rivalry between Intelligence and Operations, and the Eighth Air Force Operations guys on Guam complained to the Operations guys here at SAC that we were sending the information to the Intelligence shop, even though they got it faster. I got caught in the middle and got in a lot of trouble."

There was another, unasked question as the preparations continued. How would the B-52 crews react to missions that bring significant losses? Could they be counted on to fly such missions in an unpopular war, to face being killed or taken prisoner for an indefinite time? Would they persevere in the face of heavy defenses? How solid would their resolve be in the face of losses, perhaps severe losses, when few of the crewmembers had ever experienced losses before?

ON THE MORNING OF DECEMBER 17 (early in the morning of the 18th at Andersen), the Joint Chiefs of Staff sent the final attack message:

"You are directed to commence at approximately 1200Z, 18 December 1972, a three day maximum effort, repeat, maximum effort, of B-52/TACAIR strikes in the Hanoi/Haiphong area. ... Objective is maximum destruction of selected targets in the vicinity of Hanoi/Haiphong. Be prepared to extend beyond three days, if necessary."

At five o'clock in the afternoon of December 17, the briefing for all the Andersen B-52 aircraft commanders began at the Arc Light Center. Bill Buckley's aircraft commander, Lt. Col. Don Rissi, and another aircraft commander, Captain Steve Smith, went to Mass off base and had not gotten back in time for the meeting. Buckley and Smith's copilot, Bobby Thomas (one of the few African-American B-52 crewmembers), decided to stand in for their aircraft commanders. Buckley remembered, "We were challenged when we arrived but finally they reluctantly let us stay. Of course this was the briefing where it was all presented—we were going to strike Hanoi in a series of unprecedented massive bombing raids."

The aircraft commanders were given a general overview of the missions scheduled for the next night, told to make sure their crews were available, but cautioned not to tell their crews any specifics. The aircraft commanders left the briefing sobered, and began—frantically, in some cases—to try to locate their crews. As Buckley and Thomas were leaving, their squadron commander, Lt. Col. Al Dugard, stopped them and asked Buckley what he was doing there—Dugard thought Buckley's crew had rotated out on Friday. Buckley explained. "Then Lt. Col. Dugard told me he wanted me to fly on the lead B-52G because that copilot had to go on emergency leave, then he turned to Bobby Thomas and said he wanted him to fly with my crew. We said 'OK, sounds good to us.' Little did we know what this decision would mean later."

That night, at Andersen's Top Three Club where the senior non-commissioned officers ate, the Security Police came in and announced, "All gunners stop drinking, go to quarters and stay there until further notice." Jim Short, the gunner on Major David O'Neil's crew, remembered, "I was hyped up. I figured we weren't going to bomb another cabbage patch or a swaying bamboo bridge."

When the flight schedules were published at Andersen late that evening many of the crews got the first real inkling of what was coming. There was a briefing for more than thirty crews the next morning at 10:00 A.M. and two more large briefings at 2:00 and 6:00 in the afternoon. Bob Certain and his crew were scheduled for the 10:00 A.M. briefing of the first raid.

ON DECEMBER 18, ADMIRAL MOORER explained what was at stake in a message to Admiral Gayler, Commander in Chief, Pacific (CINC-PAC): "Linebacker II offers the last opportunity in Southeast Asia for USAF and USN to clearly demonstrate the full professionalism, skill and cooperation so necessary to achieve the required success in the forthcoming strikes in NVN [North Vietnam]. . . . You will be watched on a real-time basis at the highest levels here in Washington. We are counting on all hands to put forth a maximum, repeat maximum, effort in the conduct of this crucial operation."

LATE ON THE AFTERNOON OF DECEMBER 17 the details of the Day Two (December 19–20) missions began to arrive at Eighth Air Force from SAC. The staff saw that the second day's missions were using the same headings, times, and targets as the first day's missions. An Eighth Air Force staff officer remembered, "We were coming in the same way the second day as we had the first day, like targets in a shooting gallery. I knew then our losses were going to be a lot more than 3 percent."

FIVE

"Downtown, where all the lights are bright . . ."

The morning of December 18 was superficially quiet at Andersen, but at Eighth Air Force Headquarters the activity was frenetic as the staff prepared for the 10:00 A.M. crew briefing. SAC had continued to send a steady stream of changes to the missions, and at 9:30, just a half-hour before the first large briefing, another set of changes arrived and the briefing had to be delayed for an hour, until 11:00 A.M., while the changes were made.

At U-Tapao, Colonels Don Davis and Bill Brown, having avoided the potentially devastating race riot, discussed the upcoming raids. Brown, familiar with the psychology of heavy combat from his F-105 experiences over Hanoi, believed strongly that a senior officer should fly in the lead B-52 at the head of each wave to help steady the crews. But this officer would have to fly as an extra crewmember and sit in a fixed "jump seat" behind the pilots, not in an ejection seat. If the aircraft was hit and the crew had to bail out, he would have to walk downstairs and jump out through an open hatch after the navigator and radar navigator ejected. It was a time-consuming process, and if the aircraft were seriously damaged an extra crewmember would almost certainly go down with it. Still, Brown thought it was worth the risk and Davis agreed. Since General Sullivan had still not returned from leave, they called General Johnson at Eighth Air Force with the proposal. Johnson initially rejected the idea, but after Brown's third call he reconsidered and gave approval. Brown promptly made himself the leader for the first wave of the first raid.

Major Bruce Smith was a U-Tapao B-52 scheduler who had been called back from a conference on Guam when the raids were announced, and when he arrived at the U-Tapao bomber scheduling office he found his colleagues building the missions for Hanoi. Smith was an experienced Arc Light veteran and remembers thinking, "Great, we're finally going to plan something we should have done a long time ago. Then I was told, 'well, not really, actually the routes and mission planning are being done at Omaha.' Nobody at Guam or U-Tapao, especially the grunt people who had been doing this kind of planning every day, was going to be involved in the real planning.

"Then, when we got the routes, times, and altitudes and we started looking at the mission profile, we saw there was a real problem. SAC had assigned our aircraft altitudes that were too high for the aircrafts' weight. Even if they could even get to the altitude, the bombers were going to be close to stall speed as they turned south on the bomb runs. Anyone that had a bad engine couldn't catch up, and the bombers would have huge problems keeping in formation and getting their speed stabilized [a requirement for accurate bombing]. We were also concerned that the crews couldn't make any sort of evasive maneuvers because they would be so slow they would be wallowing around."

Smith brought the problem to Colonel Bill Brown. "After checking our numbers about a dozen times (nobody wanted to tell SAC they had made a dumb mistake) he went to General Sullivan, who had just gotten back from leave. Sullivan came to our office to use the 'Red Phone' and called SAC using 'FLASH OVERRIDE,' normally used only for a nuclear war. He talked to them about the problem, but nothing changed."

THE B-52 CREWS WERE USED to small missions of three or six aircraft, and the one thing that all the crewmembers remember about the first briefings was that people were wedged into every cranny in the briefing rooms. At Andersen the delay in the briefing time made the crews even more tense, but finally, at eleven o'clock in the morning, the 43rd Strategic Wing commander, Colonel James R. McCarthy, began what several crew members described as a "Twelve O'Clock High" briefing, starting with the words, "Gentlemen, the target for tonight!" as the curtains rolled back showing a bullseye on Hanoi.

As the consequences of what they were hearing began to sink in, many of the crewmembers paid little attention to the targets. They could not get past the idea that they were going to Hanoi.

"All you knew was that you were going 'downtown'" remembered Captain John Allen, "and that you might not be coming home ... all you were thinking about was, were you going to make it back or were you not ... and what about the guy sitting next to you."

Copilot Jim Farmer, who had not been enthusiastic about the earlier "press on" missions, was excited. "By God, this was a mission worth hanging your ass out for, finally!"

Bob Certain remembered: "The emotions I felt were enormous and varied—fear, anger, depression and elation. Fear of the probable danger of a B-52 strike over the capital of North Vietnam, anger because we were flying the mission on this, our scheduled day of return, depression over yet another extension to the separation from our families, elation at finally being able to be a part of an effort to force the government of North Vietnam to sign a treaty and release the POWs."

As the briefing progressed and the crews saw the route to the target, they began to become even more concerned. Steve Brown, who had barely made it back from his snorkeling trip in time for the briefing, thought that the route of B-52s looked like "a line of ants going to a picnic." He also remembered that he was most concerned about the possibility of becoming a POW: "If I was hit, I didn't want to be captured. I just wanted to be vaporized."

Jim "Bones" Scheideman, a D model aircraft commander, was not impressed with the plan. "It was clear before we ever took off that the tactics were really dumb; everyone coming in from the same direction, same altitude, and same exit routes. It was so much like the image of the British in the Revolutionary War, all lined up marching in straight rows making easy targets, that it was bizarre."

The tension increased when Colonel McCarthy, who was not flying that night, told the crews that they could not maneuver on the bomb run—they would have to fly straight and level for four minutes prior to target. The crews were stunned, because maneuvering until just prior to bomb release had been approved by SAC Headquarters the entire time they had been flying into SAM areas. They were convinced that this was a mistake. Many crews were sure that the instructions not to maneuver were simply mindless adherence to SAC directives rather that being based on knowledge, and they were right. No tests had been conducted on B-52 cell jamming and tactics against the Fan Song radar or the SA-2 missile, and SAC did not know what was effective.

It was not only the crews that were surprised. Some of the experienced B-52 staff, especially at U-Tapao, agreed. One frustrated commander commented: "One thing that was—'discouraging'—was that we couldn't do evasive action coming in to the target. We'd done this for years, and the crews were quite proficient at it, but somebody got this idea, and somebody dictated that there would be no maneuvering until bombs away. The bombing system on a B-52 is good. If the radar navigator is on the offsets and the pilot has the PDI [pilot direction indicator, a needle which the pilot followed to keep on course to bomb] centered, it doesn't make any difference what you do before you get to target, the bombs will hit."

After the general briefings were over, the crewmembers went to their specialized briefings, and the tension increased even more. The crews noted that the staff seemed to be under huge pressure, and the strain was especially obvious with the target study officers, who had to give the radar navigators the descriptions of the radar offset aim points around Hanoi where they had to place the crosshairs for accurate bomb delivery. Now, preparing to go on the most difficult and important mission of their lives, many of the radar navigators were told that there would be no target study because the target folders had not been completed. The target folders would be delivered to the aircraft just before takeoff, and the crews would have to study them on the way to the Hanoi. Only later did the crews learn that the reason for the delay was that the staff was dealing with a continuous barrage of changes to the bombing plan.

BRENT DIEFENBACH WAS NERVOUS after the pilots' briefing, so he did something seemingly incongruous—he sat down and began to shine his shoes. When his radar navigator came in a few minutes later and asked him what he was doing, Diefenbach looked up and said, "Well, you only get one chance to make a first impression."

Copilot Bill Buckley stuffed eleven sets of batteries for his survival radio into his flight suit. "I wanted to be able to talk forever. I also carried a small Bible given to me by my best friend from high school."

Bud Hughes, the former EB-66 electronic warfare officer now part of Craig Mizner's crew, noted a major change in the attitude of the rest of his crew towards him. "We were going downtown. The big Kahuna. To SAC crews, this was VERY frightening because they never thought they would fly real combat missions. So here was a real combat mission staring them in the face. Actual combat that could—would—get people killed. The crew treated me totally differently after the mission briefing that night. All of a sudden, I wasn't the secretary any more, but the guy who could make 55 square meters of aluminum disappear, thereby saving our collective butts. I was now an integral part of the crew."

AT 10:15 IN THE MORNING of December 18 a U.S. reconnaissance drone flew over Hanoi, and thirty minutes later another reconnaissance drone flew over Haiphong. North Vietnamese intelligence began to intercept messages from U.S. Navy ships, and at noon two American RF-4s flew over Hanoi and reported the weather. This was the first time an American tactical aircraft had flown over Hanoi since the October bombing halt, and it was enough for the North Vietnamese Commander of Air Defense, Le Van Tri. He immediately called in all of his commanders to tell them about these events and to prepare for an attack. Now a frantic effort began to try to bring back the members of the 261st Regiment, including the regimental commander, Tranh Huu Tao. They were on leave all over North Vietnam, some in villages where there were no telephones, and staff cars raced off to try to find them and bring them back to their units.

At 4:30 that afternoon, the General Staff received a message that "many squadrons of B-52 planes have taken off from Andersen Airport." Hanoi's air defenses went on alert at 5:00 P.M. and the Air Defense Headquarters emptied as virtually all the staff headed out to inspect the various units and make sure they were ready for combat. Six MiG-21s were put on seven-minute alert, two each at the bases of Phuc Yen, Kep and Hoa Loc.

Meanwhile, Joan Baez and her three companions were being given the full treatment by their North Vietnamese hosts. Baez remembered being disgusted and bored with the war memorials and pictures of casualties, but noted that "most of the details were directed at Telford [Taylor], who was there to determine whether or not war crimes had been committed. ... Telford was probably the most important member of our group as far as credibility at home was concerned."

MANY OF THE ANDERSEN CREWS arrived at their aircraft in a somber mood, but the maintenance personnel gathered at the B-52s buoyed their spirits. They were clearly proud to be a part of the operation and determined that their aircraft would make it. Soon the huge bombers started their engines and the crewmembers ran through their equipment checklists while the Eighth Air Force staff finished reproducing the target information, packed it into large, bulky brief-cases which were then put into jeeps and rushed out to the flight line and passed into open hatches of the B-52s. One frustrated com-mander said later, "This was the first chance the crews had to study the classified target information. This was a severe handicap to the crews because these missions were the most complex plan to date and tolerances were extremely critical."

Climbing into the very rear of the B-52Ds were the tail gun-ners, the only enlisted men on the crews and the last of a breed that went back to World War I and the gunners' glory days of World War II. In contrast with the G model gunners who sat in the front com-partment with the rest of the crew, the D model gunners sat under a glass canopy in the extreme tail of the aircraft where they had a magnificent view of the entire operation. The gunners performed a variety of functions that went beyond protecting the tail of the bombers with their four .50-caliber machine guns. Their turret had a short-range radar, and if another B-52 lost its bombing radar the gunner in the aircraft in front of him could guide him to drop his bombs. D model gunners could also see SAMs approaching from the blind spot in the rear of the aircraft, but one remembered, "We worked backwards—our left was the pilots' right, so when a mis-sile was just a few seconds away from hitting and the gunner yelled 'BREAK RIGHT,' that damn well better mean break to the gunner's left." The D model gunners could also see the engines and the trail-ing edge of the wings that the pilots could not, and when the aircraft received battle damage the gunners' observations were often critical in deciding how long to stay with the aircraft.

By 2:00 in the afternoon, as the engines began to start, word had spread around Andersen about the missions. Most of the people on the base had never seen a mass launch of B-52s, and any place where there was a view of the runway, especially the tops of buildings, was jammed with people. The base housing was on one side of the raised runway and the B-52 revetments on the other side, so even from the rooftops only the tail fins of the aircraft could be seen. Soon the fins—the high-pointed fins of the D models and the chopped ones of the G models—began to move, and the slow, steady movement looked like a stately line of sharks as they moved toward the runway. In the radio headsets of the crewmembers came the sound of music—Henry Mancini's "Baby Elephant Walk."

Overseeing the engine start, taxiing and takeoffs from a special tower was "Charlie," the call sign given to a highly qualified B-52 instructor pilot chosen for his knowledge of aircraft systems, his decision-making ability, and his coolness under pressure. Once the aircrews were at their aircraft, Charlie made all decisions. When an aircraft had a problem it was Charlie who decided what to do— take the aircraft "as is," abort it and replace it with a manned spare, or perform a "bag drag" where the crew took all of their flight bags, left the aircraft, and moved to another one to keep their place in the mission. One of these Charlies was Colonel Bob Hruby, a highly experienced B-52 pilot, Arc Light veteran and former B-52 operations officer at March Air Force Base with many friends in the crew force. Hruby had been originally scheduled to be an airborne wave leader but was pulled out to fill one of the critical Charlie slots. Hruby was well known and respected by the crews, and he would often come by the Officers' Club to pick up crewmembers and take them home where his wife Pat would cook dinner for them.

Bill Beavers, Craig Mizner's navigator, remembered Hruby as a Charlie. "He was a guy that knew his 'shit' and the BUFF quite well and spoke on the radio with a calming, peaceful but plainly urgent and respectful tone. Everyone I knew really liked and appreciated him in Charlie Tower. He just gave one the confident feeling that 'You're in Good Hands' when he spoke—when he spoke ANYTIME."

AT 2:41 IN THE AFTERNOON, the first of the 28 B-52s rolled out on the runway to begin its takeoff, accompanied by cheers from the watching crowd, looking like "a solid wall of dark flies on the walls and balconies," as one onlooker remembered. Craig Mizner, whose crew was scheduled to fly the next afternoon, looked at the people watching and cheering from every vantage point and was reminded of newsreels he had seen from World War II of Japanese carrier crews cheering as their aircraft took off to attack Pearl Harbor.

A B-52 takeoff from Andersen was always a spectacle. It began with the roar of the eight engines and thick black smoke from the water injection system as the bomber began to roll. Because Andersen's runway had a large dip in the middle, each bomber accelerated rapidly at first then, as it reached the middle of the runway and began the climb up the other side of the dip, it seemed to slow. The end of the runway had a slight dip down and a few hundred feet later was a steep cliff, and the combination of the two made the B-52 drop out of the sight of the onlookers before it climbed back into view, accompanied by an almost audible sigh of relief.

The takeoffs were especially "exciting" for the navigator and radar navigator, who sat in a windowless compartment below the pilots and who had *downward*-firing ejection seats. The two had a ground speed indicator in their position and one navigator described takeoffs from Andersen from his compartment. "On takeoff roll, acceleration was comparatively pretty quick as we went downhill, but after the dip we were rolling uphill. Many times we saw 70 knots and accelerating going downhill at the beginning and then 70 knots and DECELERATING going uphill. At the end of the runway when the pilot called 'over the cliff,' it meant we had enough airspace below us to eject."

The B-52s took off at ninety-second intervals, so it was almost forty-five minutes until the last of the bombers lifted off, leaving a cloud of black smoke that lingered for hours after they had vanished. The line of B-52s stretched for almost seventy miles as the bombers slowly formed up into their three-ship cells and began the journey to Hanoi, almost three thousand miles and eight hours away—a long time for the crews to think about what awaited them. Below them an omnipresent Soviet "trawler" at the end of the runway had noted their departure and soon the information was on its way to Hanoi, where it arrived about two hours later.

Bob Certain and his crew had some disconcerting moments during this time. "We were scheduled to fly as Charcoal 03, the fifteenth G-model in a train of 18 behind 9 D models. We were notified that one of the aircraft ahead of us had been taken out of line because of an equipment malfunction, and we would move up to Charcoal 02, the fourteenth aircraft in the queue. Tensions were rising even further. I checked the flight plans in my bag and discovered that instead of having the plans for our cell and the two cells ahead of us, we actually had the plans for the two cells behind us. We wouldn't be able to move to a cell in front of us if there were more aborts—more indications that the planning of the mission was not up to the mark."

As Certain's aircraft began to roll, the B-52 in front of them aborted and Certain's aircraft moved up to become Charcoal 01.

Steve Brown remembered the beginning of the mission as being "all screwed up, but once we got airborne and the crews took over, it was all right. We could cut it, but it was still confusing. So many people had changed position that there was a lot of 'Who are you?' When the answer came back someone else would say, 'No, you can't be that, I'm that.' It finally sorted itself out, but not until we were over Laos."

As Brown's wave of B-52s approached their refueling point, he looked out of the right window of his B-52G and saw a glowing object with a heavy contrail racing across the sky at very high altitude heading for Hanoi. Brown had seen the contrails of SR-71s before, but this one was much higher and going much faster, and the exhaust was orange, not blue like a SR-71. He wondered what it was, and then decided it was something new. We're really pulling out all the stops, he thought.

The Andersen bombers proceeded to the refueling area, then after refueling dropped off the tankers and began to head for Vietnam. They were scheduled to cross South Vietnam and fly into Laos, where they would turn north and fly until they approached the Chinese border, then turn east over the northern part of North Vietnam and finally southeast to Hanoi.

THE PRE-STRIKE ATMOSPHERE at U-Tapao had been somewhat different from Andersen. The cancellation of the missions on the 17th did not cause any undue alarm because the UT crews were used to standdowns for a day followed by a surge of sorties in a short period of time, and there was no noticeable flurry of staff activity as there had been at Andersen with Eighth Air Force.

Because U-Tapao was so close to Hanoi when the crews went into the briefing room, the Andersen B-52s were already hanging on their tankers being refueled. Colonel Bill Brown, the 307th Deputy Commander and the Airborne Commander for the first wave, started the briefing. Later he described the crews' reactions when he announced the target and the crews saw the lines on the map leading to Hanoi: "I could see the different emotions on the various crewmembers' faces. A lot of them almost cheered, and a murmur of 'it's about time' went across the room."

Major John Dalton, the aircraft commander who was leading the raid, remembered he was "scared to death" when he saw the lines to Hanoi on the map, while Captain E. A. Petersen said, "It was just kind of amazing we were going to do it. . . . I almost thought it was a joke at first."

Aircraft commander Glenn Russell said, "My crew was pretty charged up to go. I think most of us had the attitude that we just wanted to get the POWs released and then go home. My main complaint was with the planners. . . . We were all going on the same track, no maneuvering, opening the bomb doors sixty seconds prior to release, and making the same turn off the target. . . . I felt these were dangerous tactics going into such a heavily defended area."

Aircraft commander John Yuill remembered: "Usually the poor briefing officer had a problem keeping us quiet long enough for him to get through the briefing. On the night of the 18th we had a theater full of crews and the guy could have briefed in a whisper, it was so quiet. I remember looking around and thinking that this was what it was like for those guys flying out of England in B-17s in 1943, and I also thought that some of us in that room would probably be dead in a couple of hours. I think we were pleased that the decision had been made to send us downtown and finish the job. I did feel some of the tactics were wrong, i.e. common turn points before the target, breakaway turns into numerous SAM sites, opening the bomb doors one minute prior to bomb release."

Dwight Moore, an aircraft commander from Carswell, remembered being in a state of disbelief. "You could have heard a pin drop. Our target was Radio Hanoi. You get those stray thoughts—why a radio station? Then kind of a sinking feeling in your stomach with an 'Oooooh, Shit!' thought. My crew just sort of looked at each other. I sat there in a little bit of shock taking notes so I didn't miss anything important, but a bit numb and not really registering a lot. The map of the Hanoi area on a poster board in front of the briefing room showing the known active SAM sites—50 plus dots (it looked like it had measles) with the flight path line going right down the middle of all of them, then turning right about 150 degrees and coming back out through the dots. That didn't look good. The weather guy was talking about turning into a headwind for the outbound leg from the target and that didn't sound good either. The Wing staff made sure we knew it was a 'press on' mission, that we understood we needed to keep good cell formation for mutual jamming, and to be careful where we dropped because of the POW camps."

The staff at U-Tapao was as concerned as the crews about the tactics, and General Glenn Sullivan wrote a friend later: "A common bomber stream track was used for all sorties. All aircraft entered the target area on the same track and departed on the same track and no evasive action was to be taken on the bomb run. What a bunch of horse shit, huh? But the post-target turn was the murder point. Jamming effectiveness was reduced to nil and the radar surface quadrupled because of the flat surface the aircraft gave to the SAM radar in the turn."

This was the same post-target turn problem Eighth Air Force had identified to SAC in April and SAC had refused to change.

THE FIGHTER BASES ACROSS THAILAND were also beginning to find out about the missions. At Ubon, the home of the F-4s that would lay the chaff corridor before the B-52s arrived, Joe "Lurch" Richardson was called out of bed at 2:00 that afternoon. "I was part of the 497 TFS 'Nite Owls,' who flew mainly at night," Richardson remembered, "and since we rarely got up before 5 P.M. I was a bit wary. It didn't help that they wouldn't tell me what was going on until I got to the Command Post. There I was told we would be laying a chaff corridor to downtown Hanoi in support of B-52 strikes there. With a little over a month left before I went home, I felt a little short for such foolishness. We weren't virgins at laying chaff for BUFFs and they were damned scary missions. Since we had to lay the chaff corridors on precise routes and at specific altitudes, we were unable to apply normal SAM evasive maneuvers. There's not one of us who flew that hadn't seen at least one SAM come between our aircraft and a wingman's on these chaff missions. We were told if we lost an engine en route to target, we were to go on anyway. Things were real serious. We were also told there would be no SAR (Search and Rescue) operations until it was over. In other words, we were told if we were shot down to find a hole and hide until after the bombs stopped falling. It was the sort of mission that will cause your sphincter muscle to eat a seat cushion."

Bob Hipps was also scheduled to fly the first Ubon missions. "The scariest thing was when we were briefed that there would be no SAR for the first three days, at least. Now THAT got everyone's attention. You could have heard a pin drop. As we were putting on our flying gear and getting ready to head out to the jets, I could hear a guy throwing up in the latrine. It was the only time in 214 combat missions I ever encountered anything like that."

At Korat, Ed Rasimus, a former F-105 pilot now flying F-4Es, was scheduled to be Supervisor of Flying that day: "I was told that all the day's missions were cancelled and was shown a list of the B-52 sorties that night. I had a lot of POW friends from my F-105 days when the losses were brutal but surprisingly I didn't relate the Linebacker II bombing to their release. I had given them up for dead with little hope of a reasonable resolution of the situation. I was also amazed that somebody thought that the B-52 could survive in the Hanoi area."

A Korat F-105G Wild Weasel pilot, Captain Ed Rock, also had a previous F-105 tour over North Vietnam during Operation Rolling Thunder in the mid-60s, thought, "It's about time those SAC bastards got in the war."

In the Fourth Tactical Fighter Squadron at Udorn, the crews were waiting impatiently around the scheduling desk for word when Captain Jon Baker, an F-4 aircraft commander who worked in the Wing Scheduling Shop, walked in and announced in an awe-stuck voice, "It's a gigantic fucking BUFF escort."

At the same base Captain Bob "B. C." Connelly, who had been forced to cancel his Christmas leave without being told why, saw the mission schedule at the 13th Tactical Fighter Squadron. "I am on the schedule for a NIGHT MISSION! Now I am really pissed because there are plenty of people who can fly a night mission. I was so unhappy I didn't look at the schedule and notice who else was on the schedule. If I had, I might have had a clue.

"When I got to the briefing room I saw that everyone in there were 'Old Heads,' and the wing commander, vice commander, the chaplain and a lot of others who never attended a briefing showed up. Needless to say, there was a buzz in the room. The curtain was pulled back, and a collective gasp went up because all the lines were converging on Hanoi. After order was restored the wing commander said, 'That's not us, that's the B-52s.'"

Indeed, all the fighter crews were sobered when they saw the B-52s' routes. It was immediately obvious to these veterans of many missions to Hanoi that having every B-52 coming in on the same heading, and then all turning to leave in the same direction, was a bad idea. They were even more amazed when the briefers—who had the routes for all three B-52 raids that evening—told them that the three raids were four hours apart, flying basically the same routes and bombing the same targets. As they left the main briefing, the fighter crews realized the BUFF crews were going to have a long and difficult night, but there was a certain *schadenfreude* because the B-52s would be absorbing all of the North Vietnamese defenses.

The U.S. fighter bases at Thailand were fairly specialized, with each base having a particular mission and in some cases a unique aircraft. Takhli Royal Thai Air Force Base (RTAFB) was the home of the F-111s, a swing-wing, two-seat, low-level attack aircraft that was the Air Force's only true all-weather fighter-bomber. While the F-111 had been plagued by accidents and was derided by other American pilots, it was an amazing aircraft capable of delivering twelve 500-pound bombs from very low altitude accurately in all weather. It was also the *bête noir* of the North Vietnamese defenses, whose gunners and missilemen put an inordinate amount of effort in trying to shoot them down.

There were a variety of aircraft at Korat RTAFB, but the ones that were to have the most impact on the B-52 raids were the EB-66 electronic warfare aircraft and the SAM-hunting Wild Weasels flying F-105Gs and F-4Cs. The F-105G, though much older, was generally considered the most effective because it carried two types of anti-radiation missiles, the large "Standard ARM" and the smaller "Shrike." Both homed in on the Fan Song guidance radar, and while these missiles had limitations of which the U.S. crews were very conscious, the ARMs were much feared by the North Vietnamese missile crews. Korat also had F-4Es that teamed with the Weasels to attack SAM sites in "Hunter-Killer" teams, the Weasels locating the sites and the F-4Es attacking with cluster bombs.

The chaff-dropping F-4s came from Ubon RTAFB, which also supplied the "smart bomb" strikers for day missions. The "chaffers" had great difficulty with the B-52 missions because they flew at very high altitude, several thousand feet above the approved altitude for F-4s with chaff dispensers. To stay at that altitude, the F-4s had to use afterburners, which emitted a bright, highly visible flame and burned fuel quickly.

Most of the fighter escort would come from F-4s based at Udorn RTAFB. Many of these had a highly classified device called "Combat Tree," which enabled them to read North Vietnamese MiG transponders on their radars and separate the MiGs from American aircraft. Combat Tree, along with the F-4s' powerful radar and "all aspect" AIM-7 Sparrow missiles, gave the Udorn F-4s a significant advantage over the MiG-21s, but it was somewhat offset by the extreme unreliability of American air-to-air missiles.

Most of the American crews flying the missions were experienced combat veterans. By a fluke of timing, early in 1972 the Air Force had been forced to begin to send fighter pilots back to Southeast Asia for a non-voluntary second tour, because virtually the whole fighter pilot force had already completed one tour. Many of the wings had a number of these experienced pilots to lead their flights; additionally, many of the crews had flown combat missions during Linebacker I from April to October and were very familiar with Hanoi and its defenses.

Most of the B-52 crews were also very experienced, many with over two hundred missions, and the October and November missions had exposed them to SAMs—though nothing like they were about to see.

Since the beginning of the Vietnam War the Air Force had been frustrated because of politically imposed limitations. Most Air Force officers believed that the Air Force could end the war in a few days, if only the "politicians" would get out of the way and turn them loose, and now Nixon had done just that. The crews were ready to go, and while there were many conflicting individual emotions among them, the most dominant emotion this first day was "At last. Now we're going to really get a chance to show what we can do, and we'll end this thing and get our guys back." Few doubted that the North Vietnamese would crack quickly once the B-52s began to pound Hanoi.

AT 5:18 P.M. THE FIRST of twenty-one U-Tapao B-52Ds, John Dalton's Snow 01, lifted off. By now the B-52s from Andersen had already been airborne for five and half-hours, but the B-52s from U-Tapao would get to Hanoi first because U-Tapao was so close. One crewmember remembered that from U-Tapao "There was just time enough to say the Lord's Prayer, sing the Air Force Hymn and recite the 23rd Psalm, then we were on the bomb run."

Nick Whipple was sitting in his B-52 as the number one spare with engines running. Like several of the crews flying that night, Whipple and his crew had been scheduled to return to the United States two days before, but they were now the "hot spare." As he watched the B-52s roll down the runway, Whipple remembers, "My copilot, Larry Odum, was saying how much he wanted to go with them. I told him that he really didn't want to go because this time the bad guys were going to be shooting back, unlike the many Arc Light missions we had flown before.

"Everything was fine until the last airplane took the runway. As it started roll Larry and I both saw a large amount of fuel leaking from the wing. We called them and told them about the problem and the crew aborted the takeoff. A few minutes later we got a radio call from Charlie saying to take off, that we were now Brown 03. Larry would get his chance."

SIX

The Night
of the Fan Songs

Even for the northeast monsoon, the early evening of December 18, 1972, was exceptionally cold and rainy in the small village of Nghe An on the western edge of North Vietnam. Just outside of the village sat the radar vans of the 45th Radar Company, 291st Radar Regiment, Vietnamese People's Army Air Defense Corps. This was one of thirty-six radar stations that made up the first line of the North Vietnamese early warning system. Dinh Huu Than, the commander of the 45th, and his crew were hunched over the scope of their Soviet-made P-12 radar watching as a line of radar returns came into view, returns that had first been detected an hour earlier by Company 16 of the same regiment and had been passed on to Dinh. The radar images were proceeding north in a stately procession up the Mekong River dividing Thailand from Laos, surrounded by heavy electronic jamming. From the jamming patterns Dinh knew that the returns on the screen were B-52s. The 45th's operators had seen B-52 radar returns many times before but never in this number, and they watched transfixed as they moved up to Point 300, the point where the B-52s normally turned west to bomb targets in Laos' Plain of Jars or east to bomb targets in the North Vietnamese panhandle.

But tonight the B-52s moved past Point 300 and continued north and Dinh suddenly realized that they were following a course that many U.S. aircraft used when they were attacking Hanoi. He watched the returns for a few seconds longer, then, at 7:15 in the evening Hanoi time, he sent a message to his regimental headquarters. "Large numbers of B-52s have flown past Point 300. B-52s appear to be on a course for Hanoi."

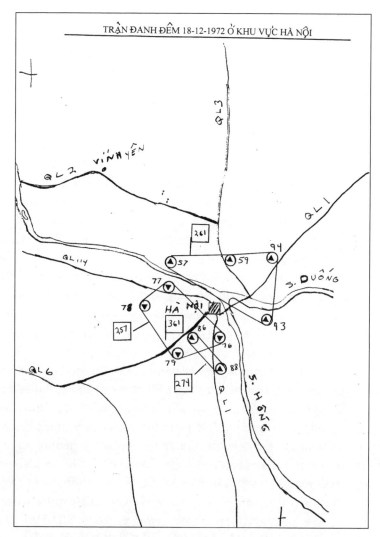

North Vietnamese missile battalion deployment, December 18: The initial deployment of Hanoi's ten missile bettalions. Note the position to the north of the capital of the 261st Missile Regiment, which was almost transferred to the south just before the raids.

The regiment quickly forwarded the message to the Air Defense Command Headquarters in Hanoi. There was a delay of a few moments then a response, almost unbelieving. "Are you certain? Comrade, do you maintain that the B-52s are striking Hanoi?"

Dinh repeated the message.

The word of the incoming raid was passed to the General Staff, who proceeded to their bunkers. The Chief of Staff of the North Vietnamese Army, General Vo Nguyen Giap, told the Air Defense Headquarters to inform him every five minutes of the progress of the raid.

BOTH THE POLITICAL CAPITAL and cultural and historical center of North Vietnam, Hanoi is located in the center the Red River Valley delta. A flat plain extends from the town of Yen Bai in the northwest to the port city of Haiphong in the southeast, an area approximately 80 by 120 miles. Hanoi means "inside of the river," and the city is nestled in the west side of the large curve on Red River where the river turns to the south from the northwest. Another smaller river, known as the *Canal de Rapides,* flows into the Red from the northeast and joins it on the journey to the Gulf of Tonkin.

Hanoi is revered by the North Vietnamese. One North Vietnamese officer described it: "Hanoi—where Uncle Ho rests in peace, where the Declaration of Independence is kept, Ba Dinh square, the Turtle Pagoda, standing on an island in picturesque Hong Kiem lake, the thirty-six wards, and the traditions of Thang Long and Dong Ho are maintained, the Ho Chi Minh Mausoleum, and Tran Quoc Pagoda." The capital had been bombed many times before, and Ho Chi Minh had used the bombing to rally his people, saying often that even if Hanoi was completely destroyed, "the Vietnamese people will rebuild it a hundred times, a thousand times more beautiful." But now the time of bravado was over. The capital would feel the full weight of American air power, and the will of the people would be tested as it had never been tested before.

DINH AND THE 45TH RADAR COMPANY were a part of simple but dense centrally controlled air defense radar network that covered North Vietnam in depth. U.S. flights were picked up by the early warning radars and reported to filter centers, which passed the information to the Air Defense Headquarters. As the targets approached the missile battalions' sites, the Air Defense Headquarters passed on information about the strike and assigned each battalion a target in the strike force. The missile battalions followed the target using the battalion commander's own Spoon Rest search radar or the information from the headquarters. When the target came in range of the battalion's Fan Song guidance radar, it began to track the target and prepared to fire when it came in range.

The hub of the Air Defense Headquarters was an amphitheater dominated by a large transparent plastic map with an overlay of grid squares where information about the incoming strikes was posted. On one side of this transparent map sat the air defense staff with telephones to the various units. On the other side of the map were plotters. As the raid moved the changing position was called out to them and they marked the progress of the raid on the map, writing the information backwards so it could be read by the air defense staff on the other side. But while the system was well organized and covered the country, it was a manual system that had difficulty coping with multiple raids or a rapidly changing situation, and the radars were very susceptible to jamming, further complicating the problems.

The Hanoi region was the responsibility of the 361st Air Defense Division. The division had numerous radars and five anti-aircraft regiments, but its heart was the three SA-2 Guideline regiments. The 261st Regiment was responsible for the area north and east of the city, while the 257th and the 274th Regiments covered the south and west. The 261st and the 257th had four battalions, but the newly arrived 274th had only two battalions ready for combat. The U.S. forces considered Hanoi the most heavily defended target in the world, but when Linebacker II began, the General Staff's decision to redeploy many of its missile battalions to the south earlier in the month meant there were far fewer missile units around Hanoi than there had been in 1967.

The Air Defense Headquarters alerted their missile crews that the B-52s were inbound, and the trucks that carried the missile control vans started up their noisy diesel engines to provide power to the units. In the command vans for each battalion, the commander moved his radar switch to the "power on" position and sent power to all the parts of the system, waiting for four minutes until the system was fully powered. The Fan Song tracking radar was now in "standby," ready to go to full power in four seconds but not giving off electronic emissions that might be picked up by a prowling Wild Weasel.

Each SA-2 battalion manned a missile site with a Spoon Rest early warning radar and a Fan Song missile guidance radar, along with six SA-2 Guideline missile launchers, each with a SA-2 missile mounted on it. Each battalion also had trucks with a single spare missile to replace a missile when it was fired. Generally the sites had a maximum of twelve missiles in their immediate area, and replacements had to be brought from the regiments' storage areas. In the storage area each regiment had a technical battalion that was responsible for the assembly of the SA-2 missiles and the maintenance of the launchers. But on December 18 the 274th's technical battalion was still in the south, so the 274th had to depend on the technical battalions from the other two regiments to supply them with missiles.

THE STREETS OF HANOI were lined with public address speakers that were easily heard in the virtually carless capital, and when the B-52s were about thirty minutes out a "pre-alert" announcement was made. As the bombers closed to within fifteen minutes of the city, the sirens began and the populace was expected to go to the bomb shelters.

Joan Baez, Telford Taylor and the other Americans were sitting in their hotel lobby watching propaganda films of American atrocities when "the electricity in the building failed leaving us sitting in the dark," Baez remembered. "Everyone stiffened, the American uneasy, the Vietnamese speaking rapidly to each other in quiet tones. ... I heard a siren coming from a distance, starting at zero base and rising evenly to a solid, high note where it stayed for a second or two and then slid back down through all the notes like a glider. All I could think of was the civilian defense drills we'd had in grammar school. ... By the time the siren began its second wail, one of our hosts had lit a candle and broken out of Vietnamese to say to us, calmly and with a smile, 'Please excuse me, alert.'" The Americans and their hosts headed for the basement bomb shelter while the reporters from *Agence France-Presse* who were also staying in the hotel walked up on the third floor balcony to watch the action.

JUST BEFORE THE B-52S ARRIVED, low-flying F-111s attacked the North Vietnamese MiG bases, including the base at Phuc Yen where

Pham Tuan, one of the North Vietnamese pilots, was sitting alert in his MiG-21. When the attack was over the runway was still useable, and Tuan was scrambled to intercept the B-52s.

It was an absolutely beautiful night, very clear with a bright, full moon over a solid white undercast at about 10,000 feet, and the spectacle gave many of the American crews a surreal feeling. A line of Andersen B-52s was moving west across South Vietnam and in the distance Steve Brown could see a line of red rotating beacons—the 21 B-52Ds from U-Tapao—heading north. Brown's cell and the rest of the 27 bombers from Andersen swung into the bomber stream behind the bombers from U-Tapao and followed them north towards the Chinese border. Dwight Moore was in one of the U-Tapao B-52s watching the Guam B-52s approach and, in front of them, the lights of the escorts. "Throughout the flight over Thailand headed north, you could see rotating beacons almost all the way to the target. There were lights all over the place—it was a zoo!"

To the east and west of Hanoi EB-66s began jamming the North Vietnamese radars. The Wild Weasel F-105Gs and F-4Cs, as well as twenty F-4s for escort and combat air patrol (MiGCAP) over the MiG airfields, moved into position. As these support forces approached Hanoi, they saw that the North Vietnamese anti-aircraft fire was exploding well below them at about 15,000 feet, the altitude of the previous Linebacker tactical strikes. The North Vietnamese were clearly not prepared for what was to come.

Just before the B-52s arrived, F-4s began laying a chaff corridor into Hanoi at 35,000 feet, and Joe Richardson was in the first group.

"We were to lay the chaff at 35,000 feet, a mere 8,000 feet above the combat ceiling of the F-4 carrying chaff dispensers, and at that altitude we were going to have to be in at least stage one or two afterburner, with a stream of flame out the back of the aircraft. So much for hiding from the MiGs under the cloak of darkness! As we began our climb to 35,000 we were told a MiG-21 was being vectored to intercept us. We saw him pass us on a parallel course, high and to our right, saw his single-engine burner light as he began his attack, but just about then we turned right towards Hanoi and he lost us in the turn. We figured the fun was just about to begin as we headed for Hanoi and expected to see many of the 35-foot-long telephone poles, with fire on one end, coming up to greet us. We were all surprised when no missiles came up, nothing but 85mm and 100mm AAA and MiGs, but they were a lot better than SAMs."

But unbeknownst to Richardson and the rest of the chaffers, the winds were almost twenty miles an hour stronger and the direction was ten degrees off from the forecast, so the chaff corridor was blown off the B-52s' inbound course. The B-52s were now solely dependent on their own electronic countermeasures to counter the SA-2s. One B-52 crewmember said later, "When we arrived we could see on the radar the chaff corridor was off our course to the right several miles. All it did was mark the run in heading for the North Vietnamese and afforded us no protection at all."

At 7:45 Major John Dalton in Snow 01, with Colonel Bill Brown sitting behind him in the jump seat as wave commander, turned Snow cell and the rest of the first wave of B-52s towards Hanoi and their target, the Hoa Loc airfield. As the B-52s turned south, the radios came alive. Thuan and one other MiG were airborne, and the American control agencies began to call out "bandits," giving their range and bearing off of Bullseye—the center of Hanoi—to guide the American fighter escorts to the attack. Off to the side and below, the B-52 crews could see the Wild Weasels firing Standard ARM anti-radiation missiles preemptively, hoping to keep the SAM radars off the air. The missiles' motors fired with a bright flash and the missiles climbed before they started down towards the ground—and, hopefully, into a North Vietnamese radar. The fire trails from the ARMs made a few of the B-52 crews think they were SAMs.

MANY OF THE CREWS from Andersen welcomed the adrenaline that was beginning to flow as they approached Hanoi. Flying in a B-52 from Guam to Vietnam and back was a miserable experience, taking roughly twice as long as a flight from New York to London, and the B-52 was very noisy and the ejection seats were uncomfortable, even compared to the narrowest airliner seats. There was little room to move, and the air conditioning was very inefficient so the compartments were not equally heated. Keeping one compartment comfortable usually meant making the others too warm or too cold. There was also the ceaseless noise from the air conditioning, the steady hum of the electronics, and drone of the eight engines, and all of these combined made the long flights from Guam extremely fatiguing.

Except for the pilots and the D model gunners, the B-52 crew compartments were virtually windowless. The B-52's radar navigator and navigator, known as the "bomb-nav team," sat next to each other beneath the pilots in a small compartment with a narrow desk and radarscope in front of each. As the B-52s approached the target, the bomb-nav teams began to run their checklists, then saw on their radars a terrain feature most had only heard about before: the Tam Dao mountains, a mile-high spine jutting out from the flat delta and running from the northwest to southeast from the Chinese border pointing almost directly to Hanoi. The mountains were a legend in the U.S. Air Force, known to a generation of American fighter pilots as Thud Ridge, "the string of small mountains that stretches like a long bony finger to the north and west of Hanoi . . . marking the route to the modern fighter pilot's private corner of hell—the fierce defenses and targets of downtown Hanoi."

Joe Richardson and the rest of the chaffers had finished their mission and were departing as the B-52s began to arrive. "It looked like we were going to waltz out of this one unscathed, but as we turned away we came nose to nose with the BUFFs who were totally blacked out and trying to enter Indian territory behind the chaff. We didn't have time to maneuver or anything, and one of our guys came within inches of becoming a B-52 hood ornament."

WAITING FOR THE B-52S were the North Vietnamese missile control crews in the command van of each missile battalion, a van that bore many similarities to the crew compartment of the approaching B-52s. The van was about the size of a tracker-trailer, and inside was a seven-man crew: the battalion commander, a fire control officer, three guidance officers, a plotter, and a missile technical officer. The command vans were tightly sealed to keep out light so the operators could focus on their radarscope, and in warm weather the unair-conditioned vans became broilingly hot. For reports on what was going on outside, the battalion commander either had an observer in a tower or, on the later model SA-2s, in a small "box" on top of the radar van.

Inside the cramped vans the battalion commander sat in front of the radar scope of a Spoon Rest acquisition radar where he could watch the targets come in while waiting for orders from the headquarters by telephone or radio. Next to him was a transparent plotting board with a map of his battalion's area of responsibility, overlaid with the same grid references as the map at the headquarters, and the plotter stood behind it.

Headquarters assigned the battalion a target by giving the commander a target number along with its range and bearing, and once the battalion commander received the target information he tried to locate the target with his Spoon Rest search radar while the plotter wrote the information on the plotting board. This insured that, even if jamming prevented the battalion commander from finding the assigned target on his radar, he could watch the target's position and course on the plotting board and tell when he could began the engagement.

As the B-52s approached, the only noise in the van besides the voices of the crew was that of loud cooling fans, necessary to dissipate the heat from the vacuum tubes of the relatively primitive electronics of the SA-2 system. The crews were accustomed to background noise and all conversation inside the van was by voice. The battalion commander's tone of voice set the tone for the crew. Each battalion commander had his own style based on his personality and this was reflected in how he trained and talked to his men. Some commanders liked a high-pitched, tense atmosphere while others liked a calm one where they talked in a normal (but loud) voice and would only shout when they needed attention.

Once the battalion commander was assigned a target and picked it up on his Spoon Rest radar, he could turn on the Fan Song tracking radar by pressing the Target Transmitter button. In four seconds the Fan Song was at full power, but emitting signals that the American Wild Weasels' electronic sensors could pick up, so generally the battalion commanders delayed turning on the Fan Songs for as long as possible and the target was well within range.

The first missile sites the B-52s met as they moved down from the northwest were the missile battalions of the 261st Missile Regiment, called the *Thang Long* regiment, the ancient name of Hanoi. As the bombers approached, the regiment was in a state of disarray while its members scrambled back from leave. The 261st's commander, Tran Huu Lao, arrived back at the headquarters at 7:30, just before the first bombs began to hit, while the commander of the 94th Battalion, Tran Minh Thang, as well as several others did not arrive until the next day. In the battalions that were missing crewmembers, some guidance officers took over as fire control officers. Even though the crews were trained so they could perform any function in the van during an emergency it added to the confusion as the battle began.

As the B-52s closed the distance, the radarscopes of the 261st were blanked by jamming from the bombers and their escorts. The official North Vietnamese history of the operation described these first minutes: "The B-52s' signals were drowned in a jumbled mass of fake signals from the B-52s themselves, the signals of the escort planes, as well as the signals of EB-66s flying outside the formation and other decoy signals. F-4s were spreading chaff over a wide corridor. These operations caused us many difficulties in discovering and striking the enemy."

Nguyen Van Phiet, the commander of the 261st Regiment's 57th battalion, had never seen anything like this in five years of engaging American air strikes. "All the radar returns were buried in a jamming curtain of bright, white fog. The screen of the guidance officer and the tracking operators showed many dark green stripes slanted together, changing at abnormal speeds, one strobe overriding and mixing with another, this stripe joining that one and splitting away. After that, hundreds and thousands of bright dots specked the screens like bunches of target blips moving sluggishly. With all that mass confusion coupled with constantly blinking signals like a downpour of rain, how were we expected to distinguish between fighter jamming and bomber jamming, or which was EB-66 jamming and which was the passive type metallic chaff strewn across the sky by F-4s?"

The North Vietnamese Air Defense Headquarters began to receive reports from the MiG bases at Yen Bai, Hoa Loc, Phuc Yen, and Kep, saying that they were being bombed by F-111s. The headquarters began to press the 361st Air Defense Division's battle watch commander, Hoang Bao, with questions:

"Have you seen the B-52s yet?"

"Have any units opened fire yet?"

"Why haven't they opened fire?"

The commander of the 59th SAM battalion, Nguyen Thang, heard a report of an F-111 inbound and turned on his Fan Song radar, then gave his fire control officer, Duong Van Thuan, the position of the F-111 so he could turn the radar antenna to try and engage the low flying fighter bomber. Thang was especially anxious to shoot down an F-111, because once before his battalion had missed an F-111 that was shot down a moment later by light antiaircraft. The downed F-111 had been the 4,000th U.S. airplane shot down over North Vietnam and the kill received great fanfare, and Thang was bitter that he had missed that opportunity.

Thuan located the F-111 on his radar screen and Thang waited for the aircraft to approach closer to be sure of a kill. Just as he was ready to fire, a call came from the regimental headquarters, "B-52s approaching from the northwest!"

Thang made a quick decision—he would fire at the F-111, then turn his radar towards the B-52s immediately afterwards. As two missiles roared off their launchers toward the low-flying American aircraft, Thang's headquarters reported that the B-52s were bombing the MiG airfield at Hoa Loc and he was ordered to take target T569, a cell of approaching B-52s. Thang watched in dismay as his missiles missed the F-111 then, when he tried to pick up the B-52s on his radar, their jamming filled the scope. He hesitatingly reported the miss to the regiment, along with his failure to pick up his assigned B-52 target. The regimental commander snarled at him, "Pay attention to the B-52s!"

Thang was furious with himself. The B-52s were attacking and he had wasted two missiles and precious moments! The atmosphere in the 59th's command van became increasingly tense.

SEVEN MILES ABOVE THE CITY, the electronic warfare officers—the EWs—of the B-52s were playing a desperate chess game against the North Vietnamese missile crews on the ground. In his narrow compartment just behind the pilots, each EW had two scopes. One, the APR-20, had a rectangular 8" x 12" screen that displayed all the North Vietnamese electronic signals, the height of the strobe indicating how close the radar was, and the EW used this scope to center his jammers over their signals. There was also a second receiver, the APR-25, that had a circular scope that displayed strobes emitting from the center of the scope outwards in the direction of the North Vietnamese radars, with the length of the strobe showing the range of the radar.

EW Bud Hughes described the silent battle. "The key is the signal strength of the enemy radar. When it gets to a certain point, or starts to change patterns, then you start to jam. They make a move and you counter. They change frequency and you adjust your jammer to the new frequency. The skill of the players becomes readily apparent. They used every trick they knew—shifting frequency, acquire from one site and shoot from another and various other ruses."

The B-52s' multiple jammers were almost all controlled manually, and each of the jammers had three knobs, so the skill of the EW in manipulating these controls was absolutely vital. Ken Nocito, a G model EW flying the first night, remembered: "There were too many knobs to turn. If you have all the time in the world, it is easy to select the correct knob and casually tune the system to cover the radar. But when someone is shooting at you, time is of the essence and there is tremendous pressure. It was not a good feeling to reach up, turn a knob and find out it was the wrong one. It could be a terminal mistake if it happened at the wrong time."

AS MAJOR JOHN DALTON in Snow 01 approached his target, there were no SAMs in the air. One minute prior to bomb release, Snow 01 opened its bomb bay doors and 60 seconds later 108 bombs began their ten-mile journey to their target. The crew felt a slight vibration, and in their lower compartment the radar navigator and navigator watched as an amber light winked rapidly over their heads, each wink signifying a bomb going out. As soon as the last bomb was gone, the doors slammed shut as Dalton yanked the bomber into the prescribed steep-banked, post-target right turn to the west to exit the target area. Snow 01's bombs were just hitting the ground as the B-52 completed its turn.

Rex Rivolo was flying one of the escorting F-4Es from Korat. Rivolo had over five hundred combat missions and was on his second tour. He and his wingman were part of a Hunter-Killer team in support of the B-52 strikes, carrying cluster bombs and flares to suppress SA-2 activity, but Rivolo was not pleased. The Hunter-Killers would be almost useless at night since they could not see the SAM sites under the clouds to bomb them visually. "We were flying with our lights off, at very low altitude and airspeed over a known cluster of SA-2 sites. It seemed very stupid to be there at such low speed and altitude, but almost immediately we realized that we were quite safe since they were having none of us—they were waiting for the BUFFs. We knew the ECM in the F-4 didn't work, but we believed that the B-52s, SAC's great pride, had 'magic stuff' unknown to us that would render them invulnerable. As we waited my back-seater and I were casually talking about the great show we were about to see as the B-52s used their 'black magic' ECM to deflect dozens of SA-2 missiles. As the first cell of B-52s arrived we heard them checking-in on strike frequency. By this time we could see missiles in the air all around us and in the distance as other cells of BUFFs were attacking other targets."

THE VANS OF THE NORTH VIETNAMESE missile battalions began to tremble slightly as the first B-52 bombs hit the MiG bases at Hoa Loc and Phuc Yen. Then bombs began to gently rock downtown Hanoi, and the North Vietnamese history of the operation noted, "The atmosphere in the command headquarters at every level was extremely strained at this time. We did not have much experience and were not effective. Almost all the missile units responsible for protecting Hanoi had never seen a B-52 signal on their screen. Though they had been trained early on paper, it was only in theory. In battle, there is a very wide gap between theory and practice."

Tension mounted as the missile crews continued trying to track the B-52s passively on their Spoon Rest search radar by following the jamming strobes instead of using their Fan Song radars in the active mode and risk an attack by anti-radiation missiles. But the passive tracking was not working—the jamming was too intense.

Nguyen Chan, the commander of the 78th, the westernmost battalion of the 361st, watched his assigned target approach on the plotting board next to his search radar set, but the radar was only showing "wave after wave of jamming. It looked like overlapping blades of a fan that came together and wiped out the whole spectrum. It was so bright it hurt the eyes, and the returns were twisted and coiled together into a clump like a tangled ball."

Chan decided to take the risk and turn on his Fan Song tracking radar to try to pick up the B-52s. He pushed the Target Transmit button and four seconds later the radar was at full power, and he and the 78th's guidance officer, Nguyen Van Luyen, began the complex process of trying to locate and fire at a B-52.

Chan gave Luyen the range and bearing from the plotting board and a few seconds later Luyen was able to break out a single B-52 jamming strobe on his Fan Song scope. He put the cross hairs on it and pressed a button. The return appeared on the radarscopes of the three guidance officers responsible for tracking the target and controlling the missiles' course in range, azimuth and elevation.

The range officer, Dinh Trong Due, excitedly called out "B-52!" and now the difficult process of tracking the return began. Each of the three guidance officers had a small steering wheel under his radar scope, and each slowly and carefully turned the wheel to track the return while twisting their gain control knobs to try to sharpen the jamming strobe into a useable target. The actions of these three guidance officers were critical. When there was no jamming the radar could be set to automatically track the target, but when the target was jamming the return was too unstable and the missile had to be guided manually. They each had to gently turn their steering wheels to keep the return centered in their scopes, so the missile could follow the radar beam to the target.

Meanwhile Due continued his excited chattering, shouting "It's really a B-52!" while Chan tried to quiet him down to keep the crew calm. The B-52 came closer and, at 7:44, Chan ordered Luyen to fire. Luyen pushed one fire button and then, six seconds later, the second. With their booster rockets burning brightly, one after another two missiles climbed through the overcast towards the B-52s. Nguyen reported the firing to the regimental HQ of the 257th as his crews continued to guide the missiles toward the target, but there was no indication of a hit on the radar screens—the missiles had missed.

Still, there was a sigh of relief at the Air Defense Headquarters—now at least they knew they would be giving the B-52s a battle. Tran Nhan, deputy commander of the 361st, felt: "It was the beginning. The news that the 78th Battalion had been able to identify the B-52's signal and fire their missiles spread rapidly, and gave great confidence in the remaining battalions. . . . They were our first reply to the insolent memorandum of Nixon who had hoped to force our surrender."

AS THE NORTH VIETNAMESE began to fire their missiles, the American crews were treated to a spectacular show. When the SAM booster rockets fired, the flare of the huge motors was diffused and magnified under the solid white undercast. One of the pilots described the scene: "An area about the size of a city block was lit up by the flash and it looked as if the whole block had caught fire. As the missile broke through the clouds, a ring of silver fire that appeared to be the size of a basketball replaced the diffused large lighted area. This was the exhaust of the rocket motor that would grow brighter as the missile approached the aircraft. From the front when the missile was pointed at you it looked like a lighted silver doughnut."

When the missile warheads exploded, they became in huge fireballs sending out ribbons of luminescent fragments. When the missiles missed and their rocket motors ran out of fuel, they arched over and dropped toward the ground and then detonated like roman candles as their safety fuses went off.

Inside the B-52s, the pilots and D model gunners had a full view of what was happening, while the other crewmembers did not. But their compartments, unlike the missile crew's command van, were not light-sealed and they could see flashes from exploding SAMs, "like flashbulbs going off outside," and feel the concussion when a missile detonated nearby. The B-52s did have a downward-looking optical viewer so the radar navigator could look below the aircraft and see the bombs hitting, but generally the RNs were too busy to look. At least one remembered that once he looked through his optics on the way to the target and "saw so many missiles coming up I never looked outside again."

THE FIRST SEVEN CELLS, all from U-Tapao, dropped their bombs, came through unscathed and turned towards home as the next group of 18 B-52s from Andersen moved in to attack the huge storage area at Kinh No, just north of Hanoi. Major Billy Lyons and his crew were flying in Lilac 01, a D model leading the second cell.

Like several others, Lyons' crew had been getting on a tanker to go back to the U.S. when they were called back to fly the Linebacker II missions. Lyons remembered: "You could take a Fourth of July fireworks show and multiply it one million times and you would have an idea of what it was like coming in on the bomb run. . . . Suddenly my copilot yelled "BREAK LEFT" and I rolled into a 50 degree left bank and I was able to move the aircraft just enough to make a SAM coming from our right side miss us. As we left the target area our gunner reported that the number three aircraft in the cell, Lilac 03, didn't make the post-target turn to the west but continued south until the gunner lost him off his radar scope. After several fruitless attempts to contact him we could only assume he had been lost over the target area. Things were quiet as we began our trip back to Guam."

Lilac 03 had been the first victim of the SA-2s. Thirty seconds prior to bomb release a SAM exploded on the left side of the aircraft, puncturing most of the fuel tanks, knocking out the instruments and electrical power and damaging its bomb-release system so none of the bombs released. The aircraft commander, Major David O'Neil, was hit by small pieces of shrapnel in his eye and arms, and the copilot, Joe Grega, was hit in both arms. With the loss of fuel in the drop tank, the aircraft began to roll rapidly to the right before O'Neil and Grega got it under control. Leaking fuel, with all of the radios and the intercom out, and with a full bomb load, Lilac 03 turned for U-Tapao. In the rear of the aircraft, gunner Joe Smart's compartment had taken a heavy hit. All of his oxygen lines were cut, and there was a hole in back of his seat the size of a small plate, but Smart was unhurt.

Once the aircraft turned towards U-Tapao, copilot Grega pulled out his battery-operated survival radio and began trying to contact friendly forces. But unbeknownst to the crew, the bleed air duct in the bomb bay had ruptured and was pouring 800-degree bleed air from the engines onto the full load of 750-pound bombs in the bomb bay.

NGUYEN THANG'S 59TH BATTALION command van was now being rocked by bombs from the B-52s. In a small control tower "birdhouse" mounted on top of the van, his observer, Quang, thought he had never felt as helpless and apprehensive as he did tonight.

Waves and waves of B-52s were filling in the sky as anti-aircraft artillery and missiles were fired, bombs exploded, and the sky took on a red glow. Quang began to describe the scene but Thang told him to be quiet as the battalion was ordered take a new target.

Thang decided to turn on the Fan Song early so that his crew could pick out the B-52's radar return in the jamming waves. His fire control officer, Duong Van Thuan, picked up jamming from the B-52 but Thang hesitated. He had already missed the F-111 and wanted to fire at the B-52s using the "half-angle" technique which led the target and was more accurate than the "three-point" technique normally used for a jamming aircraft. But the "half-angle" technique required a clear radar return, and Thang waited for almost a minute hoping that Thuan and the three guidance officers could break out the bomber.

But the jamming was too strong and his crew could not separate the bomber's return from the jamming, so Thang finally ordered Thuan to fire two missiles using the three-point technique. Again the 59th's missiles missed, and Thang was beside himself. "It was my fault again," he thought. "I waited too long. Hopefully we'll find a target in the next wave. It's not realistic to try and use the 'half-angle' technique with this jamming."

Bombs continued to explode around the missile site and the command van swayed back and forth as if it was going to tip over. Then Quang's voice came from the top of the van, frustrating Thang even further. "The 93rd and 94th battalions are launching!"

In another part of Hanoi, in the North Vietnamese POW camp known as the Hanoi Hilton, the winds were blowing through Navy Commander Jim Mulligan's cell door window as he prepared to get into a sleeping bag he had made from North Vietnamese army blankets. Mulligan was an A-4 pilot shot down and captured in March of 1966, and he wrote later, "All of a sudden the wails of the air raid siren echoed thorough the camp . . . the lights went out and we were plunged into darkness. I looked out . . . to see if I might catch a glimpse of anything. Suddenly the missiles from the SAM sites began to roar off. . . . One, two, three I counted from one site as they climbed heading north. From the southwest I saw more missiles leap skyward heading in the same general direction as the first group. Then all hell broke loose, and I heard the rolling thunder of massive string of bombs going off in the distance. The earth shook violently and the building reverberated wildly. The sky turned white ... the rolling thunder of the bombs' echoed and reechoed. 'It's a B-52 raid ...' I said to my cellmate. 'Pack your bags, we're going home.'"

On the third floor of the Hoa Binh hotel, Jean Thoraval, a reporter for *Agence France-Presse,* wrote: "Stretches of sky north and north-west of the city glowed red and white. With each explosion, doors burst open, furniture trembled and bottles fell to the floor. Blasts like immense incandescent mushrooms could be seen ... one after another as [missiles'] lighted plumes rose into the sky like a fireworks display. From time to time it was as bright as daylight."

AS THE B-52S DROPPED their loads, Ed Rock was watching the action from the cockpit of his F-105G Wild Weasel. Rock was thinking about his many tactical missions to Hanoi on a previous tour and about his many friends that were POWs, and he was taken aback by what he saw this night:

"The thing I remember most is the gigantic secondaries. It was beautiful, terrifying, and awe-inspiring. I had experienced numerous frustrations my first tour being assigned to strike dubious targets while being forced to avoid the most lucrative. It was absolutely amazing to see really meaningful targets get wiped out with overwhelming force. Why couldn't this have been done years before and thus avoided the needless pain and suffering?"

RUST CELL LED THE B-52GS to Hanoi. Rust 01's co-pilot was Bill Buckley, and as the wave turned south towards Hanoi, to Buckley's amazement Colonel Thomas Rew, the airborne commander of the wave sitting behind him, said to make a radio call to the rest of the aircraft in the wave and get a fuel check. Buckley protested, saying that it would tell the North Vietnamese exactly how many B-52s were inbound, but Rew insisted.

Bob Certain was in Charcoal 01, the lead plane in the next cell. "We were supposed to be on radio silence," Certain remembered, "and a fuel check from each airplane given in the clear would tell anyone listening how many B-52s were on the way and which way they were coming from. We were incensed."

As they approached their target, Buckley saw that the sky was full of airplanes. "I saw F-4s trolling for MiGs with their gear and flaps down and landing lights on. The SAM missiles were thick. For the first time since flying over Vietnam in 'combat,' I came to realize that those SOBs were trying to kill me and that I could die at any moment. The scene reminded me of those old World War II movies with the skies filled with flak, except this time it was SAM missiles.

"We released our bombs, then we saw a SAM on our right and made a hard right turn, far exceeding our bank limit for that weight, and we lost a lot of altitude as well as overstressing the aircraft. Then our radar navigator called and said our bombs had not released. That's why our turn was so sluggish and we lost all that altitude—we still had 22,000 pounds of bombs in the bomb bay to take back to Guam, which we did. Pretty frustrating."

Bob Certain's Charcoal 01 was at the head of nine B-52Gs in three cells attacking the Yen Vien railroad. Charcoal 01 was one of the "unmodified" G models with the lower powered ALT-6B jammers; this was the first time the North Vietnamese SAM operators had seen the lower powered system, and they were to exploit it with a vengeance. "The radar navigator, Major Dick Johnson, and I were focused on making this the best, most accurate mission we had ever flown," Certain said later. "We would be in the lethal range of SAMs for about 20 minutes, but we couldn't be distracted by the threats. Dick and I turned off our outside radios so we could concentrate only on our checklists and crew coordination. We had been ordered to take no evasive action on the bomb run and these orders seemed to become increasingly suicidal as we heard multiple SAM calls from the B-52s from U-Tapao that had entered the target zone 30 minutes ahead of us."

Steve Brown and his crew were in a cell behind Charcoal. "As we turned towards Hanoi I could see bright dots of light climbing out of the clouds, then arching over and starting down and exploding like fireworks. It was like the world's biggest Fourth of July show. Then we heard the first emergency beeper, a radio device that sounded when an ejection seat fired or a parachute opened."

THE NORTH VIETNAMESE AIR DEFENSE Command Headquarters watched three cells of B-52s approaching the rail yards at Yen Vien, then passed the first cell to Thang Nguyen and his 59th battalion as their target.

Having already failed twice, Thang and his crew were particularly anxious when they received the call assigning them target T671 at an altitude of 10,000 meters. As the target approached Thang watched both on his Spoon Rest radarscope and the plotting board next to the scope, and when the range closed he called to his fire control officer, Thuan, "Target azimuth 350, distance 30 kilometers, altitude 10,000 meters, grouped."

Thuan pushed the Target Transmit buttons to activate Fan Song radar, then manually turned the antenna to an azimuth of 350 degrees and, at a range of about thirty kilometers, saw heavy jamming on the scope, indicating a cell of three B-52s. He could not break out their range because of the jamming, and he called back to Thang:

"Target detected, azimuth 352, unknown range, altitude 10,000 meters, group, hostile."

Thang looked over at Thuan's radarscope, then back to his own, then at the plotting board. He had to make sure that they were all looking at the same radar return. Satisfied, he gave the order to fire two missiles when the B-52 was in range, and to use "three-point" guidance. There would be no delay this time.

Thuan tracked the movement of the jamming strobe on the scope, and once the return was stabilized, turned the target over to the three guidance officers to take over tracking the target manually. Now everything depended on the skill of all three of the guidance controllers and Thuan later described the problems: "It is difficult enough to guide the missiles manually under normal conditions when the targets are clearly seen. It is even more difficult looking at the silky crepe jamming of the B-52 aircraft on the radar screen. An uneven rotation or a mere jerky movement of the control wheel could cause the missiles to deviate from the target by thousands of meters or even detonate in the air."

As the B-52 approached Thuan saw the three crewmen were tracking the target well. Thuan had a template over his radar scope that indicated the maximum range of the missiles, and when the B-52's return was well inside the engraved range lines he checked the lights on his control board to make sure two missiles were ready to fire. The two READY lights were on, and Thuan pressed the FIRE button under one of the READY lights then, six seconds later, the second FIRE button.

The first SA-2 missile, 35 feet long and weighing almost 5000 pounds, was started on its way by its solid fuel booster in the tail, which burned with a very large, bright flame for five seconds. As the fuel in the booster burned out the booster motor dropped off, the liquid-fueled sustainer engine cut in and the Fan Song radar acquired the transponder located in the rear of the missile.

As each of the guidance controllers turned their wheel to keep the strobe centered, the Fan Song's computer began to direct the missile's onboard guidance system to follow the radar beam. This guidance information was sent to the missile by means of a radar signal detectable to the American EWs, known as the *uplink.* The uplink was the only signal needed to guide the SA-2, but American anti-radiation missiles could not home in on this signal.

CHARCOAL 01 WAS PREPARING to release its bombs and Bob Certain was going through his final procedures. "Fifteen seconds before bombs away, we opened the doors, and five seconds later I restarted my stopwatch as a backup to the drop should anything go wrong. Almost immediately, it did. The radar screens went blank and other instruments lost power. It retrospect, it was very strange—there was no thump, no explosion, and my first thought was that the electrical generators had been accidentally knocked off line. Before I could say anything, Bobby Thomas, our substitute copilot, was shouting over the intercom, 'They got the pilot! They got the pilot!' The EW, Captain Tom Simpson, was also shouting, 'Is anybody there? Gunner, gunner!'

"I realized that we had been hit. I looked over my left shoulder and saw fire in the forward wheel well through the porthole in the door behind me. My first thought was of the twenty-seven 750-pound bombs in the bomb bay right behind the fire, and I turned to the RN and yelled, 'Drop those damn bombs!'

"He safetied them and hit the release switch and my next thought was that the fire was also directly below the main mid-body fuel tank, loaded with 10,000 pounds of JP-4 jet fuel. Then aircraft commander Don Rissi's voice came weakly over the intercom. 'Pilot's still alive.'

"I figured it was time get out of here and I called, 'This is the Nav, escape heading is 290.'

"About 10 seconds after the first of two SAMs hit the plane when I heard 'EW's leaving!' as Tom Simpson ejected. I heard the explosion of his hatch and boom from his seat as it rocketed up and out. I looked at the RN. Our eyes met, and we both started preparing for ejection. I threw my flight case as far to the rear of the cockpit as I could, grabbed the ejection handle, looked at the RN again, and then turned to face forward. I saw the ejection light come on showing the pilot had ejected, and pulled the handle. The seat failed.

"At least, that's what I thought. The ballistic activators were supposed to blow the hatch below my seat and fire me out of the bottom of the plane in one-tenth of a second, but I was so scared that the panels in front of me seemed to be barely moving at first, then to move up in slow motion. In fact, the seat worked fine. It was just an illusion brought on by the state of shock induced from being in a burning bomber."

REX RIVOLO WATCHED the scene from below in his F-4E. "All our radar warning gear lit up and suddenly three SA-2 missiles were in the air. The BUFFs were at 35,000 feet and it seemed like the missiles took forever to arrive.... The B-52s' 'black magic' didn't work. The very first aircraft in the cell was hit and the radio immediately exploded with a dozen people trying to talk at once. We watched in amazement as the giant airplane cracked open like an egg. What followed was a surrealistic scene. It seemed like the wing was blown off and, with fuel streaming out, it rolled slowly over on its back, raining fire as the fuel burned and slowly fell toward the ground in a sheet of flame. The flames would split into two, the two into four and so on. It seemed like we were watching for minutes, but it was only a few seconds. As other missiles detonated in the vicinity of the B-52 in the light of the explosions we could see the second and third B-52s in the cell in a hard 135 degree break turn, their wings bent upward from the g-load and condensation coming off the wing tips. It was an incredible sight—we didn't believe that BUFFs could turn like that, but they did. The sky was filled with chaff and missiles and for the next 10 minutes or so, amidst great confusion, other B-52 cells arrived and dropped their bombs. We were entranced. It was really incredible that the B-52 crews did it. I don't know if I could have gone back the second night. But they kept coming."

THE B-52 BOMBING SUDDENLY stopped and the sky was quiet around the 59th's command van. A light on the control panel flashed, indicating the first missile's proximity fuse had gone off, followed by the same light from the second missile. The azimuth officer, Nguyen Van Do, called out that he had lost the strobe, followed by the elevation officer, Le Xuan Linh, excitedly reporting that the target's jamming strobe was rapidly losing altitude. Then Quang began yelling from the top of the windowless van: "It's burning! It's a big fire! There is one big cloud of smoke like the one in an atomic bomb explosion, in the north."

"You see a cloud of smoke like that looks like a mushroom shape?" Thang excitedly asked.

Then, over his headset, Thang heard the regimental commander ask, "Did you do it? Did you shoot down a B-52?"

Still unbelieving, Thang replied, "Yes, it's truly a B-52. We shot down a B-52 on the spot."

ON THE GROUND, JIM MULLIGAN saw the hit from his prison cell window. "The white sky turned yellow as a B-52 was hit and exploded, then burned wildly as it fluttered down from high in the atmosphere. Night had turned into day. The strings of bombs came on and on...."

Also coming down were American airmen, one of them Bob Certain: "The next thing I knew, I was tumbling in the cold air of the stratosphere, thinking, 'That was a dumb thing to do. I'll bet the plane was still flyable. Where is it? Maybe I can crawl back in.' A moment later, I felt the parachute opening. So far, so good. I checked for a good chute, then looked down for the first time. Between my boots, I saw the inferno that made up the three targets that we had hit over the last 20 minutes. As I watched, I saw a series of explosions walk through the target, a string of 27 bombs from Charcoal 02 finding paydirt.

"Then I saw another series of explosions—right in line with my drift. 'Oh, God, now what?' There shouldn't be another target over there; that was our escape route. As I looked down and drifted past this new blaze, I realized that this fire was shaped like an arrow—our B-52 had plowed in flames into a village. Now panic was beginning to replace concern. Where the #$%& were the clouds that had covered the ground when I first bailed out? With the full moon I could see the ground clearly all around, and the white panels in the canopy and my white helmet were not going to be assets as I slowly descended to the ground no more than 10 kilometers north of Hanoi."

EVEN THOUGH THE 59TH had reported its kill, there was an air of unreality in the North Vietnamese Air Defense Headquarters. Could it really be a B-52? Had one of these invincible aircraft really been shot down over Hanoi? The phone rang again. It was the Vo Cong Lang, the 261st deputy commander at the crash site, who said he was holding a metal placard in his hand that said "B-52G." The headquarters exploded with joy, and Tran Nhan remembered, "Commander Tran Quang and Political Commissar Nguyen embraced each other, their eyes brimming with tears, followed by speechless moments marked with the display of deep emotions and happy tears from old, hoary-eyed soldiers who had never before cried in 30 years of carrying on the resistance."

A few moments later North Vietnamese soldiers reported that they had captured Richard Johnson, Charcoal 01's radar navigator, and Bob Certain close to the spot where their aircraft had crashed.

One thing remained. One of the officers called the Chief of the General Staff, General Giap, to tell him the news, but instead of being excited Giap cautiously asked, "Is it really a B-52?" When he was assured it was and hung up, one of Giap's colleagues reminded him he had asked the same kind of question some eighteen years before, at Dien Bien Phu. At that time he had been told that one of the units that had broken into the French fortress in the final assault had captured the commander of the garrison, General Christian De Castries. When Giap was told that the French commander had been captured, his first question was, "Is it really De Castries?"

By coincidence, the 59th battalion that had shot down Charcoal 01 had also been the first artillery unit to fire on the French fortress at Dien Bien Phu, then using 75mm howitzers. Now, almost two decades later, it scored the first kill in the battle that the North Vietnamese would come to know as the "aerial Dien Bien Phu."

B. C. CONNELLY HAD TAKEN off from Udorn in his F-4 to escort chaff-dropping F-4s from Ubon. "I found them drilling along at 36,000 feet, the assigned BUFF altitude, to lay their corridor. I tried to fly with them or just ahead but at that altitude I was so slow that I was just short of falling out of the sky, so I told the chaff leader I was going to drop down to 25,000 feet where I might have a chance against a MiG. He said no sweat, so down I went.

"Now I am flying over an 8000 foot undercast and things are starting to come out of the clouds which are not fun, like significant flak. Then the RHAW—the radar warning system—lights up indicating a SAM and sure enough I see a large glow under the clouds which quickly diminishes and becomes a streak. I know this SAM is mine so I do the standard maneuver and smartly pulled up and the missile detonated a very long way away. It was obviously not aimed at me. About that time the RHAW goes crazy again, the light goes under the clouds and we watched the SAM launch. Everything looked the same as the first one, so we didn't do much maneuvering. The SAM blew up in our face, and I told my backseater we were probably going to die because I couldn't figure this shit out fast enough.

"About this time Red Crown called a MiG. We got him on radar and closed to about nineteen miles when the radar went blank. I screamed at my backseater to turn it back on, but he replied he hadn't turned it off, the radar had just died."

The pilot of the MiG-21 that Connelly was pursuing was Pham Tuan, who had been unable to locate the B-52s and was now trying to get home to his base at Phuc Yen. But even when Connelly lost his radar Tuan's problems were not over, and Connelly continues: "About that time some more F-4s showed up and got a radar lock on to the MiG so I left the fight, but due to a maintenance screw up the F-4s couldn't get a missile off the rail and the MiG escaped. One lucky Gomer! We recovered at Udorn and I figured my day was done. I walked into the squadron and asked the Duty Officer for a beer. He said 'Sir, you can't have one.' I inquired 'Why?' in less than friendly tones and he told me that I was flying in a little over two hours. My comments would melt my keyboard, but needless to say I was not happy."

Even then, Pham Tuan was not finished for the evening. After escaping for the second time a third F-4 found him and fired seven missiles at him, but none hit. As Tuan came in to land back at Phuc Yen he found that the runway lights had been knocked out by the B-52 strikes, and when he touched down he ran into a bomb crater and damaged the aircraft. American intelligence, listening to the North Vietnamese radios, gave the last F-4 that attacked Tuan credit for a "MiG damaged."

WITH HIS AIRCRAFT COMMANDER still partially blind from shrapnel, copilot Joe Grega was coming in to U-Tapao in his damaged B-52. Grega requested a straight-in approach to land, but at that moment U-Tapao's KC-135s tankers were taking off from the single runway to refuel the next missions. Nick Whipple and the rest of the B-52s from the first wave were holding, waiting for the KC-135s to take off. "As the damaged bomber approached the runway," Whipple remembered, "the tower called and told him to go out and land in the normal pattern. The young copilot called back and said he had a shot-up aircraft and a wounded aircraft commander. There was a pause and a calm voice intervened.

" 'Son, this is Charlie. You pick out any runway you want and land that airplane, and we'll talk about it later.' The aircrews in the holding pattern broke out into cheers."

The damaged B-52 landed without problems and then turned off the runway. Gunner Joe Smart remembered: "I got out in time to see the pilot rushed to the hospital. I was just looking around, glad to be alive, when I saw explosive ordnance-disposal team men running from the bomb bay calling that the 750-pound bombs were so hot from the broken bleed air duct they couldn't touch them with their bare hands. I ran like hell along with them. We later found out the ground crew quit counting the holes in the aircraft after they reached 680."

R. J. Smith, an electronic warfare officer with over 500 missions, returned to his trailer after the harrowing first raid to find his trailermate, Hank Barrows, getting up to fly on the third wave. Barrows asked Smith how it was and Smith replied, "Well, they haven't run out of missiles and we lost at least three aircraft," then went to bed.

EVEN THOUGH THE FIRST RAID was over, the North Vietnamese missile activity did not slow. As soon as a missile was fired, the empty launcher moved to a centered position so it could be reloaded and the launcher crew moved in. A truck with another missile loaded on a rack on its bed moved from a camouflaged holding area a few hundred yards away to the launcher, then carefully backed up until its rear wheels rested against precisely located wooden chocks just in front of the launcher. The missile was slid from the truck rail directly onto the launch rail, and once the missile was on the launch rail, the launch crew quickly attached the leads and prepared it for firing. The missile circuitry was checked and the launch crew commander, using a phone in the base of the launcher, called the command van and notified the missile control officer that the missile was ready. As the circuitry was checked, a green ready light came on the missile control officer's light panel. The whole process took less than ten minutes, even in bad weather, and often took considerably less time depending on the skill of the crew.

Once the missile was unloaded, the missile trucks had to go to the storage warehouses to replace the missiles they had fired with new ones. The trucks picked their way through the narrow, rain-swept streets and burning buildings, having to stop from time to time and turn back to find another route when one was blocked by debris.

While this desperate parade continued, the second American raid, an all-Andersen group of eighteen B-52Gs and twelve B-52Ds, was inbound to Hanoi. Their pre-launch experience had been somewhat different from the first wave's because the Andersen briefers had returned to their normal professional style and the crews received the well-organized briefings they were accustomed to. More importantly, the radar navigators had a chance to look at the targets they were to bomb. The briefers did not mention to the crews of the second wave that they would be going to the same targets as the first wave—in fact, the first night Kinh No was to be hit three times, the Hanoi railroad and Yen Vien twice.

As the second wave of Andersen B-52s was air-refueling, Ken Nocito, the electronic warfare officer on Aqua 01, listened to the reports from the first raid's wave leaders to the Eighth Air Force Command Post.

"The first report came in. 'Spellman [the call sign for Eighth Air Force], this a Hot News report. SAM activity extremely heavy in all quadrants. Lilac 03 is missing.'

"Our hearts sank. Then after what seemed like an eternity, 'Spellman, we have received a radio call from Lilac 03, he is heading for U-Tapao.'

"We all cheered, and then we heard the second message. 'Spellman, this is Charcoal 02, we have just come off the target and when we rolled out Charcoal 01 was missing.' We knew that Charcoal 01 was Don Rissi's crew, also from Blytheville and very good friends of ours. No chutes were seen nor was there any radio contact. The reports continued:

"'Heavy SAM and AAA in all quadrants ...'

"'...damaged ... two engines out ...'

"'... is missing ...'

"We pressed on. Our time was coming."

The final report to Eighth Air Force was that four B-52s in the first wave had been hit—one downed by SAMs, two missing, and one heavily damaged and on its way to U-Tapao.

As the second wave approached the target, they passed the first wave outbound about 5000 feet above them, and the pilots could see the lights of the aircraft in the first three-ship cell, then the next cell, and then the next. "We counted the cells as they passed overhead: one, two, three; one, two, three; one, two ... one, two.... We turned north into Laos."

WHEN THE FIRST WAVE returned to Andersen, Bones Scheideman got on the bus with the rest of his crew and sat across from his EW. "I realized we hadn't heard anything from him once we were in the target area, so I asked what he was doing back there in his little compartment. He said there was so much activity that he just turned all the jammers up to maximum and put his helmet bag over his head. I really wasn't sure if he was kidding or not."

Bill Buckley was contemplating what he had just been through. "I had found out that my regular crew was the one that was shot down in Charcoal 01, so it was a very quiet flight back to Guam.

Never before had we lost B-52s in combat. Never before had I lost friends in combat. The war all of a sudden became very personal and very real. Did they get out? Was anyone killed?

"When we landed and debriefed, I returned to an empty room. Five empty beds and I didn't know what their status was. I went next door to Steve Smith's room—he was Bobby Thomas' aircraft commander—and knocked on door. Steve was absolutely furious that I woke him up until I said, 'Bobby and my crew were shot down.' He didn't say a word, just very quietly closed the door.

"When I got back to the room, the phone rang. It was Earlene Thomas, Bobby's wife and our next-door neighbor. She had just been told by another Blytheville wife that Bobby had been shot down. I couldn't tell her anything, but I was infuriated that she had heard it from another wife instead of through official channels. What the hell was going on?"

AL BOYD WAS SCHEDULED to lead a four-ship F-105G Wild Weasel flight to escort the midnight attack. "There was a shortage of air-craft so my wingman and I took the first two F-105Gs and blasted off late, leaving numbers 3 and 4 to catch up when they could get airplanes. We arrived at the tankers and I could see SAMs in the distance, and since we were already late I asked the KC-135 pilot to take us north while we refueled so we could drop off closer to the target area. The gutless bastard wouldn't do it—at that point I distinctly recall that I really wanted to turn on my Vulcan cannon and shoot him down.

"I dropped off after I got my fuel and headed in single ship, leaving my wingman to catch up when he could. As we got up in the area of the Red River, we were over a low overcast. I didn't want to light my afterburner and I was so heavy with a full load of fuel and ordinance I ended up well below 10,000 feet, pretty low. There were planes everywhere, more SAMs than I would have thought they had and at one point I even turned on my rotating beacon as I became more concerned about a mid-air collision than being shot down.

"I saw two F-4s, two burners each, probably five miles out in front of us chasing a MiG showing a weak single burner, and I could see three missile trails going after the MiG, but I never did see what looked like a hit, and there was a cell of BUFFs above us dropping flares and making severe S turns."

This was Peach cell, a mixture of modified and unmodified B-52Gs, the first cell of the second raid, striking the rail yards at Yen Vien that had been the last target hit by the first wave four hours before. Major Clifford B. Ashley, the aircraft commander of Peach 02, had just released his bombs and begun the post-target turn when a flash and huge explosion rocked the aircraft. A SAM exploded just off the left wing and Ashley saw that the SAM had blown the wing tip and external fuel tank off the wing and set the two outboard engines on fire, so he called for help and headed for Thailand.

Behind Ashley in the fixed jump seat was the Deputy Airborne Commander, Lt. Colonel Hendsley Connor. Since the B-52s had only six ejection seats, the wisdom of carrying this extra crewmember had been a matter of some debate among the crews. If the B-52 was hit the aircraft commander had to delay his ejection until the extra crew member unstrapped, went below, then bailed out through the hole in the floor after the navigator and radar navigator ejected. Staying with a damaged aircraft this extra time was not particularly popular with the aircraft commanders, and now Ashley faced the possibility he might have to do that to allow Connor to bail out.

Connor went down to the bomb-nav team compartment to wait for the order to bail out as two F-4s joined Peach 02 as it crossed the Mekong River into Thailand. One of the F-4s said the fire was getting worse and "suggested" they bail out, so Ashley ordered the crew to leave instead of trying to make it to an emergency field. It was a good decision—the crew, including Connor, had barely gotten clear of the aircraft when the B-52 dissolved in a huge explosion. Within twenty minutes rescue helicopters picked up all of the crewmembers.

MEANWHILE, AQUA 01 and the rest of the wave were attacking Kinh No again. Ken Nocito, Aqua 01's EW, remembered: "SAC had directed us to start our jamming too far away from Hanoi and when we were jamming we couldn't see the enemy radars. After a few minutes I turned the jammers off to have a look at what radars were around, and I found that there were not 8 or 10 radars, but over 40 radars hidden under our jamming. If I had left the jammers on like I'd been told to do, I would have been jamming only a few of them. As we approached the target the pilot called a SAM in front of us— I'm not picking up the radar signal yet but I put every possible jammer on the SAM frequency, and it detonated in front and below us. Then I picked up the radar signals as we saw more launches.... They were detonating all around us. I now had over fifty enemy radar signals on my scope and five different SAM signals up, at least one in each quadrant. I could see the flash from the cockpit in front of me each time a SAM exploded near us.

"Now I had more enemy radars than jammers on my scope, then I saw a new signal that was distinctly odd, then a triple SAM launch. I pulled one jammer off and tried to break the lock of this new signal, but it persisted. After what seemed like an eternity it broke lock and the missiles exploded short. As we got closer to the target, it became harder to break lock, and still the missiles kept coming. All that was running though my mind was 'seven minutes'—that's the time we were told we'd be in the heavy SAM area. It may sound trite, but life became a luxury. All I wanted was more power on my jammers. Still they kept coming, then the radar navigator was counting '5,4,3,2,1....'

"Bombs away! Good! All bombs gone! Turn! We cranked up into a sharp bank...."

KEN HOPE WAS aircraft commander in Aqua 03, a G model just behind Nocito. "We could see the clouds light up in series of sparkles from the bombs from the first aircraft. My copilot and I had agreed that we wouldn't say anything over the intercom so the rest of the crew could concentrate on their jobs. We had a very strong crosswind and had to keep making large corrections to get back on course, but when it came time to drop only 17 of the 27 bombs released."

Two of the B-52Gs in these last two cells, Aqua 02 and Red 03, could not get on the proper bomb-release heading and did not drop, and with Hope's release problems this meant only 88 bombs of 162 planned were dropped on the Kinh No.

When Eighth Air Force and SAC found out that Aqua 02 and Red 03 had not dropped their bombs because they were off course, the question came up—was it the crosswind corrections or anti-

SAM maneuvering that caused the B-52s to withhold? Was this a sign of a breakdown in crew discipline?

But there was an even greater breakdown of discipline that SAC was not aware of. The Gia Lam International Airport was off limits to bombing because it was used for civilian flights by countries that were U.S. allies, but such diplomatic niceties were of no concern to one frustrated crew flying a Guam B-52D on the second raid. They had decided to send their own message to the North Vietnamese, and as they approached Hanoi their bomber drifted slightly, almost imperceptibly, off the west of the bomb-run heading and lined up on the Gia Lam airfield. They unloaded their bombs on the airport. Their bombing was spectacularly accurate, cratering several runways and destroying about 80 percent of the international terminal, as well as two Soviet airliners and two helicopters. This bombing would also strand Joan Baez and her party in Hanoi.

WHILE THE NORTH VIETNAMESE had not shot down any B-52s from the second raid "on the spot," to the south of the city the 77th Battalion of the 257th Regiment had made what would turn out to be a major breakthrough in North Vietnamese efforts against the American bombers. The 77th's commander, Dinh The Van, and his fire control officer, Nguyen Van Duc, had believed for some time that they could shoot down a B-52 using the automatic tracking function of the Fan Song guidance radar. While automatic tracking was very accurate, it was generally considered to be impossible to use when the target was jamming, as Dinh said later. "No one dared think of automatic tracking when discussing the techniques of fighting the B-52s because it was 'too idealistic' . . . the three radar screens had been used automatically only in 1965 and 1966, when there was no radar jamming and the enemy had not been so crafty."

Dinh and his crew were determined to try, but the first wave of B-52s had almost ended their hopes when several B-52 bombs damaged some of the 77th's equipment and wounded some of the soldiers who loaded the missiles on the launchers. A few minutes later the site was attacked by a Wild Weasel whose Shrike exploded less than 100 feet from Dinh's command van.

When the second raid attacked, Dinh could not break out a B-52 from the jamming and did not fire, but as he watched the radar returns

Dinh thought he noticed a point when the B-52's jamming dropped off. "We saw that the B-52s heavily jammed and usually whitened our radarscope . . . but we saw that the jamming did not remain heavy all the time. The main point was to calculate and determine the timing and range to expose the B-52 for us to 'kill it like a lamb.'"

AS THE THIRD RAID of Andersen B-52s approached the refueling point, Brent Diefenbach found that his air-refueling autopilot was inoperative. The air-refueling automatic pilot can be compared to power steering on a car, and while a B-52 can be refueled without it, the refueling requires considerably more skill and, often, more time. But extra time was not available that night. The KC-135 tankers were far from their bases at Kadena, Okinawa, and could stay on the track for only about thirty-five minutes before they had to break off and return to base. The B-52s were taking on a full load of gas, about 116,000 pounds, which took about twenty-five minutes on the boom, so they had to get into position quickly and stay on the refueling boom almost the whole time.

As Diefenbach pulled into position and began his difficult task, he thought "Great! I can see it now at the White House, 'Well, Mr. President, Diefenbach couldn't get his gas. . . .'" Diefenbach finished the refueling without problems and continued on with the raid to Hanoi.

As the Andersen B-52s were refueling, the third wave of B-52s from U-Tapao was being briefed for their mission. Aircraft commander Hal "Red" Wilson remembered the briefing as very serious, and when the crews left the room the commanders shook their hands, which was unusual. Wilson was on his fourth Arc Light tour with almost 200 missions and would be flying in Rose 01, targeted on the Hanoi International Radio Station. After the briefing Wilson's crew got on the bus and were joined by Bob Steffen and his crew from Grand Forks who were flying as Rose 02.

Lt. Colonel John Yuill was also scheduled to fly on the third raid and he met crews from the first wave as he was leaving the briefing. "They didn't say a word, but looking at their eyes I knew it must have been a bad day at the office."

A few hours later, at a little before 5:00 A.M., Hanoi time, Rose cell turned down Thud Ridge towards Hanoi. Hanoi Radio was located southwest of the city and the route the 21 U-Tapao B-52s would fly took them across the most heavily defended part of Hanoi and almost directly over the previously bombed targets at Kinh No and Gia Lam. The North Vietnamese defenses were ready, and Rose cell began to pick up Fan Song signals more than sixty miles from the target.

In Rose 01, Red Wilson and his copilot, Charlie Brown, saw a large number of SAMs as they approached their target. Behind them, in Rose 02, Bob Steffen was uncomfortable. "We knew we were coming in the same heading to a target that had just been bombed and we were concerned. We saw a lot of SAMs going up and blowing up in the distance as we approached."

TO THE SOUTH OF THE CITY the 77th battalion's commander, Dinh The Van and his fire control officer, Nguyen Van Duc, discussed how they were going to modify their attack somewhat as they waited for the next raid. This time they would first manually track a B-52, fire their missiles, then try to transfer to automatic tracking as the B-52 got closer. Dinh listened to Air Defense Headquarters tracking the incoming B-52s and soon the 77th was assigned a target. Dinh watched carefully as Duc and the three guidance officers tracked the B-52's jamming. "When the return appeared very clearly I immediately called for automatic tracking and all three guidance control officers' radar screens went to automatic. We picked up the return without distortion. Fire control officer Duc pushed the buttons to launch two missiles in close succession...."

The van trembled slightly and the crew heard two dull, short roars six seconds apart as the missiles blasted off from their launchers 150 meters away; then it was quiet as the crew watched their radar screens to make sure the system was automatically guiding the missiles to the target.

Above them, Rose 01 rolled into its post-target turn into the jet stream wind. "It seemed like we were in the post-target turn forever," Red Wilson remembered, "then our gunner, Charlie Poole, said, 'that's close enough, boss—one missile just went between the wing and the stabilizer.'"

The second missile fired by the 77th had reached its maximum speed of 1800 miles an hour. As it approached the B-52 the proximity fuse detected its target and the 400-pound warhead, grooved internally to produce a circular fragmentation pattern, detonated. Copilot Charlie Brown recalls, "I heard a 'puff' sounding noise followed by a rapid decompression and my oxygen mask was pulled away from my face and snapped back. I noticed that it had gotten lighter outside and we had the number 3 and 4 engine firelights on. I was in no hurry to shut down engines over the heart of Hanoi, so I leaned forward between my seat and the pilot's seat to get a closer look at the temperature gauges when suddenly I was surrounded by fire. . . . I ejected. We were at 38,000 feet and I remember tumbling wildly and seeing our airplane exploding. . . ."

In the compartment below the radar navigator, Major Fernando Alexander, found himself looking through a large hole on the left side of the aircraft at the external bomb rack and a fire on the number three engine. He immediately bailed out.

Behind them, in Rose 02, Bob Steffen watched spellbound. "I saw a fireball and at the same time my radar navigator, who was looking on his radar for Rose 01, called 'I can't see him.' For a second it didn't register, but then I did an almost instantaneous double take as we flew through billowing black smoke, like an oil fire, and then we heard the beepers. I knew immediately what had happened, but I don't think anybody else on the crew did. The radar navigator kept saying 'I can't find him, I can't find him,' and I finally said, 'He's gone. We're lead.'"

Charlie Brown was floating down in his parachute. "I believe that I must have passed out on the way down because the next thing I remember my parachute opened automatically at 14,000 feet. I saw SAM trails and explosions above me. When a SAM detonated I noticed a spherical 'halo' expand outward, and I could see the bright flashes of bomb detonations on the ground. When I landed, I was in the middle of a great air battle. The whole earth was shaking and there were bright flashes everywhere, from bombs landing to missiles launching to anti-aircraft fire. It was funny. I didn't notice the anti-aircraft fire in the air but I sure noticed it on the ground. I guess it just didn't reach our altitude. The sound and vibrations really impressed me. One thing for sure, one's senses are stimulated by air warfare."

Brown's aircraft commander, Red Wilson, was not far away. "I landed and was gathering my stuff when about a quarter of a mile away the whole sky lit up and two SAMs blasted off. It scared the shit out of me, as if I wasn't scared enough already. .... I had almost landed on the site. I hid my chute and started to walk but unfortunately walked right into some militia types."

DINH HAD FOUND a major vulnerability in the B-52s' tactics. The steep post-target turn blanked many of the bomber's downward focused jamming antennas, and the drop-off in jamming Dinh had seen occurred when the turn was made in close proximity to the missile sites. With the jamming blanked, the Fan Song radar could break out the B-52s' radar return and track it automatically. Not only that, but the headwind and the distance the B-52s had to turn meant that for about fifteen seconds *all three aircraft in the cell were in the turn,* and the cell had no jamming protection at all over the most heavily defended part of the city.

AT U-TAPAO COLONEL BILL BROWN, who had led the first raid, was trying to decide what to do. "We sat down and said that we have to something, this ain't gonna work, it's too easy for them. We're all coming in the same altitude, doing the same thing, repetitively, and we need to do something different. [Colonel] Don Davis had led the third raid and came in later shaking his head saying, 'We've got to do something different.' But we didn't know what was going to happen the next night, so no one said anything officially."

At Andersen, Bob Hruby returned home after serving as Charlie on the first raids. His wife Pat remembers, "He would never come home until the wee hours of the morning after he saw the strike reports and found out how many BUFFs had made it that evening. He told me that first night that 'they're not using evasive action,' and that really bothered him."

Bones Scheideman and many of the crewmembers gathered, as usual, at the Officers' Club at Andersen. "We bought the tactics like good soldiers, but it was clear after the first mission that it was a bad idea. I would strongly disagree with anyone who claims that morale was high after the first mission. It was very low. We were aware of the losses and highly dissatisfied with the tactics that now looked downright stupid, and we knew we would be doing it all over again in a little while." A consensus arose among the crews at Andersen. When ordered not to maneuver they saluted smartly, then went out and maneuvered anyway when it was necessary to survive. They simply never reported it to the leadership.

At U-Tapao, R. J. Smith was asleep in his trailer. "The next thing I know this Colonel comes in and says he had to seal the trailer, which meant that Hank Barrows, my trailer mate, had been shot down. I was awake, wide-awake, when the Colonel called me and said 'what's this on the mirror in the bathroom?'

"I had no clue but went in to look. Hank had written on the mirror 'R. J., if I don't come back you can have my blender.'"

While the crews were dealing with the losses, the Eighth Air Force staff had received the mission plans for Day Three. They were virtually the same as Day One and Day Two—the same times, routes, altitudes and targets. According to a member of his staff, the Eighth Air Commander, General Johnson, "just blew his cork when [SAC] wouldn't change the axis of attack."

SEVEN

The Second Day

As the B-52s retired, the North Vietnamese air defense units all over the country inundated the Air Defense Headquarters with messages asking one question: "Is it true you have shot down B-52s over Hanoi?" When the headquarters confirmed the kills, the staff and the victorious missile battalions were overwhelmed by congratulations. Tran Nhan, the deputy commander of the 361st Division, noted that "a special feeling pervaded the various command headquarters from the battalions to the General Staff, from the northern rear area to southern battlefields. The Hanoi air defenses had stood up to America's greatest weapon and had held its own; it had inspired the people and the Army."

The North Vietnamese military and political leaders were not the only ones to appreciate what happened that night. As the sun rose, curious Hanoi citizens flocked to the wreckage of the two B-52s that had crashed close to the city. One remembered, "Once the first B-52 was shot down things turned around completely. The government propaganda machine went into action and made sure that absolutely everyone knew about the achievement. The speakers on the street corners normally used to alert people of air raids were now used to let people know all the details about how the B-52 had been shot down. After this, people lost their respect for the B-52s and the idea of them being 'super flying fortresses' became a bit of a joke."

Others on the scene saw what happened differently. Norb Gotner was an F-4 backseater, one of the few American POWs captured in Laos, and was now in the POW camp known as the Plantation.

When he walked outside the next morning, he saw the prison yard was covered with chaff. He remembered later, "The psychological effect of the massive B-52 carpet bombing was strong. Although the North Vietnamese feared the fighter drops, they had confidence that the bombs would hit a specific target, and they would often sit outside and watch the attacks. They had a much greater fear now that whole sections of town were devastated by one drop. Pretty soon senior North Vietnamese officers began to spend the night at the Plantation during the raids. . . ."

The North Vietnamese leadership quickly tried to exploit six of the B-52 crewmembers they had captured. Bob Certain, Charlie Brown, and Richard Simpson from Charcoal 01 and Red Wilson, Hank Barrows and Fernando Alexander from Rose 01 were "introduced" to the foreign press at the Hanoi International Club. A correspondent noted they all seemed to be in good condition, though Captains Brown and Barrows had been injured in the ejection. On December 21 the six had their individual pictures on the front page of the *New York Times,* Barrows with his head heavily bandaged.

The North Vietnamese were not unhappy with the first night's results. They had fired fewer than 130 SA-2s, had shot two B-52s "on the spot," and their intelligence had intercepted radio transmissions that made it clear that several other B-52s had been seriously damaged, if not downed. (The actual total was three B-52s downed and two damaged). Van Tien Dung, the Chief of Air Defense Staff, was satisfied but realized that there were decisions to be made. Clearly the Americans would be coming during the day with their laser-guided bombs, and around-the-clock operations would put a strain on the North Vietnamese defenses. To minimize the load, Van ordered the air defense system divided. The SAM battalions would take major responsibility for the expected nightly B-52 raids while the day missions would be left to the MiGs, which had not been successful against the B-52s but had good results against American F-4s during previous daylight attacks. From this point on, there would be occasional attempted intercepts at night by the few night-qualified MiG-21 pilots and an occasional SAM firing during the day, but basically this division of labor would last for all of Linebacker II.

Meanwhile, there was a steadily developing crisis with the supply of SA-2 missiles. Each battalion had begun the first night with twelve missiles, six on their launchers and six more on trucks that quickly moved in and reloaded the launchers after the missiles were fired. But because of a lack of planning by both the General Staff and the Air Defense Headquarters, there were very few pre-assembled missiles in storage warehouses, and after the first night's battles many of the battalions were short of missiles. The SA-2 missiles were capable of being fully assembled and stored for long periods (up to a year) and a reserve of assembled missiles could have been stockpiled around Hanoi. The failure to store assembled missiles was to prove a critical mistake.

As the sun came up there were long lines of trucks outside the technical units' warehouses waiting for new missiles. Reports began to come in of problems during the seemingly interminable waits at the missile warehouses. At one point, arguments erupted between the drivers and the soldiers distributing the missiles, and a North Vietnamese newspaper reporter described this scene:

"There are no more missiles now, guys."

"You have to continue to work. My battalion has fired its last missile!"

"Well, we don't have any now."

Then, when a missile finally did come of the line, there were more problems.

"You must give us this missile!"

"No, you have to wait. When it's your turn you'll get the next one."

"Just because the 77th Battalion shot down a "fat calf" [slang for a B-52] on the spot, you favor them, and I know it."

"Don't say that! We all have to work together."

While the 257th and 261st Regiments each had a technical battalion that was responsible for assembling the missiles, the newly arrived 274th Regiment's technical battalion was still straggling in from the south. Now, at the critical point of the battle, there were only two technical battalions to supply missiles for three regiments, further increasing the strain on the system.

THE NEXT MORNING, December 19, Bob Steffen was to call to the wing headquarters at U-Tapao to discuss the loss of his leader, Rose 01, the night before. Steffen was gratified by the wing leadership's response.

"The meeting was aircraft commanders only; myself, the aircraft commander of Rose 03, the third aircraft in our formation, and aircraft commander of the number three aircraft in the cell in front of us. It was a Brigadier General [Sullivan] and some colonels, and they asked us a lot of questions—actually quizzed us. It was a 'lost aircraft investigation,' kind of like an accident investigation. Their whole thrust was 'we lost an airplane last night, and we want to know why.' They were very serious, they wanted to talk about tactics, they were really interested in what happened and what suggestions I had for that night's mission. I told them that coming in all in a straight line was really dumb, we had to have room to maneuver, and all that."

A total of five B-52s had been hit and three downed, all by SA-2s, and while the losses were a shock to the crews, they were about the number that had been expected. Now the focus turned to preventing more. Of the five B-52s hit, three were hit just prior to the target and the other two in the post-target turn, the two times in the raid that experienced crewmembers believed the B-52s were most vulnerable. This was the time when the B-52s were closest to the SAM sites, and the Fan Song radar was believed to be capable of overpowering—"burning thorough"—a B-52's jamming, and when the B-52s opened their bomb bay doors it increased the B-52s radar signature tremendously, making the Fan Song's task much easier. Then, just when the bomb bay doors closed, the bombers went into their post-target turn and blanked their jamming antennas. The post-target turn was made even worse because it was made into the jet stream winds that slowed the bombers' ground speed by 100 knots, holding them suspended over the heavily defended target area. Many of the crews believed this was the reason the two bombers were hit in the post-target turn.

Another cause for concern was that two of the three aircraft lost had been G models—two thirds of the first night's losses, even though they were only about one quarter of the force. Although SAC had told Eighth Air Force that tests showed that the unmodified Gs were just as effective as the modified Gs, Eighth had already expressed doubts about the tests and was watching the unmodified G models carefully.

A different concern was that two crews had failed to drop their bombs because they were too far from the target when it was time for bomb release. Maneuvering on the bomb run had been expressly forbidden. Had the two crews disobeyed orders? If so, it was a disturbing breach of discipline that raised serious questions. Were other crews maneuvering? What if a B-52 dropped its bombs on a residential area or a POW camp as a result? Was this a harbinger of a larger breakdown of discipline? And the leadership was not even aware of the most serious breach of discipline at Gia Lam.

The number and type of B-52s that were sent to the various targets augured ill for the future. Many of the U-Tapao D models with their heavier bomb loads had been assigned to attack unimportant targets such as the four airfields, while major targets were assigned to the B-52s from Andersen with smaller bomb loads. The first night, U-Tapao Ds hit the North Vietnamese airfields with over 2100 bombs, doing little damage, while the Andersen aircraft attacked the large, heavily defended complexes at Yen Vien and Kinh No. Fewer than 1000 bombs were assigned to Yen Vien, and Kinh No was hit by less than 1200. Because they had been so lightly damaged, Yen Vien and Kinh No had to be hit again and again, and the defenses around these two targets would be responsible for most of the B-52 losses.

But for all the problems, American intelligence had intercepted North Vietnamese radio transmissions calling for more missiles, and that indicated that the North Vietnamese might be missile limited. The first and third waves had been heavily engaged by SAMs, but the second raid of B-52s attacking targets close to Hanoi reported lighter SAM activity. Why wasn't the second raid more heavily engaged? Was it a fluke or a symptom of a problem with the North Vietnamese SAM defenses?

FOR SEVENTH AIR FORCE in Saigon, the major problem was that the mission plan had arrived late, and even when it arrived it did not include the B-52s' entry and exit headings, which had a serious impact on the SAM suppression operation. The Wild Weasels needed to fly parallel to the B-52s' headings so they would be pointed at the SAM sites, in a position to launch their anti-radiation missiles as soon as a Fan Song radar came on. Without the B-52s' headings, the Weasels could not parallel the bomber stream and were at a disadvantage. The Weasels also suspected (correctly) that the B-52s were not meeting their scheduled time over the target. The upshot was that the Weasels had been forced to fire most of their anti-radiation missiles preemptively, based on the planned B-52 time over target, hoping that a Fan Song would come on the air while the ARM was in flight and, in Weasel parlance, "eat the missile." Seventh Air Force sent messages to Eighth Air Force about the late arrival of the plan and the omission of the bombers' inbound and outbound courses but it was ignored by Eighth, which was having enough problems of its own trying to deal with SAC.

The F-4 escorts reported that only a few MiGs were airborne, and none close to the B-52 formations despite the fact that the B-52s had reported a large number of MiGs. It appeared that some of the B-52s were in a "MiG panic," and the tail gunners immediately fired on any aircraft that drifted close to the bomber stream. At the same time the gunner fired, the bomber dropped flares to decoy the MiGs' ATOLL heat-seeking missiles, but these flares allowed the North Vietnamese to follow the track of B-52 cells simply by following the path made by their flares. When a B-52 gunner fired at an F-4, the fighters dove away from the B-52s; after the mission, several B-52 gunners claimed "MiG kills," saying that as soon as they fired "the MiGs dove towards the ground." The fighter crews were not the only ones who believed that the B-52 gunners were over-enthusiastic. One of the Guam wing commanders later said, "I think there were only three or four MiG engagements. ... There were several others where crew members thought they were MiGs but later proved to be other B-52s that crossed the formation or F-4s that were dodging SAMs themselves and actually came into the cone of fire of the B-52s."

The F-4s that tried to engage the few MiGs that came up had problems getting clearance to fire, either because of the large number of friendly aircraft in area or because the radios were so clogged that the control agency that had to confirm their target was in fact a MiG could not break through the chatter. On the two occasions when F-4s were cleared to fire, their missiles failed and the MiG escaped.

NIXON HAD DECIDED at the beginning of the operation that the administration would not publicly discuss the bombing, because he under-

stood that the North Vietnamese would never return to the negotiating table under public pressure. The administration did not
announce the beginning of the raids, and it was not until the international press reported the attacks that the American people found
out about the operation. As expected, there was quick and sharp
outrage in the press. Most commentators and politicians asserted
the bombing would be counterproductive and pointless, that it was
an open-ended tactic, and used the administration's silence on the
aim of the raids to support this argument. But Nixon was used to
denunciations from opponents of the war, and he and his staff realized that there was no chance of a reasonable discussion of alternatives. The president was more concerned about the reaction of
Congress and his own staff. As Alexander Haig remembered: "Some
legislators said they were going to cut off all funds to Southeast Asia
if he continued the bombing. A second group said they were going
to start an impeachment process. These two things left most of the
president's advisors with their knees knocking."

Nixon, with Haig's encouragement, was determined to stay
the course, and he also expected the outrage of the "chattering
classes" to be matched by support from the "silent majority" of the
population. For whatever reason—the winter weather, the approach
of the Christmas holidays, satisfaction that the U.S. was finally
doing something, or simple war weariness—Nixon was right. There
were no massive demonstrations and public polls showed little
strong feeling about the bombing, to the disgust of the anti-war
activists.

Meanwhile, Haig was anxiously following the details of the
raids, speaking regularly to Admiral Moorer and one of Secretary
of Defense Laird's deputies, as well as reading the reports of the
first night. Losses had been heavy but under the 3 percent predicted.

In the Pentagon, Air Force Lieutenant Colonel Jack McDonald was responsible for watching the North Vietnamese air defense
systems for the Defense Intelligence Agency (DIA). McDonald had
been an electronic warfare officer in SAC and from 1958–1962 was
a member of SAC's Test & Tactics unit that tested new, experimental
electronic warfare equipment for SAC aircraft and helped develop
tactics on how best to survive in a radar air defense environment.
He also helped develop the "Basketweave" flight paths that would

bring SAC bombers to their targets from different directions in the event of a nuclear war.

During Linebacker II, McDonald was responsible for giving the daily intelligence briefing to the Chairman and the rest of the Joint Chiefs, and he remembered, "The normal Chairman's briefing was between 0800 to 0830 in the National Military Command Center briefing room in the Pentagon. The first night of Linebacker II the first raid was just coming off their Hanoi targets about the time of the Chairman's briefing, so we postponed the brief until we knew about the results. The last raid was off target right after noon and we would brief the Chairman again, then we spent the afternoon and evening attempting to piece together a picture of the whole night. That was pretty much the briefing schedule for all of Linebacker II.

"I will never forget my dismay when I saw the SAC mission routes and timing. They had three-ship cells coming in on exactly the same entry routes exactly three minutes apart. After the first raid was through, exactly four hours later, the second raid arrived, again on identical entry routes and spaced exactly three minutes apart. The third raid arrived four hours later doing the exact same thing and with the same timing. Tuesday night was a repeat of the first night—I couldn't believe it—the same thing again.

"I was more than a little upset that everything that we had learned and tried to apply to increase survivability of the aircrews was being ignored. I'm afraid some of my bias might have crept into the briefings I was writing and giving to the Joint Chiefs of Staff."

ON GUAM, THE EIGHTH AIR FORCE staff was becoming more and more concerned about the continuing delays in getting information about the upcoming missions from SAC. The first mission had been a "shakedown cruise" and delays were understandable, but Eighth had expected that SAC Headquarters would be quicker providing the needed information for the second and third nights' missions. Instead, the information continued to be late, and when it arrived changes quickly followed, disrupting the planning process and delaying the dissemination of the plan to Seventh Air Force and the other units.

The Eighth Air Force staff could not understand what the problem was. SAC should have had no problems with tactics or route planning, which were the same for every mission; for each raid all the staff had to do was select several targets from the JCS-approved target list, assign a certain number of B-52s to each target, then send the list on to Andersen. What was holding this up? The Eighth staff complained about the delays to the Eighth Air Force Commander, but General Johnson told them that while he was aware of what was happening, "I can't do anything."

The reason General Johnson could not do anything was because he knew the problem was his superior, General John "J. C." Meyer, the Commander of SAC (CINCSAC). General Meyer was, like Johnson, another World War II fighter ace who seemed typecast. After World War II he had been a fighter wing commander early in the Korean War and had a reputation as an aggressive and decisive combat leader. One of his staff remembered him as tall, with a "movie star persona," relaxed but with a cockiness that came very close to being arrogant.

But now the fighter pilot Meyer was in charge of a massive bombing operation that he had absolutely no idea how to execute, and he had become Hamlet. General Harry Cordes, the SAC Chief of Staff for Intelligence, said later: "General Meyer took the task of running Linebacker as a personal responsibility as the commander. His reluctance to make the major decisions was frustrating to SAC Headquarters, but even more so to General Johnson."

To make things more difficult, Meyer did not have the confidence of his staff, despite—or perhaps because of—his fighter background, his combat credentials and education (he, like General Vogt at Seventh Air Force, was a New Yorker and Ivy Leaguer [Dartmouth '39]). In fact, General Meyer was viewed with some disdain by the SAC staff because he had no experience in bomber operations, and one SAC general said later, "All J. C. Meyer cared about was that Gabby Gabreski [another WWII ace] got more kills than he did and kept needling him about it."

A member of the SAC staff observed, "General Meyer was a fighter pilot, not a professional bomber guy like the SAC Deputy Commander for Operations, General Pete Sianis, and everybody was conscious of that fact. The main concern of the staff was to 'manage the CINC' so that he didn't go off half-cocked and give an order that would cause a lot of disruption."

As soon as the operation began Meyer presided over a series of daily SAC staff meetings, one early in the morning when changes in the following day's missions could be made and one later in the day when the plan was almost completed, but in fact the meetings were overlapping and often there was no real break. The meetings were not held in a formal briefing room but in a conference room in the first-story basement of the SAC Headquarters building. One of the regular attendees described the scene:

"There was a big oval conference table with General Meyer at one end with the senior staff sitting around the table and the other participants in chairs off to one side. Most of the briefings were hand written on 'butcher paper' and displayed on a briefing stand at one end. When photographs were used they were 30'x40' boards with information noted on them. The uniform was formal Class As—no shirt sleeves."

General Meyer was the central figure at the meetings, but his entire combat career had been in fighters, where decisions were made at the lowest possible level, and now he was in charge of a leviathan whose corporate culture was exactly the opposite. He had a staff that believed that everything had to be done from the top and expected him to make all the decisions. Meyer began to hesitate, exhibiting a syndrome common to successful front-line combat leaders forced to command a battle from the rear. One military historian wrote that in this situation "a leader might realize failure may mean dismissal and the end of a career unstained by any hint of personal inadequacy. As a result, the anxiety he faces may make him prefer the safety of inaction to the dangers of doubtful action."

The results were predictable. A staff member said later, "I clearly remember that General Meyer never showed anxiety or awareness of urgency, but he seemed more clueless than someone who was trying to keep calm in a tense situation. That's what drove everybody wild."

Adding to the strain was the senior SAC staff's lack of combat experience. Meyer's deputy was General Glenn Martin, who had flown a few missions in World War II. He was well regarded by some for his political acumen but in the words of one observer, "he was known to have some bizarre ideas about how bombing should be conducted and was always coming up with some idea about how to 'win the war.'"

General Pete Sianis, the SAC Director of Operations, was another important player with little combat experience—about twenty missions in World War II and about ten in Korea. It was Sianis' staff who had put together the stereotyped plan the B-52s were to use the first four nights, but Sianis, short, stocky and physically unimpressive, was well regarded. "Sianis had real bomber knowledge (unlike the CINC, who was a fighter re-tread)," a colleague remembered, "and he was generally considered the smartest guy on the staff. Sianis sat next to Meyer, and it was his job to present the operations clearly and precisely so as not to give the CINC room to exercise his considerable imagination."

The other main participants were Brigadier General Harry Cordes, tall, gaunt and ascetic, who "exuded intelligence"— but one who had no combat experience at all. Major General George McKee, the Director of Logistics, was "a man of very few words but was always listened to because he knew all the details—how long to get the bombs to the loading area, how long it took to load bombs on one cell of aircraft, how long to change the fuses if the bombs were loaded. In general, what was possible and what was not." McKee had flown 35 combat missions in 1944 but had not seen combat since then.

Since General Meyer knew nothing about bomber operations and none of the generals had ever flown combat operations in jet aircraft, much less in a surface-to-air missile environment, the staff expected them to ask a few questions so they could understand the rationale behind the plan, then sign it off so it could be quickly sent to Eighth Air Force.

This did not happen. Feeling great pressure from Washington, in unfamiliar territory with a staff that had little faith in his judgment, Meyer groped for control. General Cordes described the problem: "General Meyer was a very deliberate (often slow) decision maker. ... [His] thorough nature ... dictated his personal review and approval of each phase of the mission. ... [He] liked to war game each situation, trying to sense the reaction of all parties, political and military. The staff meetings went on for hours and hours, with thorough and complete review and with some changes and adjustments. General Meyer personally participated in the mission planning process in sessions up to 18 hours long with 8th Air Force waiting nervously for the key information they needed to . . . brief crews and launch. . . . It was an agonizing process to get a final firm decision."

Meyer often focused on minutiae instead of the serious questions that had to be answered. One example is especially illustrative. The missions the first few nights were flown under a full moon, but no one seemed to be able to tell Meyer accurately what time the full moon would rise and set over Hanoi, or what the duration of twilight was at the B-52s' altitude. Suddenly, in General Meyer's mind this information became a matter of critical importance, so instead of discussing tactics or the bombing plan the staff had to turn to the issue of "twilight time." General Cordes remembered: "Many hours and much effort were spent on this problem, on who was responsible for figuring this out, and much blood was let in the planning room."

Cordes also noted other reasons for the delays. "Often, General Meyer would consult with Admiral Moorer. . . . General Meyer wanted to be able to stand up and say to the NCA [National Command Authority, i.e. the president] that he and his staff had done the best possible job of target and mission planning." In fact, if this was Meyer's intention, it had the opposite effect. This compulsion to control and micromanage every aspect of the operation would virtually guarantee that the strikes would not have the flexibility to be successful in a high-threat combat environment.

The lower ranking planners in the SAC staff—and, indeed, some of the generals—watched in dismay as these delays and side issues started a chain reaction that resulted in Eighth Air Force and the other units getting the mission plan late, and often incomplete, with amendments to come. It was widely felt that General Meyer and the senior staff's actions were going to lead to a disaster unless they could be changed, but the subordinates had to be circumspect. SAC was still a "top down" organization and General Meyer controlled their careers, so no one was willing to push too hard.

ON NIGHT TWO, NINETY B-52 missions were scheduled against Hanoi and the first raid would be entirely from Andersen: 9 Gs and 12Ds. The briefing was once again a sobering time for crews that had never expected to be in real combat, and took place before the third mission of the first night had landed, an example of the long lead times involved in Andersen missions. Still, the first two raids had already returned and many of the crewmembers in the briefing room had heard the rumors of losses and stories of "wall-to-wall SAMs."

The Andersen crews had a mix of emotions in the briefings. Some were conscious that others had "seen the elephant," and felt left out and slightly envious that they didn't have war stories. Others were very apprehensive. Even in the same crew, emotions varied between crewmembers. One G model crewmember noted a range of reactions on his crew. The aircraft commander was very quiet; the copilot wanted to go but had "bad vibes," especially when he found out they were flying an "unmodified" G; the electronic warfare officer was comfortable because he was sure the three B-52s in the cell would give each other mutual electronic countermeasures support; the radar navigator—who had already flown a combat tour in AC-119 gunships—thought their chances were good with the B-52s' jamming systems.

The target for most of the first raid was the Kinh No complex, which had been bombed by each of the three raids the night before. There were virtually no changes in the mission pattern other than variation of a few thousand feet in altitude and different spacing between the cells, nothing the North Vietnamese would even notice. Then, at the end of the briefing, the airborne commander of the first raid, Colonel James R. McCarthy, stunned the crews when, apparently on his own initiative, he told them that any aircraft commander who maneuvered to evade SAMs prior to bomb release would be court-martialed. The crews were stunned, and one later said, "I don't know why he issued the order that there be no evasive on the bomb run under threat of court martial, but someone with experience in a position of authority should have pointed out the stupidity to higher HQ."

The six-hour flight over the Pacific to Hanoi gave the Andersen crews on the first raid time to think about what lay ahead, and while the first raid of the second night was heading for its targets, the crews of the second raid—21 Gs from Andersen and 15 Ds from U-Tapao—began their briefing with some good news. The briefer told them that evasive maneuvering was now approved as long as the bombers were straight and level at bomb release. It was almost surreal. The crews of the first raid went to Hanoi under Colonel McCarthy's threat of court-martial if they maneuvered, while the second raid crews four hours later were encouraged to maneuver.

At U-Tapao this announcement was offset by the mission profile. Unlike the Andersen crews, the short missions from U-Tapao meant that their crews flew every day, and the second night's missions included many of the same crews that had flown the first night. After the first night's losses it was chilling for these crews to see that the whole force was coming in on the same headings, the same altitudes, bombing the same targets, and using the same post-target turn in an area where the crews noted that the SAMs seemed heaviest.

SURPRISINGLY, THE NORTH VIETNAMESE air defenses were less organized on Night Two, perhaps because the headquarters of the 361st Missile Division was moving to a different location to avoid an American air attack. That layer of control was missing, but this did not appear to be important to the Air Defense Headquarters personnel watching the chain of twenty-one B-52s of the first raid turn south down Tam Dao Mountains and head for Hanoi, following the same route they had followed the night before. They heard a gentle thunder in the distance as F-111s attacked four MiG bases, and the radar operators saw the chaff corridor pointing like an arrow to the center of Hanoi. As the bombers approached, the North Vietnamese could see that the B-52s were not in the chaff corridor—once again, the narrow corridor was being blown away by high winds. They were confident they were going to inflict severe losses on the B-52s.

Then, surprisingly, the North Vietnamese missile crews faltered badly. In the twelve-minute raid all the SAMs missed—not a single B-52 was even damaged.

The unscathed first raid was well on its way back to Guam when the second raid arrived over Hanoi four hours later. Nine Gs were targeted on Hanoi Radio, in the heart of the SA-2 batteries and where Red Wilson in Rose 01 had been shot down the night before. Once again the missile crews faltered, and only one G model was slightly damaged on the way in.

These Andersen Gs were followed over Hanoi Radio by six U-Tapao Ds that received a different reception. Major John Dalton, who had flown the first B-52 over Hanoi the previous night, was again in the lead position in the first D cell as Ivory 01. As they approached the target, the North Vietnamese defenders went back to the tactics that had been so effective the first night, waiting for the B-52s to go into their post-target turn. Dalton saw no SAMs on the bomb run but as soon as he rolled his post-target turn, the electronic warfare officer called that three SAM sites had locked on and he detected an "uplink," the guidance signal to the missile that meant SAMs were on the way.

Dalton's aircraft was now facing into the jet stream, slowing down rapidly and hanging in its steep turn. Then the first SAM hit. The force of the missile blast almost stopped the B-52 in mid-air, as one crewmember remembered later: "You could feel the concussion, then you heard it. I never realized that you could hear them explode like that . . . you get static electricity raising the hair on your arms."

Ivory 01 was in serious trouble. One engine was on fire and the other engine in the pod had flamed out, an alternator was running away and overspeeding, the cables for the rudder and right elevator were severed and both drop tanks had fuel pouring out of holes the missile had blown in them.

Dalton headed for the nearest emergency base, the Marine airfield at Nam Phong, Thailand, nursing the damaged bomber along until he finally saw the lights of Nam Phong ahead and lined the B-52 up on the runway. As he lowered the landing gear and the huge, wide-spread landing lights came on, several Marines standing outside the radar-approach trailer to watch the landing were so shocked they dove off the trailer for cover.

Just as Dalton was about to touch down, the damaged bomber lost its electrical power, went dark and lost the stabilizer trim—necessary for a normal landing—as the aircraft began to flare. Dalton forced the big plane down into a hard landing that blew out two tires, then ended a night of superb flying by getting the damaged bomber stopped before it went off the runway. The crew slowly emerged to a large crowd of awestruck Marines, who later decorated the aircraft with the Marine insignia and a note, "To the Boys in the Air Force From the Men in the Marines."

The remaining five B-52s in the second raid escaped without damage, and this was to be the last B-52 raid on Hanoi Radio. In two nights almost 2900 bombs—bombs that could have been used against more lucrative targets—had been dropped on the station, and one attacking B-52 had been shot down and two damaged. The station had been knocked off the air for a total of nine minutes.

FOUR HOURS AFTER the second raid, the third arrived, consisting of 6 Gs and 15 Ds from Andersen and 15Ds from U-Tapao. The B-52s were again revisiting targets, one of them the Yen Vien complex where Bob Certain and his crew had been shot down the night before, but the nine B-52Ds that struck Yen Vien found the North Vietnamese response anemic—only ten SAMs were counted, and no B-52s were hit. The other twenty-seven B-52s bombed a safe target far from Hanoi, the Thai Nguyen thermal power plant, with little North Vietnamese reaction and no damage to the bombers.

As the third wave of fifteen B-52s returned to U-Tapao leaving a wake of high-altitude contrails, at Nam Phong, John Dalton and his crew went outside to look for the returning force. He counted fifteen contrails and knew that all the U-Tapao aircraft were returning without loss, and Dalton said later it was "one of the greatest moments of my life."

EIGHT

The Slaughter
of the Gs

The North Vietnamese official history of Linebacker II reports that the Air Defense Command staff in Hanoi was "worried and pensive" after failing to shoot down any B-52s on Night Two. Other sources suggest that a better word is "apoplectic." Despite having been in battle all night, the Hanoi area missile battalion commanders were called to the Air Defense Headquarters and, according to North Vietnamese sources, the discussions involved "self-criticism and criticism ... held in an animated and scrupulous manner at all levels."

Beyond the revolutionary rhetoric, it is clear the session was brutal. One by one, the exhausted and humiliated battalion commanders had to stand in front of their counterparts and the staff and explain the techniques they had used, why they failed, and what they planned on doing to improve their results. The Headquarters staff listened then gave the commanders a simple message. Most of them were babies in 1954, the time of the Dien Bien Phu battle that evicted the French from their country, and now they had a chance to fight their own great, decisive battle, an "aerial Dien Bien Phu." They must not fail—like their fathers at Dien Bien Phu, they would have to find a way to defeat the enemy. The commanders were then sent back for a few hours' sleep.

But after years of combat, Air Defense Command leaders knew it was not enough to find fault with the battalion commanders— the staff itself had to take action, even with their limited resources. Unlike SAC and its "zero defects" culture, which discouraged leaders from reporting difficulties and looking for collective ways to cure them, the Vietnamese Communists realized that sometimes "objective circumstances" were responsible for military failures.

Military officers were allowed to fail as long as they did their best and were trying to improve. More importantly, the review system was very democratic, and encouraged criticism from colleagues and even subordinates—something SAC would never have tolerated.

In analyzing the battles the staff members saw that the B-52s had used the northwest to southeast route to Hanoi the two previous nights, and the leadership decided to take a gamble that the U.S. would repeat the same routes and tactics it had used the first two nights. The Air Defense Command moved two SAM battalions from the south to the north of the city so that their missile sites would form a triangle around Hanoi with the point to the northwest, instead of being laid out in a circle around the city. This would allow the missile sites to fire at the B-52s coming down from the northwest much further out, but it would leave the south relatively unprotected.

At the same time, the headquarters' SA-2 technicians, experts and training officers examined each of the battalions' engagements. After analyzing the results, they decided that techniques that took advantage of the B-52s' standardized tactics appeared to offer the best chance of success, and a variation of the automatic tracking technique the 77th had used the first night appeared to be the most promising. They saw that at a certain point close to the sites the B-52s' jamming decreased and the radar return became clear, though they did not know exactly why. (This was when the B-52s opened their bomb bay doors, then continued when they went into the post-target turn). The problem was that the jamming usually did not decrease until the B-52 was very close to the missile site, too close to fire. The experts recommended firing the missiles initially with manual guidance at the jamming strobe, and then attempting to transfer the missile guidance to automatic tracking while the missile was in the air when the bomber's radar return became clear. If the crews were unable to transfer to automatic tracking, they could still continue to guide the missiles manually. The technical officers also realized that the closer the B-52 was to the missile site, the better the chances of going to automatic track, so they told the battalion commanders to hold their fire until the bombers were close, going "face to face with the B-52s" as one described it later. The Air Defense Staff's technical officers then departed for the

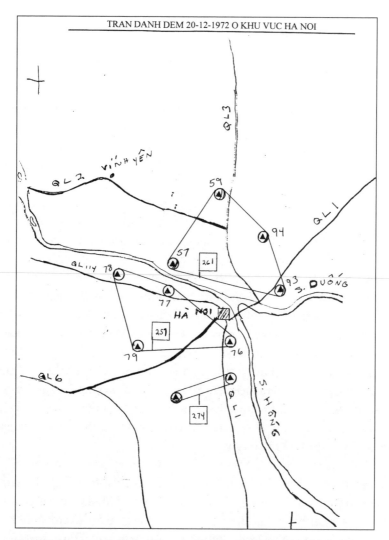

North Vietnamese missile battalion deployment, December 20: Note how the battalions of the 261st Missile Regiment had moved to a triangle pointed north to engage the B-52s further as they repeated their attacks from the northeast for the third straight night. Six B-52s were shot down that night.

battalions' missile sites late that afternoon to explain the new techniques to the crews and practice them on the SA-2's built-in target simulator.

But new guidance techniques could not solve the biggest problem the North Vietnamese had, the shortage of assembled missiles.

The battalions had fired too many missiles during the first two nights, and the number was running low. As the stocks dwindled the fear of running out of missiles began to obsess the crews, a phenomenon that they called "missile fever." One missile man recalled: "Searching for a missile was like the starving searching for food. As soon as the assembly line completed a missile, a truck was waiting to take it away. In the light of exploding bombs, the new missile was put onto the launcher and within a few minutes was roaring into the sky towards the B-52s. Never before had the 'lives' of the missiles been so short."

The North Vietnamese official history was more measured but it still showed the urgency of the situation: "The most pressing technical problem of the campaign was the próblem of supplying missiles to the units, and a special section was set up with the sole responsibility of ensuring the supply of missiles and improving both the assembly stage and the distribution stage. But the missile crews were still afraid of running out missiles. On December 19–20 [Night Two] the number of new missiles the SAM battalions received did not make up for the number of missiles they had fired the first night, so they were not firing as many missiles in a salvo." This was a special problem, because Soviet tests and combat experience had shown firing three missiles at a jamming target vastly improved the chances for a hit. Now the North Vietnamese barely had enough missiles to fire two at a target.

Actually, the issue was not the lack of missiles, but the lack of assembled missiles. Each SA-2 missile arrived in North Vietnam packed in several storage containers. The containers were given to the technical battalion in each regiment who was responsible for their assembly. Missile assembly was not a quick or easy process. The main missile and the booster stage were packed separately and had to be removed from their boxes and fueled, the main missile with solid fuel and the booster stage with liquid fuel, a delicate, hazardous process that required the crews be dressed in full protective suits. Next, the missile was filled with the compressed air that powered the control surfaces, then all of the components— wings, autopilot, warhead, etc.—were fitted to the missile. At that point, different frequencies and transponder codes had to be set into each missile's guidance electronics so they would follow only the signals from their designated site's radar, the booster section was connected, then the missile went through a final check. On a good day, all the Hanoi technical battalions together could assemble about forty missiles.

By the afternoon of Day Three, December 20, the 274th's technical battalion had finally arrived in Hanoi and been sent to the warehouse of the 257th Regiment's technical battalion, the 80th, increasing the number of assembly lines from three to five. Still, even after they had assembled missiles nonstop for three days, the supply of missiles was far below what was needed; all day, trucks waited in long queues outside the warehouses for new missiles.

The missile battalion crews woke in the afternoon and met the technical officers from the headquarters to discuss and practice the new techniques. The crews and the headquarters experts began to carefully go through the jamming patterns and formations that the B-52s had used the previous two nights and the experts showed the crews the new techniques they had developed at the headquarters. Using the SA-2's built-in target simulator, the crews practiced the new procedures again and again under watchful eyes as darkness approached.

WHILE THE NORTH VIETNAMESE were making adjustments in light of their experience the previous two nights, the American forces were not. The SAC leadership was satisfied and felt things were going as planned. B-52 losses were about 1.5 percent, below the 3 percent that General Meyer had projected. SAC believed the low losses validated the concept of planning at headquarters rather than in the field.

The SAC staff still considered General Meyer's slow decision making (which some on the SAC staff privately called "dithering") the major problem, and there were hints that General Meyer believed that more of the decisions should be made in the field, much to the chagrin of the staff. On Day Two a senior SAC staffer remembered that Meyer apparently became uncomfortable that the B-52s were coming in from northwest every raid and began to ruminate on the possibility that the bombers should come in from another direction. General Sianis, the Director of Operations in charge of planning the missions, was taken aback by the suggestion and told Meyer:

"Even as we speak, the crews are climbing the ladders at Guam."

"General Meyer replied, 'Well, tell them to come in from the south if they can hack it.'"

"Needless to say, General Sianis ignored these instructions, and the routes stayed the same."

After this incident it became clear that the staff had to "manage the CINC" better and Brigadier General Harry Cordes remembered how the staff finally got control of General Meyer. "One of the most difficult tasks during Linebacker II was getting . . . General J. C. Meyer used to the long lead time for mission planning. After two days of clock fighting, including handing bags to crews as they were taxiing out, we set up a 20 foot long critical path chart, displayed prominently in the briefing room, with each decision milestone highlighted, to demonstrate this to General Meyer and to help 'stimulate' him to a decision. General Sianis would say, 'General Meyer, we are *here* in the planning process, prepared to brief you on the targets, axes of attack and tactics. We must have your approval by (such and such a time) for 8th AF to complete mission planning and meet the TOT [time over target] schedule.' Or, 'General Meyer, we are at the target review point for tomorrow and day-after-tomorrow's missions. We must also select the TOT for tomorrow so the Maintenance can schedule aircraft, bomb loading, etc.' . . . It was a constant battle with the clock—we always seemed to be behind."

WHILE SAC WAS SATISFIED with the results of the first two days, the staffs and crews in the combat zone were not. Even though no B-52s had been lost the second night many of the crews had received a heavy dose of SAMs and they saw little slackening in the North Vietnamese defenses. At U-Tapao, General Sullivan, Colonel Davis and Colonel Brown had been working hard with the crews trying to find out what the problems were with the tactics and had begun informally forwarding suggestions to Eighth Air Force, but so far there had been no changes or even feedback. The lack of feedback showed the huge distance—both physically and physiologically—between SAC Headquarters and the combat zone. SAC did not understand how important immediate feedback was in combat and there were no mechanisms in place to take crew inputs. The crews knew when they saw the plan for the first time what most of the problems were, but they could do nothing—all recommendations for changes still had to go up the chain of command and then be digested by the SAC bureaucracy.

The SAC leadership's lack of recent combat experience magnified the problem. They never appreciated that the North Vietnamese were a formidable opponent. As one Air Force general said after the war: "for every action we took there was a reaction by the North Vietnamese. They never waited to make some corrective action when they felt like they had failed the course. If they were provided with more modern equipment they could [have] certainly been able to make us stop and think about the worth of the continued bombing of the North."

Most of the U-Tapao crews had flown both nights, and there was an undercurrent of discontent because they knew the mission profiles had been identical each night. The crews were also concerned about the post-target turns, where most of the B-52s had been hit. Some suggested the raids continue straight ahead out of Hanoi heading south to the Gulf of Tonkin, which was only five minutes away. This would not only avoid the dangerous, speed-killing post-target turn into wind, but also if a bomber was hit the crew could bail out over water where rescue was all but assured. This recommendation was forwarded to Eighth and on to SAC, where it seemed to disappear.

At Andersen the G wing had lost two aircraft the first night, and there was considerable apprehension about their limited electronic countermeasures suite, as well as a certain amount of frustration that they were going to Hanoi with only twenty-seven bombs. This frustration was exacerbated by the regular failures of the Gs' release system—the first two nights five Gs had some sort of a bomb-release problem. Still, the second night only one G had been lightly damaged and the crews were breathing a little easier.

The Andersen D wing, which had flown the fewest missions, was relatively calm. The wing had only had two aircraft damaged and no losses, and they saw no problems on the horizon. Indeed, the B-52D wing commander at Andersen, Colonel James McCarthy (who had earlier threatened maneuvering crews with a court-martial), agreed with SAC and was unwilling to support changes in the tactics, saying later: "To have made battlefield modifications any more rapidly than was actually done would have meant doing them on gut reaction or impulse."

But the Eighth Air Force staff was disturbed that the third night's raids would be identical to the first and second nights. Eighth felt that the B-52s had just been lucky the second night, and that "the separation of the waves gives the [North Vietnamese] an ample chance to deal with 18 to 21 bombers at a time, instead of all at once, allowing them to concentrate all their defenses at just one point in the sky."

Eighth called SAC several time to make that point. SAC listened to the Eighth staff's concerns "politely," as one Eighth staffer remembered, "then told us equally politely to go to hell—no changes," stating "the route was justified because of the targets' orientation and avoided or at least minimized exposure to known SAMs sites." Eighth knew that each of these assertions was patently untrue, but could do nothing.

Things were tense, and E. A. Orgon, the Eighth Air Force Public Affairs Officer during the operation, remembered one staff meeting during this period.

"After the first crews were shot down, some appeared on North Vietnamese television talking about the operation. What they said was pretty innocuous but at the next morning's staff meeting there was some discussion about this and General Johnson, the Eighth Air Force Commander, asked, 'What instructions are we giving the crews if they are shot down. What can they say?'

"There was a pause. One of the colonels said, 'Well, the Code of Conduct, you know, name, rank, serial number.'

"Another colonel said, 'No, that changed after the *Pueblo*' [a U.S. surveillance ship captured by the North Koreans in 1968]. A discussion began, and you could see General Johnson was getting pissed because the back of his neck was getting redder and redder. We were now three days into the operation, had lost several aircraft and it was clear the crews hadn't been told anything about how to behave if they were shot down!

"Suddenly General Johnson slammed his notebook down, and the sound was like a shot. 'When you f . . . g guys figure it out let me know,' he said, and stormed out. Needless to say, there was pandemonium in the room."

When the crews from U-Tapao and Andersen went in for their briefings for the third night's missions they saw that SAC had changed the attack patterns slightly—for the worse. The attack headings were coming in and exiting the same way, but were now entering in a narrower cone than on the previous two nights, making it even easier for the North Vietnamese to track the B-52s.

The first raid of the third night consisted of 33 B-52s in eleven cells, with nine of the first eleven cells targeted on Yen Vien, which had been hit both the first and second nights. The first two cells over Yen Vien would be from U-Tapao, followed by nine cells from Andersen, led by Quilt cell.

That night Terry Geloneck's crew from Beale AFB, California, was flying its first Linebacker II mission in Quilt 03, a G model. They knew from talking to other crews that the first night was "bad," but that there had been no losses the second night. They were cautiously optimistic when they climbed into their aircraft, but then they found found two disturbing things. First, the electronic warfare officer, Captain Craig Paul, announced to the crew that they were flying an "unmodified" G model without the ALT-22 jamming systems. Second, and even more disturbing, the radar navigator, Captain Warren Spencer, started to set in the coordinates for the offset aiming points for their target at Yen Vien and found that the coordinates were already set. They were going back to the same target the aircraft had bombed on its last mission.

The Anderson B-52s made the long flight over the Pacific and into South Vietnam, then turned over Laos and dropped in behind the two cells of B-52s from U-Tapao into the long, orderly procession of bombers moving north up to the Chinese border and down Thud Ridge to Hanoi. Over Laos, there was another indication of trouble. Quilt 01 reported that his unmodified G model had two jammers out, and Craig Paul reported the same thing to Terry Geloneck in Quilt 03.

As Quilt cell turned south towards Hanoi they saw several Wild Weasels move forward as they detected North Vietnamese Fan Song radars and began to fire their anti-radiation missiles, and as Quilt approached the target area they saw the bombs of the first two B-52 cells from U-Tapao begin to detonate. There were no SAMs in the air, and the crews began to breathe a little easier. Maybe it would be like last night.

Unfortunately, the Wild Weasels that Quilt cell saw were not firing at active SAM sites; instead, they had fallen for a North Vietnamese ruse. At 7:42 P.M., the Hanoi Air Defense Headquarters received reports that the Wild Weasels were approaching, and under a pre-arranged plan two SA-2 battalions turned on their radars briefly to attract the Weasels and entice them to fire their anti-radiation missiles. As soon as the missiles were fired, the radars went off the air, causing the missiles to lose guidance and explode harmlessly far from the sites.

The North Vietnamese defenders watched on their radar scopes as a narrow chaff corridor unfolded and once again the strong winds blew it through the area rapidly. The corridor showed that the B-52s were heading for Hanoi again, and at the Air Defense Headquarters, General Tran smiled with satisfaction when he saw "an extraordinary thing. The enemy continued to concentrate his attacks on Hanoi, using the same old tricks and jamming techniques."

All the Hanoi missile battalions watched the raid approach and waited anxiously for orders to engage, but none more anxiously than the members of the 93rd Missile Battalion. The night before, they had tried to engage several B-52s with three-point guidance and manual tracking, but they had not scored a hit. The guidance crew had been harshly criticized for its tracking techniques, and all that afternoon a specialist from the headquarters, Nguyen Xuan Minh, had gone over the new tactics with them. They had practiced launching missiles on their simulator using the manual guidance, then changing from manual to automatic tracking when they could see the target clearly on their radar. It was complicated and required skill and timing, but after three full practice engagements and critiques the battalion felt they were ready.

As Minh sat in the 93rd Battalion's command van and watched the B-52s approach the same way they had the previous nights, he was both pleased and amazed. "The extraordinary thing was that tonight the B-52s followed exactly the same flight path as the previous nights. They never thought that in one day their adversaries could change their tactics."

While the B-52s approached, the headquarters ordered the 93rd to engage the third cell of B-52s, designated target T621. The 93rd fired two missiles at long range, but the jamming remained strong as the

B-52s approached and they could not go to automatic tracking. Both missiles missed. As the B-52s approached to twelve miles the 93rd fired two more missiles and then, while their missiles were in flight, they broke out one of the B-52s and went to automatic tracking, then watched their radarscopes as the missile trace closed on the target.

QUILT 03 LINED UP for its bomb run on Yen Vien and Geloneck's radar navigator and navigator calmly ran through their check list, identifying aim points to make sure they were on the right target. About a minute away from the target the electronics warfare officer, Craig Paul, reported that missiles were on the way.

Despite the fact that the incoming SAMs were closing fast, Geloneck rolled his wings level to stabilize for the bomb run. Suddenly the inside of the cockpit was filled with light from a missile's rocket motor. The missile's proximity fuse failed and it passed a few feet away, then vanished into the night. The bomber gently shuddered for what seemed like an eternity—actually about fourteen seconds—as the twenty-seven bombs dropped away. As the bomb bay doors snapped shut Geloneck rolled the B-52 into a steep post-target turn, unknowingly directly into the 93rd's site and the two new missiles that were approaching.

Geloneck picks up the story. "We had been turning about ten seconds when there was a bright white flash and a metallic WHAANG! The control column snapped forward and snapped back again. We were still in that steep turn—very uncomfortable now—but the engines were still going and we were holding our altitude. The compartment where the electronic warfare officer and the gunner sat had taken the main hit—Roy Madden, the gunner, said he had been hit in the leg and that Craig Paul, the EW, was hit and bleeding all over. We were heading for Thailand now but starting down fast and the control column was all the way back in my lap, so I knew the hydraulics were gone. It was time to leave, so I hit the abandon light and heard ejection seats go, then looked over at Bill Acuri, the copilot. He nodded, so I pulled the handles.

"There was a bright full moon and as I floated down I watched SAMs break through the undercast heading up. All I was thinking was 'this can't really be happening.' I went through undercast and landed very close to our target, and that was the end of the war for me."

At Beale Air Force Base, Geloneck's wife, Jane, who was six months pregnant, had a premonition: "For the only time in Terry's Air Force career, I called him when he was away. I knew when they took off, I already figured out how long it took to fly the mission, debrief, and knew when they SHOULD be back. The phone rang in their room, but there was no answer. I tried five times then was afraid to call anymore for fear of what I would learn. I started to worry then. I remember vacuuming the living room in case someone from the base came—I didn't want Terry to be embarrassed."

The news that the 93rd had shot down a B-52 both exhilarated and relaxed the headquarters staff. They knew that they had solved the previous night's problems, and they quickly passed the word to the other battalions that one B-52 was down, then continued to assign the battalions' targets as the procession of bombers continued into the fire zones.

AS BRASS CELL TURNED south towards Hanoi, SAM and MiG warnings saturated the radio and the emergency beepers from Quilt 03 began to sound. On John Ellinger's aircraft, Brass 02, the conversation turned tense.

"Only two beepers. What about the other four?"

"If you brought some rosary beads, better get them out."

"Brass has visual SAMs two o'clock."

"Brass Cell, left, NOW."

As Brass 02 began to maneuver Ellinger's radar navigator remembered: "Fear? You bet! In our navigator stations, the SAMs exploding looked like distant flash bulbs going off, and if they were really close you could hear the detonations. When we started to maneuver the radarscope gyros would cage and not provide stabilization and big blank spots would appear on the radarscope. It was tough to pick out the offsets, and it was even worse because of the high ground speed caused by the jet stream tail winds. Things really moved fast. To keep the radar signature to a minimum, I held off opening doors until fifteen seconds from the target—not SAC procedure, but. . . ."

But Brass 02 had three jammers out, and that was all the 94th Missile Battalion needed. The site launched two missiles in rapid succession using automatic tracking. Brass 02's EW quickly picked up the launch.

"SAM uplink, three and a half rings."

"Got two visual SAMs, let's get the bombs out!"

"SAMs coming with very strong guidance."

As soon as the bombs dropped away from the aircraft Brass 02 rolled into a right post-target turn, but suddenly the copilot realized they were turning in the wrong direction to defeat the missiles.

"BREAK LEFT!... Keep going left."

(Fifteen seconds later) "Roll out. [It's] still on us; break right!"

"They're still coming right at us."

"Roll out, pilot, wing level, and...."

KABOOM, total darkness, then three seconds later, another KABOOM. The 94th's two missiles had detonated to the inside of Brass 02's turn, the first off the right wing, the second just off the right side, and had done fatal damage. The B-52 had no electrical power, no radios, damaged controls and the four engines on the right side out. The radar navigator called:

"If it's flyable, make your heading 270 [towards Laos and Thailand]."

"How's it look, pilot, we going to bail out?"

Ellinger began a slow descent heading for Thailand into the strong headwind, while the gunner, realizing that the aircraft's radios had been knocked out, took out his battery-operated survival radio and began to broadcast MAYDAY calls.

Captain Rex Rivolo in his F-4E quickly located the stricken bomber. Rivolo pulled next to them, saw that the bomber was on fire, and called to the crew to bail out. But Ellinger did not want to bail out over Laos and dragged the B-52 towards the border. Rivolo watched the B-52 drop through the undercast, then a minute later saw an explosion on the ground and was sure all the crew were killed.

In fact, as the bomber dropped down under the cloud deck, Ellinger saw the Mekong River and the lights of the American base at Nakon Phanom just beyond and ordered the crew to eject as the stricken bomber passed through ten thousand feet. All were recovered safely.

Glenn Russell's crew was one of the next B-52s over the target. Russell's electronic warfare officer, R. J. Smith, was a combat veteran with almost five hundred Arc Light missions to his credit, probably more missions than any other Arc Light crewmember. For good luck Smith carried a whistle he had gotten from a U.S. Army officer at a fire base in South Vietnam, a cross and a small golden Buddha a Thai had given him, and at the moment he needed them all. He was looking at three North Vietnamese Fan Song radars in front of his aircraft, and was twisting the jammers' knobs to refine his jammers manually as the pilots called to him that missiles were on all sides. He could feel the missiles going off nearby, and as more SAMs came up, Smith had enough. He pulled out his lucky whistle, adjusted his radio so he could transmit outside the aircraft, then blew the whistle as loud as he could and yelled, "Time out!" Then, as if on command, there was a pause in the missile firings as the crew continued on the bomb run.

As Russell began the post-target turn, two more SAMs closed on the aircraft. Smith—in direct violation of SAC directives—pumped out chaff that the B-52 carried and the missiles turned and followed the chaff. A few seconds later Russell made an evasive turn to avoid another missile that Smith thought "would pull the wings off," but nothing happened and they returned to U-Tapao safely. But the other aircraft in the wave had heard Smith's whistle and "time out" call, and a legend was born.

MEANWHILE, BACK OVER HANOI five cells of B-52Ds from U-Tapao began their attack on Yen Vien. The 76th SAM battalion stayed on the air too long and was knocked out by an anti-radiation missile from a Wild Weasel, but the other North Vietnamese missile crews continued to hammer away. This time it was the 77th Battalion's turn. It was assigned Orange cell, the third of the five cells, and fired two missiles. As the cell opened its bomb doors and the radar returns mushroomed, the 77th was able to break out a radar return and went to full automatic tracking. The first two B-52s were in their post-target turns when the 77th's missiles arrived, but the missiles were headed for Orange 03, hitting it squarely in the bomb bay just before the B-52 released its bombs.

Dwight Moore, an aircraft commander from Carswell AFB, had just taken off from U-Tapao as part of the second wave of B-52s scheduled to attack that night. "We were a long way away—not in North Vietnam or even close—when we looked over towards Hanoi and there was a ball of fire in the sky close to our altitude. The ball

Top: A D model taxiing out while a G model lands. Note the G model's shorter tail and white underbelly camouflage scheme. *Middle:* SA-2 launch during the day. During Linebacker II the flame of the booster rocket was diffused under the clouds and made a spectacular display. *Bottom:* John Dalton's B-52 after it has returned from the Marine base at Nam Phong. The caption reads "To the Boys in the Air Force From the Men in the Marines."

Top: A night shot of a North Vietnamese SAM crew. The phone was used to report the status of the launcher to the missile battalion commander. *Bottom left:* A shot of a missile battalion commander at his post in front of his Spoon Rest radar scope. The telephone was the commander's primary link to headquarters, but radios were also used. *Bottom right:* Posed picture of the guidance officers of the 79th missile battalion in action. The battalion commander would normally be seated in front of the radar scope at the top left. Note the single large control wheel each crewmember has to send guidance signals to the missile.

Top: 77th missile battalion, which shot down at least three B-52s. Sitting from left are range tracker Pham Hong Ha, elevation tracker Luu Van Moc, and azimuth tracker Do Dinh Tan, and on the far right, fire control officer Nguyen Van Duc. Directly behind the crew is the commander, Dinh The Van. The unidentified officer in the rear is probably the missile panel control officer. *Bottom:* The remains of Tan 03, a B-52G shot down on the third raid of Night Three. Only one crewmember survived.

Top: Ebony 02 explodes. This is probably where gunner Jim Cook was blown out of the aircraft. *Bottom left:* Flaming pieces of Ebony 02 fall to the ground. *Bottom right:* As pieces of Ebony 02 hit the ground, burning fuel hangs in the night sky.

Top left: John Mize, a B-52 aircraft commander whose B-52 was hit three separate times and was shot down once. He later received the Air Force Cross. *Top right:* General Glenn Sullivan, commander at U-Tapao and the man who turned the operation around with his message to General Meyer after the losses of Day Three. *Bottom:* Crew of Straw 02, shot down on Night Three. From Left: Derverl Johnson, aircraft commander; Vince Russo, navigator; Frank Gould, radar navigator; Jim Farmer, copilot; Paul Fairbanks (in rear), EW; Walt Barcliff, gunner. Gould remains missing.

Top: Peter Giroux's crew of Scarlet 01, shot down on Night Four. Kneeling: Master Sgt. Louie LeBlanc, gunner; Captain Peter Camerota, EW; Major Jerry Alley, RN. Standing: Giroux; Captain Rob Howe, navigator (replaced by 1st Lt. Joseph Copack); and Captain Waring Bennett, copilot. Alley, Bennett and Copack were killed, while Camerota escaped capture for almost two weeks. (Pete Giroux) *Top:* Crew of the 57th Battalion that shot down Tan 03 on Night Three and Peter Giroux's crew on Night Four. Kneeling are (l.) Fire Control Officer Nguyen Dinh Kien and (r.) Commander Nguyen Van Phiet.

Top: An example of the destructive power of the B-52s on a large target. The Kinh No complex before Linebacker II. *Bottom:* The Kinh No complex after the bombing.

Top: The Gia Lam International Airport. Despite being off limits, the airfield was deliberately bombed by a B-52D from Andersen on Night One. SAC later used the attack as an example of precision bombing. *Bottom:* Bob Hope performing at U-Tapao on Night Five. Hope's visit "saved a lot of people," remembered one crewmember.

grew larger then smaller as it headed earthward. The fireball was elongated like maybe the airplane or parts were in it, and a large flaming piece was falling faster, while a sheet of burning fuel was between them. We could see the fire all the way to the ground. It seemed to descend very, very slowly until it impacted with a smaller fireball on the ground."

It was not until Moore returned to U-Tapao that he learned what he had seen. The explosion was also seen by an American RC-135 orbiting more than eighty miles away over the Gulf of Tonkin. Amazingly, two of the crew of Orange 03 survived. This was the last raid against Yen Vien and the fourth attack in three nights. In all, the target had cost the U.S. five B-52s.

AS EACH OF THE B-52S was going down, a female voice announced the kill over a loudspeaker at the Air Defense Command Post. Meanwhile, North Vietnamese intelligence "listeners" monitoring the American radio frequencies reported that the B-52 formations were becoming disorganized and were making panic-stricken radio calls requesting rescue for the downed crew members. Then, "amid the joy of victory permeating the command post, everyone was caught by surprise by the voice of the duty officer of the technical section— the 77th battalion was out of missiles! This announcement was immediately followed by the report that the 94th battalion was also out of missiles! The two battalions that guarded the vital northern approaches and had fought very effectively in the latest round were in risk of being out of action. This 'deadly news' quickly spread throughout the various communications lines, creating real repercussions for the other units. The 'missile fever' reached an alarming state. We were worried to death waiting for the second B-52 raid on Hanoi, expected at midnight, as was the case the previous two nights." But nothing happened at midnight. Some B-52s were bombed well to the north, but Hanoi was untouched.

AT SEVENTH AIR FORCE HEADQUARTERS in Saigon there was profound shock when the support flights reported that three B-52s had been lost in the first raid. General John Vogt, the Seventh Air Force Commander, quickly called his old flying school classmate, General Gerald Johnson at Eighth Air Force, told him about the losses and recommended SAC cancel the rest of the missions into the Hanoi area until they could solve the defenses. Johnson told Vogt he could not stop the missions on his own, but immediately called SAC and told them the situation. Almost 10 percent of the first raid had been shot down, including two of twelve G models. Now the second raid of twenty-seven B-52s, including six G models, was on its way to North Vietnam. In an incredible example of poor planning, the six Gs were to attack the Hanoi railroad yard alone while the twenty-one D models had been assigned to targets away from Hanoi. The railroad yard was in the heart of Hanoi's defenses and had been bombed twice the first day and by the first raid earlier that night. General Johnson called General Meyer at SAC, told him the situation, relayed General Vogt's concerns, and told Meyer that there was still time to recall the second raid.

Johnson's phone call and the early loss reports shocked the staff at SAC Headquarters, and General Meyer made frantic phone calls to the Chairman of the Joint Chiefs of Staff, Admiral Moorer, and the Air Force Chief of Staff, General Ryan, to discuss the situation. They told Meyer the decision was up to him, and Meyer ordered the recall of the six Gs targeted for Hanoi back to Andersen. Though they did not realize it, the North Vietnamese defenses had done something that the Germans, Japanese, Soviets, Chinese, and North Koreans had never been able to achieve. They had made an American bombing raid abort a mission for fear of losses.

But in Hanoi the North Vietnamese spent little time pondering their luck, and instead redoubled their efforts to resupply the missile sites in case the third raid did arrive. Soon more trucks began to arrive at the missile battalions with completed missiles. Ironically, if the second wave had continued, the Gs would have met empty missile launchers and the North Vietnamese's worst fears would have been realized—the U.S. forces would have had found out they were out of missiles.

BRENT DIEFENBACH AND HIS crew returned to Andersen after the first raid, and he remembered: "It was really bad. After we landed, my radar navigator jumped out and kissed the ground he was so happy to be back. We debriefed and I made an unusual decision for me—I headed for the Officers' Club for a planned drunk.

"I had just arrived and gotten my first beer when the club loud-speaker announced calls for some of the aircraft commanders that had flown that evening. I had another beer and during the next few minutes there were several other calls for other aircraft commanders that had flown on the first raid. Then the loudspeaker said 'Captain Diefenbach, phone call on line two. Captain Diefenbach, line two.'

"The guys I was sitting with said, 'Brent, don't answer it.'

"That seemed like a pretty good idea, so I had another beer. But the calls kept coming and they asked for me a few more times, so I finally answered the phone. The guys were right, I shouldn't have answered. It was the Command Post, and they told me to get my crew together with all our flight gear and be at base operations in two hours. I had no idea where the rest of the crew were but I got three more beers, opened one, put the other two in my flight suit pockets and headed out to find them."

Two hours later Diefenbach, his crew and ten other Andersen D model crew, were on a C-141 transport headed for U-Tapao.

DERVERL JOHNSON AND HIS D model crew were scheduled to fly from Andersen as Straw 02 on the third raid. The radar navigator, Major Frank Gould, was in a good mood after the briefing because his bombing radarscope photographs from the first night's mission had been shown as an example of "how to do it." But Johnson's copilot, Lieutenant Jim Farmer, was not as upbeat because they were going back to the Hanoi railroad yards, the same target they had bombed the first night, and they were the second airplane in the second cell. The word was the North Vietnamese missile crews were letting the first cells go through and firing at the second, so Farmer stuffed a pair of socks, extra water, and a ham sandwich in his flight suit before he headed for the airplane.

Two G model crews, Captain Tom Craddock's flying in Aqua 01 and Captain Bob Panza's crew flying in Aqua 02, joked to try to break the tension as they shared a crew bus ride to their aircraft. Craddock's crew was dropped off first and the two crews agreed to meet at the Officers' Club after the mission.

Aqua 02 was the first crew for Panza, a junior captain. The crew had been scheduled to return home on December 30 after flying 40 missions since the beginning of July, but their return was canceled because of Linebacker II. While Panza was young, most of the rest of the crew were very experienced. The copilot, Captain Ed Wildeboor, and the electronic warfare officer, Captain Tom Mulligan, had just come from combat tours, Wildeboor in C-123s and Mulligan in EB-66s, where he been exposed to plenty of SAMs. Lieutenant Tom Cannon, the navigator, was a recent graduate of navigator school but had a degree in applied physics and was regarded as "a quick study." The radar navigator was very senior, Lieutenant Colonel Bob Cooper, who Wildeboor noted was "a very mellow guy who probably wondered what he did to get on a crew of kids."

As Panza and his crew preflighted their aircraft, they received a call from Charlie that Captain Craddock and his crew had to change aircraft and move to become Tan 03, the last aircraft in the G group. Panza was told to move to Aqua 01, a change that did not concern the crew because they had led cells many times before.

As Aqua cell proceeded to the refueling point Wildeboor tuned the radio to the first raid's frequency and copied the post-strike report. He decoded the message and realized that several B-52s had been shot down. "Everyone on the ground was ready and waiting while we were going to fly the same routes, altitudes, and airspeeds we had in previous days. We were going to be like the targets in a shooting gallery, and there wasn't even a pretense that this would be a surprise."

The fate of Aqua cell and the other B-52Gs from the third raid was now being decided in Omaha. After General Meyer's cancellation of the second raid of G models, the question still remained about what to do with the Gs in the third raid. From Washington, Admiral Moorer and General Ryan again told General Meyer that the decision was up to him.

Militarily, the decision was an easy one. The third raid had four cells of G models, a total of twelve aircraft, which would only be dropping 324 bombs, the same number of bombs as a single cell of B-52Ds. All were scheduled to hit the Kinh No complex just a few miles north of Hanoi, and the Gs' post-target turns would take them over the heaviest concentration of North Vietnamese SA-2 sites. A post-war official U.S. Air Force history noted: "It was apparent after the first raid losses that the unmodified Gs were neither protecting themselves nor the formations adequately, and were bearing the brunt of the losses inflicted by Hanoi's SAM sites." It was clear that sending the Gs on the third raid to Kinh No was close to a suicide mission for very little return.

But the SAC staff was clearly disturbed that General Meyer had listened to General Johnson and worse, Seventh Air Force, and canceled the second raid. General Harry Cordes, SAC's Chief of Intelligence said, "We wanted to prove that SAC could do the job," and the SAC staff pressed General Meyer to send the G models to attack. Cordes discussed the pressures General Meyer faced and the arguments to continue:

"[Fighter] General Vogt at 7th AF was furious that the B-52s had taken over the primary role [of attacking North Vietnam] and that SAC was selecting their own targets.

"The Navy was miffed that SAC and the B-52s had been given the mission to end the war.

"PACOM [Pacific Command] was miffed at the loss of control.

"General Clay [the 'fighter general' commander of the Pacific Air Forces] was personally concerned at the loss of crewmembers and aircraft."

The staff's implication was clear—if the B-52s were recalled, there would be a further diminution of SAC's credibility and reputation both in and out of the Air Force. Then, according to Cordes, the staff offered a final, seemingly incredible rationale, telling Meyer, "never in the history of the United States Air Force had a bomber attack been turned back by enemy action." This completely ignored what had happened just a few hours before when Meyer had turned back the second raid's G models, and also ignored SAC's policy for most of the war, to turn the B-52s back when they were threatened by North Vietnamese defenses. But the selective memory lapse served its purpose—General Meyer ordered the G models in the third raid to continue.

AS AQUA CELL TURNED south toward Kinh No above the solid undercast, on Aqua 01 copilot Ed Wildeboor looked ahead towards Hanoi and saw "small, bright dots on the horizon that were rising and falling. I knew that they were SAMs. I remember constantly hearing beepers on our guard channel—definitely not good news."

On the ground below, despite the best efforts of the technical battalions, both the 94th and 59th battalions were still out of missiles. But the rest of the missile battalions had been at least partially resupplied as the North Vietnamese watched the third raid move down towards the Hanoi railroad yard from the northwest.

In Straw 02, copilot Jim Farmer remembered, "The night was clear, except for a low cloud deck. SAMs were lifting off everywhere, and they were very interesting, almost beautiful, to see. At first they were a broad dull light until they pierced through the clouds, then they changed to a large bright light flying up from down below."

As Straw 02 rolled out straight and level on its bomb run, Farmer saw a missile take off and began to move straight for them. Farmer did not know that Straw 02 was ten miles away from the chaff corridor, and that fifteen miles away the 78th missile battalion of the 257th regiment had been able to break the B-52 out and fire a single missile in full auto-track.

As the bombs fell away, Paul Fairbanks, the EW, called out that a missile was tracking the aircraft. Farmer saw the missile out of the window and warned the crew they were going to be hit. The missile seemingly passed through the string of bombs and hit about a second after the last bomb dropped away. The explosion ripped through the front lower part of the B-52 and knocked out all the aircraft's power. Derverl Johnson, radar navigator Frank Gould, and navigator Vince Russo were all seriously wounded. Straw 02 turned for Thailand while Farmer tried to make a "Mayday" call by opening his side window and using his survival radio as the aircraft began a slow descent. The badly wounded Gould kept joking about the inadequate first aid kit as the bomber, streaming fuel and with only limited flight controls, struggled west. A few minutes later, very close to the North Vietnam-Laos border, the engines flamed and the crew made a controlled bail out. Johnson, the aircraft commander, was the last one out, but not before he noted that he was one of the few people to fly a B-52 solo.

As the G models headed south towards their targets, the pilots looked down and saw Straw 02 streaming fuel and heading northwest. One minute later Olive, the first G model cell, began its bomb run on Kinh No. The cell had completely fallen apart before it arrived over the target and was several miles to the right of its scheduled inbound course, and somehow Olive 3 had moved two miles ahead of Olive 02 at release point. Spread out like this, the cell had no chance for any mutual jamming coverage. When Olive 01 rolled into his post-target turn the B-52 was targeted by the North Vietnamese 77th battalion, which had just been resupplied with missiles. The 77th's missile exploded under Olive 01 with stunning effect, and the tapes of the voices in one of the aircraft behind it show the reaction.

"Good Lord, what was that?"

"Jeez, that was Wave Lead."

"Must have been a direct hit."

"My God, what a fireball!!"

Olive 01 went down like a torch about nine miles north of Hanoi and only two of the six crewmembers survived. This was the third kill for the 77th battalion, but—fortunately for the Americans—the site had been only partially resupplied and had used its last missiles to down Olive 01.

Aqua 01 led the next cell into the target. Copilot Ed Wildeboor remembered: "As we got closer to the target run I was looking forward and down to the right to look for SAMs called by our EW, but North Vietnamese radar discipline was good and sometimes a SAM was fired without our EW calling it until the last second. I counted about 12 SAMs in our vicinity, and because we were flying at about 33,000 ft and the undercast was about 15,000 feet below us, it gave us a real problem—the missiles were going full speed by the time they popped out of the clouds and we had just a few seconds after we saw it to decide if it was really a threat and what to do about it. Eventually we realized that not every SAM was a threat to us, and while we saw a lot but only had to dodge two, one that went above us and one that went below us. Meanwhile, our electronic war officer, Tom Mulligan, had his hands full and his prior experience in EB-66s was proving invaluable. Our gunner told us later that Tom was on the edge of his seat 'playing his receivers and jammers like a pinball machine' while we concentrated on the bomb run.

"After 'bombs away' we began our post-target to the right into that 100 knot wind (and at that point I realized that there went the ol' chaff corridor). It seemed like we hung there forever, and this was just having flown for 30 or 45 seconds with the bomb bay doors open, increasing our radar return by 400 percent or so. I knew that our ECM would essentially be ineffective during the post-target turn because the antennas were pointed away from the threat."

BEHIND WILDEBOOR AND the rest of Aqua cell, Tan cell was having problems. The cell was well off course as it approached the target when Tan 03, Tom Craddock's unmodified G, suffered a complete failure of its bombing radar. Standard procedure called for the gunner in the Tan 02 to use his radar to keep Tan 03 lined up behind the cell, but the procedure broke down and Tan 03 drifted off to the left, diverging from the rest of the cell and losing mutual jamming support.

On the ground below, the 57th battalion had only one missile left. The battalion commander, Nguyen Van Phiet, watched as his fire control officer, Nyugen Dinh Kien, began to break out a single jamming strobe on its radar. The guidance officers tracked the strobe and were able to go into full autotrack as the B-52 approached to twelve miles. Hopefully, Kien pushed the fire button and the 57th's last missile roared off into the overcast.

Tan 03 was still far from the rest of Tan cell when the 57th's missile stuck the forward fuselage. The bomber pitched down, then the nose came back up for a moment. The gunner bailed out and then, a few seconds later, a missile from another site hit and the B-52 disintegrated. The gunner was the only survivor.

A few moments later Ed Wildeboor saw an explosion on a ridgeline and noted its position so he could report it to intelligence when the crew landed at Andersen. He did not realize until later that the explosion was Tom Craddock's crew, the crew they had shared the bus out to their aircraft with, and that they would not be meeting them at the Officers' Club for their post-mission drink.

Just after the loss of Tan 03, four cells of B-52Ds attacked the Hanoi petroleum storage area just a few miles away from Kinh No. The D models had more effective jamming and the North Vietnamese sites had only a few missiles left, so only one B-52D—Brick 02, piloted by Captain John Mize—was hit. A SAM detonated close to Mize's aircraft in his post-target turn but a quick check indicated that there was no obvious damage. Mize, a sturdy Midwesterner who claimed he spent his whole Air Force career on a diet, headed back for U-Tapao. A few minutes later, as the sun came up, the EW called to Mize "I've got a hole in my compartment—I can see light through it." After they landed Mize found that the B-52 had nineteen holes in it and that a large piece of shrapnel had gone through the EW's station at head level—had he not been leaning forward over his jammers, he would have been decapitated.

In far western North Vietnam, the crew of Straw 02 was on the ground along a six-mile line that followed their dying aircraft's course. At first light the first wave of rescue forces, A-7 "Sandy" fighter-bombers—commonly known as SLUFFs, short little ugly fat fuckers—headed in to locate the crew. The Sandys contacted the crew and soon escorted the rescue helicopters in to begin to pick them up. "After I was picked up we were told that another chopper had been sent to pick up Frank Gould, the radar navigator, who was badly wounded," copilot Jim Farmer remembered. "We headed back to the chopper's base at Nakon Phanom where our arrival was a big deal, lots of brass and champagne. SAC had a KC-135 there to whisk us back to their control, and we didn't have a chance to adequately thank our rescuers, nor did we have a chance to talk to the people coordinating the search for Frank. Perhaps we could have told them that we went out in a straight line and they should look at a spot between where the EW and I were found."

Frank Gould's body has never been recovered.

Farmer and his EW were flown back to Guam and told they were to brief the staff on what happened. "We were told not to come in flight suits, so I had to scrounge around and borrow a blue uniform. Welcome back to SAC's idea of combat reality. The briefing room was large, and I had never seen so many full colonels in my life."

The colonels listened to Farmer with "disbelief and great respect," but there were no questions about tactics or how losses could be reduced. Farmer did tell them that SAC had directed the crews' helmets be painted a gloss white, which made them easy for the North Vietnamese to see in the jungle, and so he had thrown his away. The next day all the helmets were painted brown.

THE NIGHT'S SCORECARD was sobering. Of the twelve B-52Gs on the third wave that were sent to Kinh No to preserve SAC's reputation, two were shot down and nine of the twelve crewmembers were killed. The four cells of G models had dropped fewer than three hundred bombs on the target, and Kinh No would have to be revisited again many times.

As the last U-Tapao crews were coming in, the staff acted just the opposite of the staff on Guam. "Things were just not going too well," Brigadier General Glenn Sullivan said later. "I said that enough's enough, let's make some changes. We've got to get rid of these tactics, so let's get some crew members in here and figure out the best way to do this thing. Get rid of the single-file bomber stream, get rid of other things—that's your charter. Let's do it another way. You tell me and I'll sign off on the message and we'll see what we can do.

"Don Davis, the 307th Wing Commander, and Bill Brown, Davis' deputy, held this little session. They got seven or eight crews together that morning—it was about 5:00 A.M.—who had just flown and they made some great recommendations. One was 'Let's run in head on.' The bomb release point was six miles from the target and that's twelve miles separation between the airplanes, so why not run in head on with altitude separation? It's got to be confusing as hell for those guys on the ground. And let's do a chaff blanket instead of a narrow corridor."

R. J. Smith was one of the crewmembers. "General Sullivan called me in with other high-time people and asked what we needed to do to cut our losses. We all had similar points—change the inbound routes, change the altitudes, no post-target turns, straight out to the Gulf of Tonkin, and I told them about how I had used chaff and how it worked. (SAC had forbidden us to use our own chaff). We asked for about ten specific things of the General that morning."

At 9:30 that morning Sullivan had a message outlining the tactics changes. "I sent the message directly to General J. C. Meyer, the Commander of SAC, and just sent an information copy to my boss at Eighth Air Force, General Jerry Johnson. A lot of people told me this was probably not a very good thing to do, that I should have sent it to Johnson first, but I wanted to get to Meyer where we could get some action, and I didn't want it to have to go through General Johnson and have him say 'I have to check on this' before he sent it to SAC."

When General Johnson received a copy of General Sullivan's message to General Meyer, he passed it to the B-52 wing commanders on Guam and the Eighth Air Force staff and they had their own meetings. That afternoon Eighth Air Force sent a "we agree" message to SAC.

News of U-Tapao's message requesting tactics changes spread rapidly around Andersen, along with the rumor that the UT crews were refusing to fly unless the tactics were changed—a "revolt" that was greeted approvingly by the crewmembers on Guam. Eventually, the "revolt" became one of Linebacker II's "urban legends" and many Andersen crews believe it today. In fact, according to crews who were based at U-Tapao at the time, there was no threat of "mutiny"—just a strong desire for sensible tactics.

In Washington, Jack McDonald remembered: "When we briefed Admiral Moorer, the Chairman of the JCS, that six BUFFs were lost on the third night's raids he picked up the phone in the briefing room and called the SAC Command Post. I really don't know if he was talking to Gen. Meyer or not or just the Senior SAC controller, but his message was certainly clear—he said 'they're setting their God-dammed watches by the timing of your bombing runs!'"

THE NEXT DAY IN PARIS, the remaining North Vietnamese and Vietcong delegations walked out of the peace talks. It was clear that Hanoi thought they were winning and saw no more reason to talk.

NINE

Dien Bien Phu
of the Air

As the third B-52 raid departed, the North Vietnamese missile crews were ecstatic. In less than ten minutes they had shot down three B-52s using only thirty-five missiles, while overall that night four of the giant bombers had crashed in the Hanoi suburbs and two in Laos and Thailand. Once again the missile crews were swamped by messages of patriotic support and congratulations from other missile units around the country and in South Vietnam.

The 77th battalion, situated almost directly under where the B-52s were doing their post-target turns, had done most of the damage. Using automatic tracking, the 77th had shot down two B-52s before it ran out of missiles. The 57th battalion, located just across the Red River, hit the last two B-52s that night, downing one and damaging one. These had been the battalion's first hits, but would not be their last.

As soon as daylight arrived on December 21, the North Vietnamese leadership seized the propaganda initiative by fanning out with groups of international newsmen and camera crews to visit areas that had been struck by B-52 bombs. At the same time, the leadership issued ringing declarations about how the North Vietnamese people would not be cowed by the "terror bombing." But behind the leadership's rhetoric there remained great concern about both the slow rate the SA-2 missiles were being assembled and the ability of the missile crews to keep fighting. They had been very lucky the Americans had not attacked at midnight when most of the battalions were out of missiles, and they knew it. They also knew that if the Americans found out they were out of missiles, they would redouble their efforts and the battle could well be lost.

The two Hanoi-based technical battalions were doing the best they could. Supplied with "pep pills" and special food, the assembly crews were working night and day and were producing almost twice as many missiles as normal. But the total number produced remained at about forty per day, or what the Hanoi SAM battalions normally fired at a single raid.

The night of the 21st, the fourth night of the bombing, would be critical. The defenders only had enough missiles to engage one raid, and if the Americans attacked in three raids as they had the past three nights, they would certainly find out that the defenders were out of missiles and press their advantage. One North Vietnamese remembered: "'Missile fever' was increasing. Many units had fired their last missile. . . . Everyone was nervous thinking about the night of the 21st which was expected to be the most difficult night. The missiles from the Than Hoa missile units in the south would not arrive in time, and there was the fear that the B-52s would attack in even greater numbers, but it was impossible to increase the number of missiles."

The General Staff ordered two Haiphong SAM battalions, the 71st and the 72nd, to move to the capital, but they would arrive too late to participate in the battle that night. The General Staff also worried that the severity of the U.S. losses would lead them to attack the SAM sites and warehouses, and they began to consider additional ways they could protect their missile sites.

AT BEALE AIR FORCE BASE, California, most of the married aircrew lived in the same area on the base. The afternoon of December 21, even though it was almost Christmas, it was warm enough for Steve Brown's wife Rita and her children to be outside when she saw several staff cars filled with senior officers in their Class A uniform, driving up the street. She knew what the convoy meant so she grabbed her children, went inside and locked the door, then took the children to the back of the house so she couldn't hear the knock she was sure was coming.

The staff cars did stop in front of the Brown's house, but the officers and their wives, including the Wing Commander and the Chaplain, got out and walked across the street to Terry Geloneck's house to see Jane Geloneck.

"I answered the door to find about 10 officers in dress blues and their wives there," Jane remembered. "Instinctively knowing that they were not coming to wish me a Merry Christmas, I closed the door in their faces and went to the bedroom. They came in anyway and 'captured' me in the bedroom. They told me that Terry's plane had been shot down and that he was missing in action.

"I just remember time standing still. Very still. Very still. It was if I was in a vacuum. I asked them to excuse me for a few moments, then after I composed myself I came into the living room. I asked the squadron commander three questions. Was there any search and rescue being conducted? Were there any chutes spotted? What happened to the rest of the crew?

"To all three questions he asked, 'Why do you want to know?'"

Since Geloneck was an aircraft commander, everyone on the street knew that the families of the other members of his crew were getting a similar visit.

Meanwhile, SAC Headquarters was still stunned by the third night's losses: six irreplaceable B-52s shot down and one damaged—well over 6 percent for the night, or twice what General Meyer had forecast as maximum losses. In one night, the North Vietnamese had shot down 3 percent of all the B-52s in Southeast Asia.

To make matters worse, the SAC staff was completely befuddled by the losses, which was very disconcerting to the combat units who were used to SAC Headquarters being the experts on everything. Colonel James McCarthy, the D model wing commander at Andersen, said later: "We had the Air Force's leading expert on ECM at the time there at SAC Headquarters. I remember that after the third day he was completely shaking his head because he couldn't tell us why our ECM wasn't effective."

At the same time SAC was trying to deal with the losses, Admiral Moorer had notified General Meyer that the bombing operation would go on indefinitely. A chilling statistic surfaced—if the losses continued at the Night Three rate, almost a third of the B-52 force in Southeast Asia would be destroyed in the next ten days. Despite the intercepted radio transmissions that indicated the North Vietnamese were almost out of missiles and the president's orders to keep the pressure on, the heavy losses of the third night forced SAC to a critical decision based on what had been a central institutional premise: *conventional "little wars" were unimportant compared with keeping SAC strong.*

SAC's decided that their categorical imperative now was to cut B-52 losses, rather than to continue to attack Hanoi and force the battle to a conclusion as the president wanted. General Meyer ordered that only thirty B-52s would raid Hanoi the fourth night, sure that the smaller number of B-52s would mean fewer losses. It would also mean much less pressure was being put on the North Vietnamese, but there is no record that General Meyer told Admiral Moorer that SAC was cutting back on its attacks.

At the same time, Meyer attempted to shift the blame to Seventh Air Force for the losses. He sent a stinging message to General Vogt: "[I] consider the SAM suppression effort ... to be the highest priority and essential in minimizing future losses. If unable to provide SAM suppression as requested would appreciate you letting me know in some detail [why not]."

A few hours later Vogt fired back, pointing out: "As you know, night operations against SAM sites leave a great deal to be desired. The effectiveness of such a campaign is questionable." Vogt then threw in a dig of his own, criticizing the way SAC was splitting its forces: "I have a keen appreciation thus far for the magnitude of considerations in planning and conducting your strikes: however, the ... limited assets with which [Seventh Air Force] operates become ... critical items when target changes occur at late dates. This is particularly true where chaff and [Wild Weasels] are concerned."

Vogt also suggested that he might stand down night operations for the fourth night—an empty threat, but one that gave an indication of the depth of the division between the tactical and strategic forces about the most effective way to conduct the operation.

THE THIRTY B-52S for the fourth night's raid were all to come from U-Tapao, and that meant that some crewmembers at U-Tapao would fly to Hanoi four nights in a row while few of their counterparts on Guam had even flown two missions. To ease the pressure, Brent Diefenbach's crew and nine other B-52D model crews had been sent to U-Tapao from Andersen, where they arrived on the morning of Day Four after an all-night flight.

"We were completely exhausted," Diefenbach remembered. "We'd flown a mission to Hanoi the day before, then hopped on a

C-141 and flown all night to get to U-Tapao, and once we got there we were herded into a briefing room and told to go into crew rest because we were going to be flying that night. We were too tired to say anything but as we finished up some colonel stuck his head in the room and asked the briefing officer who we were. The briefer told him we were the crews from Andersen and that we were going to fly that night. The colonel looked at us and said 'Bullshit. Look at these guys! They'll have an accident just starting their engines. Send them to bed and use them tomorrow.' That was it."

On the fourth night the U-Tapao B-52s were to hit three targets, two of them near the center of Hanoi, very close to the targets that had been bombed the previous nights. The plan called for the same, single file northwest to southeast route to Hanoi the B-52s had used the first three nights, but General Sullivan's message had an effect and finally there was a major change, the first in the B-52 tactics since the operation began. Instead of their steep post-target turn back into the jet stream wind, after bomb release the bombers would make smaller turns and fly out of North Vietnam over the Gulf of Tonkin, known as a "feet wet" exit.

Peter Camerota, the electronic warfare officer on Captain Pete Giroux's crew from March AFB in California, was one of the crewmembers scheduled to fly that evening. Camerota's wife Joy was five months pregnant and living with him just outside of U-Tapao, but he assured her that everything would be fine, just like it had been for the other two Linebacker II missions he had flown. They made plans to meet at his trailer the next morning to go shopping.

John Yuill was the aircraft commander of the most senior crew flying Linebacker II missions. He and two others were lieutenant colonels and his crew, like Camerota's, was on their third mission to Hanoi in four nights. Yuill noted gratefully the changes in the exit route, and one other briefing item caught his attention: "We were told that six crewmembers shot down on the first night were POWs. I didn't think that the North Vietnamese were taking any prisoners, so I had told my crew we weren't leaving the aircraft until it came apart. This news made me reconsider that."

During the briefing Yuill's navigator, Captain Bill Mayall, remembers having special feelings of apprehension that night. "We started out as wave lead, but they moved us to the eighth cell and we became Blue 01. We didn't have a good feeling about this. If you were going to be in a line of 30 B-52s all bombing the same target, it was better to be in the front than in the back."

THE MISSILE BATTALIONS around Hanoi considered their meager stock of missiles —just enough to fully engage one wave—and waited anxiously for the first of the three B-52 raids they expected to come at eight in the evening. Nothing. Then they waited for the midnight raid. Again, nothing. The tense headquarters breathed a sigh of relief. For the second time, the Americans had missed an opportunity to attack Hanoi when it would have been defended by empty missile launchers.

At about 3:00 A.M. the North Vietnamese began to detect preparations for a raid, and a half an hour later they watched as cell after cell of B-52s followed their standard path down from the northwest, headed for the center of the city. Each cell was tracked and assigned as targets to the missile battalions.

Pete Giroux's B-52, Scarlet 01, was the first B-52 cell inbound to Hanoi but was in trouble from the time it turned southeast towards the target. In the turn, Scarlet 01 had lost its bombing and navigation radar and was forced to execute a complicated maneuver where the bomber moved to one side, let the other two aircraft in the cell pass, then dropped back to the end of the formation where it could be positioned to bomb by another B-52 gunner's radar. But the maneuver had to be done quickly, because while the B-52 was out of formation it was away from the combined jamming support, and if it was in range of the Hanoi's SA-2 sites it would be an easy target.

As the other two B-52s passed, Giroux's tail gunner, Louie LeBlanc, detected an aircraft behind the B-52, yelled "MiG," and called for evasive action maneuvers. Giroux was in an impossible position—the B-52s were entering the range of Hanoi's missiles and maneuvering would force him further away from the formation's jamming, but if he stayed he might be shot down by an air-to-air missile. Giroux elected to follow LeBlanc's directions and began to weave the B-52 back and forth while the gunner fired.

On the ground, the commander of the 57th battalion, Nguyen Van Phiet, watched as Giroux's radar return moved away from the formation. Phiet's battalion was on a hot streak—it had scored the last two hits of Night Three and now it was trying for three in a row. Another battalion fired two missiles as the 57th's guidance control officers were manually tracking Scarlet 03's return, and a few seconds later the fire control officer, Nguyen Dinh Kien, pushed the fire button once, then six seconds later pushed it again, and sent the two missiles into the night. As the missiles were in flight, the 57th's controllers broke out a clean radar return and went to automatic tracking as the missiles approached their target.

As the other two B-52s in Scarlet cell watched mesmerized, two missiles roared past Giroux's aircraft without exploding, followed by two more from the 57th. This pair appeared to passing well below the B-52 when, suddenly, about a mile below the aircraft, the missile's automatic tracking cut in and the two missiles pitched sharply upward. They exploded under the B-52's right wing. Radio calls flooded the air:

"Oh, no, Scarlet"

"[Scarlet] two, [Scarlet] one, Scarlet three's been hit by a SAM. . . ."

"Oh, my God. . . ."

The B-52's right wing was engulfed in flames and the bomber began a slow, almost leisurely, roll to the right when the burning wing folded over the top of the aircraft and the B-52 plunged towards Hanoi.

Giroux tried desperately to save the doomed aircraft. "I stood on the rudder and tried differential power . . . but the bank angle was increasing. I looked at the hydraulic panel and saw there wasn't much hydraulic pressure left and it didn't look like we were getting out of this turn. I turned on the Emergency Bailout Light . . . then heard an ejection seat go immediately, and two more followed as the aircraft depressurized. The next thing I knew I was upside down in the aircraft. All I could see was the shattered window directly in front of me. I was hanging by my ejection seat straps. The world began to come apart and I reached for the arming levers on the side of the seat, pulled them up and tried to pull the trigger to fire the seat. Nothing happened. I squeezed again as hard as I could and the seat fired."

Meanwhile, Giroux's EW, Pete Camerota, could tell that things were not going well. "The intercom quit so we couldn't talk, and I knew we had two engines shut down, so when the Emergency Bailout Light come on I was history. The hatch exploded open and it felt like the plane dropped away from me, as opposed to me going out of the plane."

The other two aircraft of Scarlet cell lost sight of the stricken B-52 and, as they cleared the target, tried to locate their cellmate:

"Scarlet 03, ground radio check."

"Scarlet 01 copies loud and clear."

"This is Red Crown. Is Scarlet 03 still up there?"

There was a pause, and an escorting F-4 called in. "OK, Red Crown, this is Lair. Your first BUFF is on the ground. He blew up."

Ironically, there were no MiGs in the area. Giroux's gunner had probably fired at an F-4 escorting the cell.

Peter Camerota remembered: "I was really surprised when my chute opened automatically—that meant I was below 14,000 feet, much lower than I had thought. My first thought was 'OmiGod, I'm hanging in the straps, and my wife is pregnant and in Thailand, ten thousand miles from home.' My second thought was that we must have had an electrical problem that shorted out the bailout light and that I had ejected from a (relatively) good aircraft. So I was the only one dumb enough to eject, and the other guys were safe. Then I saw three chutes clustered together a couple of hundred meters away with the guys flashing their emergency beacon lights. I slipped into the undercast and, since I knew we had been heading for the coast, prepared for the inevitable water landing.

"I started to break through the cloud layer and could see water! Great!! Except when I descended lower, I could see I was going to land in a rice paddy. When I hit I heard a great deal of shooting and shouting in one direction, so I took off running the other way as quickly as I could. I dropped my chute so all I had left was my survival vest with its minimal equipment."

About an hour later, as dawn was breaking, Camerota found a small cave in a rock formation, crept inside, and went to sleep. "When I woke up at first I wasn't sure it hadn't all been, and still was, a bad dream. Nope. Much too lifelike, especially the rice paddies below and the people and animals working in them.

"The cave was my home for the next three days or so. I had lost my water bottles, probably in the ejection, and I was afraid to drink the paddy water since I would (probably/hopefully/maybe) be rescued soon. I would come out of my cave at night and try to contact someone on the radio, but no luck."

ABOUT FOUR MINUTES after Giroux was hit, Blue cell, led by John Yuill in Blue 01, moved in to bomb the same target: "About fifteen seconds from bombs away I saw a SAM directly ahead and just under us," Yuill said later. "There was no time to do anything and the next thing I knew we were in 30 degrees of bank, all windscreens shattered, engines three and four on fire. . . ."

In the navigator's compartment below, Bill Mayall felt a large explosion and a fireball leapt out of the equipment bay in front of him. He felt something spray up his legs and arms and called over the intercom that he'd been hit, then felt the aircraft start down and then back up, then there was a second explosion. "The Emergency Bailout Light came on and the radar navigator motioned for me to go. I pulled my ejection handle but nothing happened; the handle had broken free and I was holding a fist full of ejection handle and wire. The radar nav was frantically motioning for me to eject, but when he saw the broken handle in my hand he realized what happened and he ejected so I could unstrap and go out of the hole left by his seat. I unstrapped from the seat, went over and knelt by the hatch, hoping the aircraft was slow enough that I wouldn't impale myself on the lower ECM antennas, then cannonballed out."

Yuill's crew was lucky—they all survived, the only time during Linebacker II that an entire B-52 crew survived the bailout over Hanoi. After his capture, Yuill was put in solitary confinement for seven days leaving him plenty of time to wonder if he hadn't bailed out too early. "Each day that wing fire became smaller and smaller until it no longer existed. When they took me out of solitary and put me in with Bill Mayall and another member of my crew, and I told them that bailing out was a big mistake. Then Bill told me about his seat and how he and the gunner—as best we could determine the last two out of the aircraft—both saw the B-52 explode as they were making their 'nylon letdown.' I felt better about my decision after that."

Back at U-Tapao, Joy Camerota was waiting for her husband Pete in his trailer to go shopping. She had heard on the way to the

base that one or two airplanes had been shot down and was a little worried, but sat down to read and wait. About an hour later, she
heard a key in the lock and a lieutenant colonel opened the door,
looked at her, and said "Oh, no!" As Pete remembered later, "Being
quick on the uptake, she realized that things had not gone well for
our crew. The Air Force did good work for her. They took her to
the hospital, got a chaplain and got some nurses to take care of her.
Everyone was concerned primarily because of her pregnancy, and
they made sure she got to meet Bob Hope at the Christmas show."

TRAGICALLY, BOMBS FROM one of the downed B-52s fell on the
Bach Mai hospital, causing considerable damage and giving the
North Vietnamese a propaganda victory to go with their very real
combat victory. The North Vietnamese leadership rushed foreign
reporters to the scene, and by that afternoon pictures of the damaged hospital were appearing in newspapers around the world,
along with the descriptions of the damage in rest of the city. The
North Vietnamese also took several large parts of downed B-52s
and put them in the center of the city and surrounded them with
floodlights so that day or night the population could see evidence
of their victories.

The Bach Mai hospital bombing killed twenty-five members
of the staff, including fifteen nurses. That, along with pictures of
wrecked B-52s and of new American POWs being paraded through
Hanoi, stoked the ongoing outrage of Congress and added to the
vitriol the press directed against Nixon. Now he and Haig stood
virtually alone.

The cost to the U.S. forces—eight B-52s in two days, a loss
rate twice what SAC had predicted—sent shock waves through the
administration. Nixon had been prepared for losses, but not such
a large number, and they increased the pressure on Nixon from
within his inner circle. Just after the raid Secretary of Defense Laird,
who had been against the bombing from the start, received a message from Admiral Noel Gayler, the commander of the U.S. Forces
in the Pacific, saying that the bombing should be halted. The message was exactly what Laird wanted and he took it to Nixon to make
the case that the bombing was not working and must be stopped.
General Alexander Haig remembered later, "After the losses of the

fourth night it was clear we couldn't continue at this rate. The message from Gayler came in ... and Laird brought it to the President to make it very clear that the head military man in the Pacific was opposed to the bombing. I felt I had to go to directly to General Meyer at SAC and asked the President to let me talk to him. General Meyer told me that they had to modify their tactics and they were doing it, but that we should certainly continue to bomb."

Haig relayed the information to Nixon, who was furious. Nixon knew that Hanoi would not give in until the B-52s inflicted a high level of damage *at low cost,* and that the heavy B-52 losses were creating the opposite of the psychological impact that he wanted. He said later, "[Our] initial heavy losses turned out to be rooted in faulty tactics ... the routes flown by the bombers were too predictable. I raised holy hell that they [the B-52s] kept going over the same targets at the same time. ... Finally we got the military to change their [tactics]." But even with the losses Nixon, stiffened by Haig's strong support, ordered the bombing to continue.

IN OMAHA, GENERAL SULLIVAN'S message about modifying tactics had come just in time. SAC had not known what to do about the B-52 losses, and their distance from the combat zone and bureaucratic layering meant that they were just beginning to get feedback from the B-52 electronic warfare operators that had flown the first missions. The members of the SAC's electronic warfare staff still had no idea about how to counter the North Vietnamese missiles, and SAC's failure to test its jamming techniques prior to the missions was coming back to haunt it. Sullivan's message and General Haig's call galvanized General Meyer into action, and finally—a week after the operation began—he ordered a B-52 be sent to Eglin Air Force Base in Florida to test the bomber's electronic countermeasures against the Fan Song radar site.

The SAC staff had to consider another non-technical problem as well. How were the crews dealing with the losses? The staff was aware of the morale problems in October, before the crews suffered heavy losses. Would they be able to stand up under the strain? SAC could not take the chance. Hanoi was removed from the target list, and the fifth night's raids were changed to the port city of Haiphong, heavily defended but nothing like Hanoi. Neither Nixon nor Haig knew that SAC was taking the pressure off the North Vietnamese by moving their attacks away from Hanoi.

THE LOSSES HAD A DEEP psychological effect on the U.S. airmen. None of the escorting U.S. fighter crews had seen bombers pressing on through heavy enemy defenses as their predecessors had in World War II, and they were as impressed as the previous generation of fighter pilots had been at the courage of the bomber crews. There would be no more sniping or suggestions of cowardice from the fighter forces—in fact, just the opposite. There was nothing but admiration as the B-52 crews braved the SAMs night after night.

But at the B-52 bases, the losses came as a very severe shock to the crews themselves. After years of flying missions with virtually no risk, suddenly many of their friends were gone—a few known to be alive, but most simply down in Hanoi with no information about their fate. After their return from these missions, the crews indulged in a ritual recognized by combat soldiers for thousands of years, one known to the ancient Spartans as *hesma phobou,* or "fear shedding." One Andersen pilot remembered, "By the second day you would walk in the Officers' Club and just smell the fear. Guys were hanging on each other and just revalidating the fact that they're still alive, and they were getting all that fear out in the open." Adding to the problem was that the crews were never told how many aircraft had been actually shot down and, since Guam aircraft diverted into U-Tapao if they were damaged, rumors abounded of even heavier losses than had been officially acknowledged.

The strain showed in other ways. At the Anderson clinic the number of people at sick call almost doubled, from 30 to 40 a day to 55 to 60 a day. At U-Tapao, one copilot had directly refused to fly early in the operation and after two more losses on the fourth night, the stress was showing on some of the other crews. Many of them had flown three missions the first four days when losses were the highest, and after U-Tapao had to fly all the missions the fourth night it was clear now that they, not Andersen, would have to carry the full load of bombing the dangerous targets. The tension was palpable, and one U-Tapao staff officer noted, "The adrenaline and the bravado had worn off. The crews now realized that they were going to be doing this for a long time, maybe a very long time, and this was very sobering."

Fortunately U-Tapao had strong leadership, and from the beginning of the operation the high-ranking officers on the staff—Sullivan, Davis and Brown—as well as many of the other senior officers, had shown a keen interest in the missions and in the crews' suggestions for improving operations. The crews appreciated how their commanders stood up for them, especially after Sullivan sent his message to SAC Headquarters saying the tactics needed to be changed, a message that the crews knew could spell the end of his career.

One aircraft commander summed up the feelings of most of the U-Tapao crews:

"We felt that the Wing Commander at U-Tapao was on our side. He and the rest of the colonels worked hard to try to keep us informed about how the campaign was going, intelligence on the SAM sites, how they were splitting our workloads to try and make it fair for all, the latest rumors, etc. The Wing leadership talked personally with the aircraft commanders after the mission debriefings, both informing and asking for problems, etc."

Additionally, the strong personal rapport that the leadership had built up with the crews began to pay dividends. Colonel Bill Brown remembered one junior aircraft commander came in to him and said, "I just don't think I can fly."

"I said 'sure you can,' but he said 'I've just got so much to live for.' He had a beautiful young wife, and she was there at U-Tapao with him, and I knew that was part of the problem. I told him 'I know that, I know how you feel, but what will your wife think of you if you didn't fly? How could you ever live it down? You'll loose the respect of your peers. I just don't think you can do that.' He went off and flew."

General Glenn Sullivan had a slightly different experience when an aircraft commander come in after the first two nights and said, "I'm scared, I just can't do it."

Sullivan replied, "'OK, you don't have to fly tonight,' and after he left I called the wing commander and told him to leave him off the schedule but to put his crew on with a spare aircraft commander. He came back about 4:30 that afternoon and, in a not very military fashion, said 'You lied to me.'

"I told him that I said that HE didn't have to fly, but that his crew wasn't mentioned. He said, 'They can't go without me,' and

I said that was up to him. He flew the mission, and he came back about 3:30 the next morning, plopped down on the couch I had in the office and told me, 'I know what you did, and I know why you did it, and I really appreciate it.'"

AFTER THE FOURTH DAY'S losses, Seventh Air Force in Saigon convened a conference to discuss the problems the B-52s were encountering and invited the B-52 force to send a representative. Eighth Air Force declined.

Most Seventh Air Force discussions revolved around electronic warfare. The Wild Weasel SAM hunters reported almost a complete absence of signals from the Fan Song SA-2 guidance radar. Additionally, the Air Force Special Communications Center, a highly classified organization that was responsible for monitoring and classifying North Vietnamese radar signals, had concluded that a new, unjammable North Vietnamese radar signal, designated T-8209, was being used to guide missiles from an SA-2 site designated by the U.S. as VN-549. VN-549 had been given credit for five kills the first three nights and been dubbed the "killer site." To counter this, the U.S. decided to make a major effort to knock out site VN-549 with Wild Weasels, and eventually B-52s.

In fact, the analysis was completely wrong. The North Vietnamese had learned from years of combat to minimize their emissions by getting the B-52s' predictable track from other radars, then turning on the Fan Song briefly to fire their missiles just before the post-target turn made the jamming disappear and allowed automatic tracking. It was the SA-2 crews' skill, not a new radar, which was frustrating the Weasels. The electronic warfare officers on the B-52s were getting a normal range of Fan Song signals. The B-52 electronic warfare officers could have pointed this out to the Weasels, but without B-52 representatives at the conference the information was never passed. For the rest of the operation the Weasels were trying to detect and knock out phantom North Vietnamese "super" radars.

Not only was there was no special guidance signal, there was no "killer site." Post-war research indicates that the site might have been occupied by the 77th battalion of the 257th regiment, a very efficient unit—it shot down three B-52s—but it was far from the "killer site" that U.S. intelligence credited it with being. The idea that an "unjammable radar signal" was being used to shoot down the B-52s seems to have been nothing more than a reluctance on the part of the Air Force to believe that third-world missile crews could perform well enough to shoot down America's premier strategic bomber.

Chaff corridors were another topic at the conference. Seventh Air Force realized that the narrow chaff corridors were being blown away by the high-altitude jet stream winds. All the B-52s shot down so far were at least five miles from the chaff corridor, some as far as ten miles. Now that SAC was sending only one wave of B-52s, the planners at Seventh Air Force decided to concentrate their chaffers and lay a chaff blanket directly over the target, rather than hoping the B-52s could stay in the narrow corridor.

FOR NIGHT FIVE, December 22, U-Tapao was once again scheduled to fly all thirty missions into North Vietnam. It seemed that many of the crews must be reaching the end of their tether, but fortunately that afternoon several events came together to reduce the pressure.

First, Sullivan got part of the response from SAC he was looking for. "It was two o'clock in the afternoon and we didn't have a mission order yet," he said later. "We didn't know anything, then about 3:30 in the afternoon I got a phone call on the secure phone and they say we want you to try these targets and there are some big surprises. When we finally got the attack message there were some big changes."

The biggest change was that the bombers were not going to Hanoi but to the port city of Haiphong. This made a huge difference because the strike would come in from the south over the Gulf of Tonkin, bomb, then turn and exit over the Gulf, spending just a few minutes over land. The crews were relieved. They knew that U.S. rescue forces waited in the Gulf of Tonkin, and as one said later, "We knew there would be missiles, but the mission didn't bother me. If we got hit, no matter how bad, we could make it to the water and get rescued."

Additionally, a single raid of B-52s meant the tactical support force would be larger, about twice what a normal night's raid received, and Seventh Air Force would be trying the new chaff tactics. Two flights of eight F-4s each would fly an elaborate pattern to lay a chaff "blanket" thirty miles by twelve miles that would drift over Haiphong before the bombers arrived, and at the same time Navy aircraft would attack all seven SAM sites in the Haiphong area.

By now, word had spread around U-Tapao about the arrival of eleven Andersen D model crews, with twelve more to follow, to help fly the missions. This meant that the hard-pressed U-Tapao crews would only have to fly one night out of every two instead of three out of every four, as they had done the first four nights.

December 22 was Col. Bill Brown's birthday, but he knew that this was a critical mission and he designated himself the airborne commander flying in the lead airplane. Brown was known to the crews as "a good guy but a no bull-shit type of leader," and at the mission briefing he told them in no uncertain terms what was expected of them. "Col. Brown knew how to lead the wave," one of the pilots later remembered. "He was a flying leader; he knew what it was like up there. . . . He was aware that people were maneuvering on their own and breaking up the formation's jamming. He pointed out people, called names and said you will not do that, you will do it this way. This is what you did wrong, this is how you're going to do it right."

The final bit of good news on Day Five was the arrival of the Bob Hope Christmas show. Hope knew when he arrived at U-Tapao that the base had suffered heavy losses, and before the show he personally went to meet the crews that were going to be flying the mission that night. The crewmembers were flattered and very appreciative. As one said later, "It was really grand of him to take the time to come in and talk to us. He was very sober about it: he didn't tell any funny stories. . . . He just showed his appreciation by taking the time just to come in there and say hello to us."

Another B-52 pilot recalled, "The best thing that happened during the operation to take the pressure off was the Bob Hope show. It saved a lot of guys."

THAT NIGHT'S RAID CAUGHT the North Vietnamese off guard. The 363rd Air Defense Division, the unit that was protecting Haiphong, had little time to get organized and fire its missiles. The chaff blanket confused their tracking radars, and the rapidity with which the

B-52 force struck and departed disrupted their manual tracking process that had been successful over Hanoi. For the first time since Linebacker II began a night passed without a B-52 being hit.

But while they had not shot down any B-52s the North Vietnamese leadership thought the raid on Haiphong was a sign that they had won a victory. The change of targets meant that the Americans were unwilling to risk more losses over Hanoi, and, in an article published after the war, a North Vietnamese military analyst wrote, "If Nixon had continued to send the B-52s to Hanoi we would have been in big trouble. Where would we have gotten the missiles to fight back? . . . When the B-52s stopped coming after the fourth night, the greatest trial of the Hanoi missile troops was over. They fought to the last missile and made the difference between victory and defeat. It was the 'Dien Bien Phu of the Air.'"

TEN

Holding On

O n Night Six, SAC moved even further from the
North Vietnamese defenses, sending thirty B-52s
against a storage area and railroad repair shops
in deep canyons close to the village of Lang Dang,
about fifty miles northeast of Hanoi near the Chinese border. Twelve
Andersen crews would be going back to North Vietnam for the first
time since Day Three, joining eighteen of the hard-pressed UT crews
who had flown the last sixty missions. The SAC staff considered
Lang Dang a "minor target," but what was important at this point
was that they not suffer losses while continuing to bomb North
Vietnam in accordance with the letter, if not the spirit, of the president's orders. Lang Dang was expected to be a classic "milk run,"
and adding to the crews' confidence were some real changes in the
attack plan that reflected the U-Tapao crews' suggestions. The
bombers were told to delay their post-target turn to clear the target
defenses, then make two small turns rather than one large one, and
to fly in a significantly larger altitude "block," from 31,000 to 38,000
feet, varying their altitudes as they approached the target, then
changing altitudes again after they dropped their bombs.

With the specifics of the mission settled, the Andersen commanders turned to the most important event of the evening—the
Officers' Wives Club Formal. The wives had told their husbands
that they were not going to cancel their Christmas party over such
a minor matter as a war and, declaring "the poor visiting crews will
enjoy it," the party was on. (In fact, the visiting crewmembers were
only allowed to come if they had a "mess dress" uniform to wear,
the military's equivalent of black tie, which none of the crews had
brought.) The senior officers—few of whom had flown any

Linebacker II missions—dined and watched the floorshow. It had just begun when calls came in on the commanders' personal radios and they hurriedly departed for the command post.

At the command post they were faced with a disaster in the making. The mission plan had arrived late at the fighter and support wings in Thailand, so the support forces were running behind, and to compound the problem there was bad weather in the refueling areas over Laos where the fighters had to refuel prior to their rendezvous with the B-52s. Only the F-111s (which did not need air refueling) were certain to offer full support of the raid. The B-52s might be on their own with no chaffers, fighter escorts or Wild Weasel SAM-suppression. The Andersen commanders notified SAC about the situation but recommended that the bombers continue on to their targets. SAC concurred, and the commanders returned to the party.

Luck was with them. The raid was well outside of SAM coverage and such raids were allocated to the MiG force. A relatively large number of MiG-21s—at least four—roared off to probe the B-52 formations, but the MiGs were cautious and it took some time before they realized they were unopposed. The brunt of their attack was on Topaz and Copper cells, and the MiGs fired four missiles as the B-52 tail gunners blazed away. One gunner on Copper 3 claimed two MiG kills (not confirmed) but no bombers were hit. The failed attacks highlighted the MiG-21s' very limited night interception capability, even in good conditions, and for one of the few times in the operation the North Vietnamese did not make the U.S. forces pay for a mistake. All the bombers returned safely, and the Officers' Wives Club Christmas Party was considered a huge success—at least until later. Once the senior staff left, the returning crewmembers appeared at the club and threw all the Christmas decorations into the pool. The next day several of the wives complained vehemently to General Johnson, but at that point Johnson—who had just been notified of what was to happen after Christmas Day—simply let it go, remarking "boys will be boys."

The B-52s had been lucky not only with the mission, but also with the results. The SAC staff was worried about bombing Lang Dang because the radar offset aim points around the village were very poor, and in fact many of the bombs missed the caves and valley they were aimed for and instead hit the center of the village that the Americans thought was a market square. But later, when photos of the bomb damage arrived, the SAC staff found that the bombs had blown the covers off storage areas and exposed huge amounts of military stores in the square, and the cliffs were honeycombed with caves and additional storage.

On Night Seven, thirty B-52s, all flown by U-Tapao crews, bombed railroad yards well away from Hanoi's defenses. Once again Seventh Air Force chaffers laid down a chaff blanket, and this time the B-52s dropped chaff in their small post-target turns to further disrupt the North Vietnamese defenses—a useful tactic but one that had been previously forbidden by SAC, apparently because the chaff was difficult to load into the B-52.

While the targets were far from Hanoi's SAM sites, they were not undefended. John Mize and his crew were flying in Purple 02 attacking the Thai Nguyen railroad yard when Mize felt a huge bump in the back of the airplane and heard his gunner yell. A 100mm anti-aircraft gun shell had exploded below the aircraft just in front of the tail and had severely damaged some of the B-52's systems. One engine was knocked out, but more importantly the stabilizer trim was damaged and fuel was trapped in some of the fuel tanks, a combination of problems that meant the Mize would not be able to raise the nose high enough to land the aircraft unless something was done. An emergency tanker was launched and Mize slipped the damaged bomber in behind it to take on enough fuel to alter the aircraft's center of gravity so he could land, then he headed for U-Tapao. There was some thought of telling the crew to bail out but Mize was an Arc Light veteran who had had a very good reputation with the U-Tapao leadership, and he was allowed to continue.

Once Mize set up to land, he could feel that the aircraft was unstable and warned the crew to be ready to bail out because he felt it was too badly damaged to go around and try again. Mize was able to set the damaged bomber down successfully and he and his crew—who had been hit by a SAM on an earlier mission—achieved some notoriety as being the first crew to be hit twice by North Vietnamese defenses.

The U-Tapao crews were back on the base by midnight and joined a huge, raucous and richly earned Christmas party. The party was highlighted (or lowlighted) by a raid on a closet that held the New Year's Eve fireworks, and soon the fireworks were whistling across the club, while the crewmembers yelled "SAM, SAM," and dove under the tables. The party was also fueled by the knowledge that the crews would not have to fly the next night because President Nixon ordered the JCS to take a 36-hour bombing halt for Christmas, from Christmas Eve until 6:00 A.M. on December 26, Hanoi time. A Christmas cease-fire had been a consistent feature of American operations in Vietnam, and with the domestic pressure against the bombing there was no consideration of continuing the operation over the holiday. But notwithstanding Christmas parties, the bombing pause generated some bitter reactions from the B-52 crews, who felt that it gave the North Vietnamese an opportunity to continue to reinforce their defenses.

The crews were right. The North Vietnamese Air Defense Command was already using the break in the attacks on Hanoi to improve the capital's defenses. They believed that Hanoi would still be the B-52s' main target and expected the entry and exit routes could be changed, radar-jamming increased, and as a desperate measure to increase the pressure, the B-52s might shift their focus to residential areas.

A final wave of evacuations began to remove as many civilians as possible, and to counter the expected changes in the B-52 attack patterns the Air Defense Command began to rearrange its missile battalions, moving some to the northeast and southwest of Hanoi to form a circle around the capital. They also moved in two additional missile battalions, raising the number protecting Hanoi to twelve, so that several missile units would now meet an attack from any direction.

While the North Vietnamese busied themselves with their military preparations, they did not ignore their propaganda campaign. Joan Baez and her three American companions had been trapped in Hanoi since the Gia Lam airport had been bombed, and early Christmas Eve their hosts encouraged Baez to sing at a gathering in the lobby of the hotel for the Western guests. Baez, who had a cold, was singing the Lord's Prayer when F-111s raced over the capital and the group had to scramble to shelters, causing Baez to grouse, "Those bastards, if there's one thing I can't stand it's being interrupted in the middle of a performance." Later that evening the group went to a midnight mass that Baez said was "awful ... there were roving cameras with bright lights." But another member of her group remembered moving renditions of Schubert's "Ave Maria" and Gruber's "Silent Night," sung by a choir that included a boy soprano with a remarkable voice.

WHILE THE PAUSE HELPED the North Vietnamese, it also allowed the American staffs both in the combat theater and at SAC to try to solve the problem of the B-52 losses. The first four nights the B-52s had flown about 300 sorties into the Hanoi area and had lost 11 aircraft, a loss rate of about 3.7 percent, and all the losses had come while bombing targets within ten miles of the center of the capital. The unmodified Gs had proved to be very vulnerable and after the third night SAC decided they would not be sent to Hanoi again. From now on only D models would be used, and this had the added benefit of putting more bombs on the important Hanoi targets.

The tests in the United States at Eglin against the captured Soviet SA-2 site showed that, as the crews had suspected, the post-target turn did blank the B-52s' jamming antennas, but by then most of the post-target turns had been significantly reduced as a result of Sullivan's message to SAC.

The tests showed other problems. For years SAC procedures called for the B-52 EWs to jam a part of the SA-2 system known as the *beacon,* the electronic signal from the SA-2 missile down to the Fan Song radar telling the crew where the missile was. This was a very serious mistake, but SAC Intelligence was not alone—an electronic warfare officer from the Air Force Staff, Dave Brog, had told SAC to jam this part of the system in a meeting at SAC in November 1972. At the Eglin tests SAC learned that the B-52 beacon jamming was not effective against the beacon of the current Fan Songs, because in 1969 the Soviets had modified the beacon so that it was essentially unjammable. The North Vietnamese had been using this unjammable beacon on their Fan Songs since about 1971 and Seventh Air Force had reported the SA-2 beacon was unjammable for the past year, but SAC and Air Staff had either not read the Seventh Air Force reports or not paid attention to them. SAC hastily told the B-52 electronic warfare officers to change their jamming procedures and to use their jammers on other parts of the SA-2 system. The tests also showed that jamming protection was seriously degraded when there were only two B-52s in a cell, but this problem—the degraded jamming of the two-ship cell—was treated with less urgency and not forwarded to the combat zone because of the need for "further study."

Analysis also made it clear what was already brutally obvious to the B-52s crews—the northwest to southeast route of flight to Hanoi the first four days was a serious mistake. Despite SAC's insistence that the northwest-southeast routes avoided the bulk of the North Vietnamese defenses, the route had carried the B-52s right over the best North Vietnamese SAM regiment, the 261st, which was to score eight of the fifteen B-52 kills in the operation.

In Saigon, Seventh Air Force continued to be frustrated with how SAC was conducting the raids. General Vogt had been trying to juggle a twenty-four-hour-a-day operation with limited resources, supporting the B-52s at night and launching tactical strikes during the day, despite being severely hampered by bad weather. Working with this tight schedule, SAC's chronic late delivery of the bombing plan had been causing Seventh tremendous problems.

General Vogt also felt that General Meyer and SAC were trying to use Seventh Air Force as a scapegoat for the B-52 losses, and his frustrations came out in a message he sent to General Meyer. "Since the beginning of LBII we have made every effort to support B-52 operations.... [But t]here is inadequate time from receipt of essential SAC information to adequately plan. Often we receive final information on ingress, egress, spacing between cells, etc. after our [orders] should have been disseminated. This severely constrains us in planning optimum tactics and the Wings have inadequate time to prepare for the missions.... We must regroup after the brief Xmas standdown ... if I am to meet my commitment for LBII day strikes and provide ... support for your forces."

FOR NIXON AND HIS STAFF, the situation Christmas Eve was grim even though the losses had dropped off. The North Vietnamese remained intransigent despite the attacks. The angry rhetoric of those opposed to the bombing continued, and Congress would be back in less than two weeks in a fighting mood. Nixon was almost

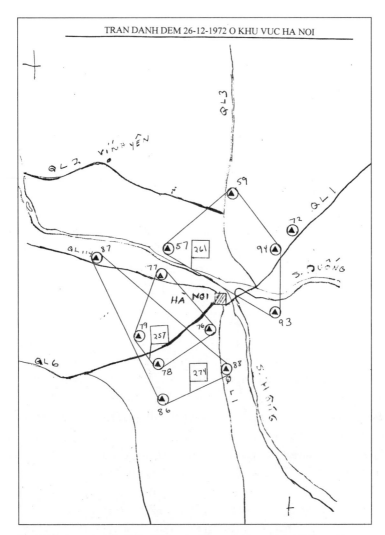

North Vietnamese missile battalion deployment, December 26: Expecting
the U.S. to change tactics, the North Vietnamese reverted to surrounding
Hanoi with missile battalions. Two new battalions had been added by this
time, bringing the total number to twelve.

out of time. If the North Vietnamese did not agree to return to the
peace talks immediately after Christmas, then his gamble would
fail and the war would be lost.

To make matters worse, reconnaissance photos finally arrived
and showed that the amount of damage done by the raids had been
vastly exaggerated. It was clear the North Vietnamese had not been

hurt as much as SAC had claimed, and on December 24, Nixon rolled the dice for the last time and ordered the Joint Chiefs to conduct a massive attack on Hanoi on December 26, as soon as the Christmas cease-fire was over. Admiral Moorer passed the order on to General Meyer at SAC to plan a large mission for that date.

The battle would be won or lost on the night of the 26th. If the raids suffered heavy losses, there was no reason to expect that the North Vietnamese would return to the peace talks. Congress would convene, cut off money for the war, and South Vietnam and the American POWs would be abandoned.

In fact, the situation was even grimmer than the White House knew. When the B-52s stopped bombing Hanoi, the North Vietnamese were sure they had won a victory, an "aerial Dien Bien Phu." They had caused U.S. heavy casualties and they knew that in the United States dissent was mounting. It was only a matter of holding out a little longer.

STILL SMARTING UNDER THE CRITICISM of its routes and tactics, when the SAC staff received the order to return to Hanoi they bowed to the inevitable and took themselves out of much of the mission planning. They gave Eighth Air Force general instructions incorporating the lessons of the first four nights, junking the three separate waves spread over eight hours and replacing it with a single attack of 120 B-52s in fifteen minutes to overwhelm the defenses and not give the missile sites time to reload. Most of the rest of the planning was left to Eighth, including the precise axis of attack, target routes and tactics inside the target area, but SAC would still choose the targets.

Buttressed by the experiences of the first six days, the Eighth Air Force staff set about modifying the plan they had originally developed in September, incorporating many of the changes suggested since then by the B-52 crews. There would be no more "line of ants" crawling predictably down the enemy's radar screen. The B-52s would fly on four routes, two raids coming in from Laos and exiting over the Gulf of Tonkin and two raids entering from the Gulf of Tonkin. As the B-52s approached their target area, the raids would split into seven waves to attack ten targets, seven in the Hanoi area, two around Haiphong and one near Thai Nguyen. Seven of the ten targets would be hit simultaneously by B-52s flying at different altitudes on different routes of attack, and the attack patterns, altitudes and spacing of each cell would be different from the one in front. Some of the B-52s' flight paths would actually cross, though with several thousand feet difference in altitude.

Post-target tactics also changed dramatically. After dropping their bombs, the B-52s would change altitude and, except for a few cells, there would be no large post-target turn to blank out the B-52s' jamming antennas over the SAM sites. The whole raid would last only fifteen minutes.

Seventy-eight of the B-52s would come from Andersen, and most of them—forty-five of the vulnerable G models—were sent to targets outside of Hanoi. As usual, U-Tapao did the heavy lifting, sending forty-two Ds to the dangerous targets around the capital.

The compression of all the B-52s into a single raid allowed Seventh Air Force and the Navy to provide a massive support force of over 110 aircraft for the mission, and Seventh in particular made several changes to increase the pressure on the SAM battalions. For the first time, F-111s would attack SAM sites, and the force would have ten pairs of Wild Weasel Hunter-Killer teams to visually attack the missile sites, though the weather was expected to limit their effectiveness.

Seventh also continued to tweak its chaff procedures. Twenty-four F-4s would lay a massive, U-shaped chaff blanket over the target areas. With the blanket, the B-52s would not have to worry about staying in a narrow corridor, and the wide dispersion of the chaff complemented the tactic of using multiple-attack headings. The compressed target times for the B-52s also solved the problem of the wind blowing the chaff away because this night the chaff only needed to be in the target area for fifteen minutes, instead of the fifty minutes required on the earlier missions.

But SAC still had control over the target selection and the number of B-52s assigned to each target, and once again problems arose. A little over an hour after sending the first target list to Eighth, SAC issued a major revision. Then, two hours later, SAC ordered Eighth to incorporate two new targets into the raid, and two hours later these new targets were cancelled and the time of the entire mission moved back by three hours. The changes continued almost until takeoff, but the most important change that could have been

U.S. routes, December 26: After the heavy losses on
Nights One to Four, SAC finally turned the Hanoi mission
planning over to Eighth Air Force. After staying away from
the capital for five days, the B-52s returned en masse and
attacked from all angles in a fifteen-minute blitz that overwhelmed the North Vietnamese defenses. Compare the
routes with those of December 18–21 (p. 66).

made was not—no B-52s would attack the SAM storage and assembly areas, the key to the North Vietnamese defenses.

At the briefings, most of the B-52 crews were elated when they
saw the mission routes laid out for them, but a few were worried
about collisions with cells coming in from different directions. As
the crews came out of the briefing late on the afternoon of the 26th
and headed for their aircraft, the word quickly spread around the
base at Andersen that this was "the big one," and when the B-52s
began to taxi once again a huge crowd was watching.

The spectacle did not disappoint them. Seventy-eight B-52s
roared off one by one in a launch that took well over two hours to
complete. One observer remembered realizing that what he was
seeing "was unique in his lifetime and probably would not be dupli-
cated in the lives of his children." Indeed, what the people at Andersen saw may have been the last mass launch of heavy bombers in
the history of warfare.

At U-Tapao, Bob Morris and his crew had volunteered to be one
of twelve crews that came to reinforce U-Tapao on Christmas Eve. That
night they were scheduled to fly their first mission from there as Ebony

03, but just before they were to taxi they were told that Ebony 02 had aborted and they became Ebony 02. They were also told that there were no spares and there would be no Ebony 03. As Morris taxied out his gunner, John Schell, called and said he was sick and would have to be replaced. This was a severe breach of the "gunners' code," and another gunner said later, "You flew unless the flight surgeon grounded you, no matter how bad you felt. You didn't let someone else go into combat for you unless you couldn't do anything about it. Also, when the engines started and you began to taxi, you went no matter what."

But Morris had no choice and called for a replacement, and the U-Tapao command post called the gunners' quarters where a spare gunner was supposed to be available. Jim Cook answered the phone and looked around for the "spare" gunner, but he had left when the bombers began to taxi. Cook offered to fly the mission then grabbed his equipment, forgetting his lucky flop hat, and started to leave. As he passed through the gunners' lounge, another gunner said "see you later," but Cook had a strange feeling and replied, "Maybe."

Bob Hudson, Morris's copilot, remembered. "A truck pulled up and a guy got out and ran to the rear of the aircraft. I got a 'Door Open' light from the gunner's position and John Schell said he was leaving. The "Door Open" light went out and a strange voice said, 'I'm in, let's go.' He never introduced himself and he didn't know where he was going or what to expect."

The maintenance crews of the B-52 force at U-Tapao had been doing a magnificent job, but the aircraft had been stretched to the limit and finally began to break. Six bombers aborted on the ground; there were only two spares, so only thirty-eight B-52s from U-Tapao flew the mission. With the aborts the U-Tapao aircraft now had four cells of two rather than three aircraft, and there was some discussion about whether to fly the two-ship cells alone or to move them up and add them to a three-ship cell, making a five-ship cell. The argument for the value of the combined jamming of a five-ship cell would seem to have made the choice an easy one, but SAC had no procedures for five-ship cells. Rather than do something wrong, Eighth opted to do nothing and four two-ship cells from U-Tapao— Ash, Rainbow, Brown, and Ebony—headed for Hanoi.

As Ebony 02 climbed out, the engine fire light came on for engine number seven, and copilot Bob Hudson looked outside and saw that the engine was on fire. The new gunner, Jim Cook, confirmed that "crap" was coming out of the engine. "We pulled out of the formation," Hudson remembered, "took care of the problem and started talking about what to do. The discussion centered on the fact that if we aborted Ebony 01 would have to go alone, almost sure suicide because they needed our jamming support. We decided we needed to press on. We had to cut back the second engine in the nacelle back to 60 percent power, and we finally caught up to Ebony 01 just as he turned towards Hanoi."

EVEN THOUGH SEVERAL NEW SAM battalions had arrived in Hanoi, the North Vietnamese were still concerned. They had watched the gradual change in U.S. tactics before the Christmas pause, and anticipated an even more dramatic change in the next battle plan. The North Vietnamese official history reported the Air Defense Staff "knew that the U.S. . . . . would change their plans for the next wave of action. They would not come from the same direction and would not split into three groups . . . but send a big group of B-52s at the same time striking straight at Hanoi. From our side, the preparations for the attack made the atmosphere at the Air Defense Headquarters quite tense."

The tension mounted when two reconnaissance drones flew over Hanoi about noon, followed by a tactical fighter raid an hour later. This was too much for one of the newly arrived missile battalions from Haiphong, the 72nd, which fired two missiles at an F-4, disobeying orders to wait for the B-52s expected that night. The battalion's commander, Chat Pham, was called on the carpet, chastised thoroughly and told again that all the missiles had to be saved for the B-52s.

The strong rebuke Pham received highlighted the continuing North Vietnamese problem with missiles. During the break every possible measure had been taken, but the assembly of the missile was still agonizingly slow. The night of December 26 the Hanoi defenders would have just over a hundred missiles available, about half the number they had at the start of the campaign.

ELEVEN

The Eighth Night

Just before ten o'clock the night of December 26, the North Vietnamese early warning radar crews reported to the Air Defense Headquarters that they were seeing the standard beginning of the U.S. battle pattern unfold—fighters and Wild Weasels refueling over Laos, EB-66s moving into position to start their jamming, and F-111s approaching at low altitude. Half an hour later, sixteen F-4s began to lay their chaff blanket just north of Hanoi, and then five minutes after that, eight more F-4s did the same north of Haiphong. The high winds, which had done much to neutralize the corridors the first seven nights, now blew the chaff together to form a huge, dense blanket over the two cities.

Craig Mizner's crew was leading a wave of 18 Andersen B-52s in from the east to North Vietnam. They flew from Guam, turning north over the South China Sea towards the Communist Chinese island of Hainan, where they were to turn short of the island and head into eastern North Vietnam, then turn west towards Hanoi.

Bill Beavers, Mizner's navigator, was carefully watching the approach to Hainan because the Chinese were quite sensitive, and several U.S. aircraft that had violated Hainan's airspace over the course of the war had been shot down. There was an international twelve-mile "no fly zone" around Chinese territory, and Beavers had planned to turn the cell well short of the line and proceed to North Vietnam. As they approached Hainan, Beavers and Mizner were dismayed to hear a call on Guard frequency, a universal distress frequency, from Red Crown, a U.S. Navy cruiser in the Gulf of Tonkin that American aircraft used as a radar control agency.

"B-52s approaching Hainan, this is Red Crown on Guard, turn left now."

What was going on? Here was the largest American raid of the war whose outcome might well depend on tactical surprise, and an American air traffic controller was telling the North Vietnamese that B-52s were coming in from the east!

Mizner and Beavers talked quickly, and Beavers assured him they were on track and that an early turn would make the next turn towards Hanoi very sharp, which would "crack the whip" throwing the whole wave out of line. With over 120 aircraft converging on Hanoi at the same time, this could be disastrous.

Once again the call came, "B-52s approaching Hainan, this is Red Crown on Guard, turn left now."

Mizner was torn, but Beavers convinced him to hold on and a minute later, when the wave hit the turn point, they turned northwest.

Notwithstanding this warning, what was unfolding was the North Vietnamese defenders' worst nightmare. As the B-52s approached from four different directions, a chaff blanket 40 miles by 23 miles completely covered the Hanoi area and a similar one covered Haiphong. As F-111s roared in to attack SAM sites around Hanoi for the first time, Navy attack aircraft began to simultaneously attack SAM sites around Haiphong.

As the North Vietnamese official history described the situation, "The enemy had altered many of his tactics. They also changed the direction of their bombing, changed the flight paths in and out of the bombing area and began to collectively and unceasingly bomb a large number of targets at the same time within a short period.

"The initial situation was very complicated. There was much radar jamming and 'fake B-52s' [chaff] as well as squads of Wild Weasels continuously launching guided anti-radiation missiles. The enemy sent many groups of B-52s into the area simultaneously. All of the groups arrived at their bombing targets at the same time and this simultaneous attack from many directions caused us many difficulties in focusing our firepower, so we were not able to fire at all of them in time. The enemy split into many groups and many tight formations they did not stay in the range of our missiles for long."

The Air Defense Headquarters was so badly overwhelmed that the 361st's Division Command Post had to take over allocating targets to the missile battalions. As the early warning system broke down further, the SAM battalions had to use their own Fan Song radars to search for targets, a technique that not only was inefficient but also vastly increased their vulnerability to prowling Wild Weasels. The heavy chaff also forced the missile crews to abandon their automatic tracking and fall back on the less efficient three-point manual guidance.

As the North Vietnamese missile crews tried to cope with the new situation, six B-52 cells attacked the Giap Nhi railroad yard from the south, exactly the opposite direction from which they had attacked previously. As they approached, the six cells then split into two groups, one of two cells and one of four cells, and attacked from different directions.

Unfortunately, the new tactics were negated to some extent by their limited jamming in the two-aircraft cells. Ebony was one of these, and Bob Morris and his crew in Ebony 02 were approaching the target when both the 76th and 78th Battalions of the 257th regiment tracked them. Each battalion fired two missiles and manually tracked the B-52 as it approached. As Morris rolled out to stabilize the B-52 on the bomb run, the 76th's first missile narrowly missed, but as the aircraft steadied the crew heard Nutter Wimbrow, the electronic warfare officer, said calmly, 'We're going to be hit.'"

The second of the 76th's missiles exploded in front of copilot Bob Hudson: "It blew off the radome and the radar. All the windows upstairs were gone. The explosive decompression sucked out everything in cockpit past my head. The initial explosion killed Bob Morris—I could see part of the hydraulic panel blown through him. I had my left sinus collapsed by the overpressure, my left arm was broken, and I had multiple puncture wounds from glass and debris. I sat there in a daze until the RN called and said we had to get the nose up so we could get the bombs off. I got us centered on the target and we dropped the bombs."

A few seconds later a missile from the 78th hit the dying aircraft. "We took another missile in the left wing," Hudson remembered, "and it flipped the aircraft over on its back so I gave the order to bail out. The nav bailed out immediately and I thought the gunner went too. Nutter told me he was ejecting and I heard his seat go. The radar navigator said he was ejecting. I looked over at Bob Morris, my best friend. I could see he was dead, and then I too stepped over the side."

In the tail of the aircraft, substitute gunner Jim Cook had heard the conversation over the intercom and knew the aircraft was in serious trouble, and he began the cumbersome task of jettisoning the rear turret. Cook leaned forward and grabbed a yellow "T" handle just above his left foot, then pulled it toward him, and with a "whish" four explosive bolts fired and the entire back end of the B-52—the radar console, the guns, everything—fell away and disappeared and Cook was staring at thin air. Cook unstrapped from the seat, grabbed the cloth handles on either side of the compartment, and tried to pull himself forward though the open hole in the back of the aircraft. What Cook did not know was that the aircraft was now upside down and falling. He could not pull himself out, so he rocked back in his seat and tried again.

A brilliant flash lit up the sky as the bomber blew up in midair, and large pieces fell burning to the ground in a scene described later as "looking like fire being poured out of a pitcher." There were a few seconds of stunned silence from the American forces. Then, "miraculously," as one crewmember recalled, emergency beepers from the parachutes began to sound.

The explosion had blown Jim Cook clear of the wreckage. "I woke up on a riverbank in two feet of water, coughing. I had come down headfirst because my legs had been tangled in the chute risers. I hurt all over, and later I found out both legs had been shattered below the knee, my back had been fractured, and my right shoulder and elbow had been broken. The North Vietnamese found me and interrogated me for twenty-four hours, breaking five ribs in the process."

Cook was one of four Ebony 02 crewmembers who survived and were captured. Nutter Wimbrow, the EW, was apparently killed in the ejection.

Bill Beavers, Craig Mizner's navigator, described the scene as it sounded on the radio: "There were MiG calls as we went in and

out, SAM calls as some fool (we never did figure out who) kept calling, 'SAM, SAM vicinity of Hanoi,' as they were salvoing two, four
or six missiles. Emergency locator beacons were screaming on
GUARD channel and you KNEW it was too many beepers to be a
single or dual seat fighter going down. One or more BUFFs had
been hit and was going down over Downtown. Visual reports came
in from BUFF cellmates:"

"'Ebony Two is hit and going down on fire.'"

"'How many chutes?'"

"'Four' comes the reply. . . ."

At the same time, Beaver's EW, Bud Hughes, had his hands
full on the run in to the target. "You get to a certain point in target
penetration where the signal strength of the SAM radar is sufficient
to burn through the jamming emanating from your aircraft. You just
can't carry that much power with you. Try as I might, I couldn't
deny the enemy radar information. At one time I counted six SAM
radars painting our BUFF from all around us. There was no way I
could address them all, especially when they were shifting frequency. I would jam one and move on to the second and third, then
go back and check the first and find out he had moved out from
under my jamming."

For the sixth time the B-52s attacked Kinh No, whose defenses
had already brought down three of the bombers. Two of the three
cells going against Kinh No had only two B-52s in the cell, and
with limited jamming coverage the defenses again scored against
one of the B-52s, Ash 01. Copilot Bob Hymel heard the gunner call
"'We have SAMs coming up from the rear,' and I could see two
SAMs coming up behind us side by side. The pilot put the plane
in a descending turn and one of the SAMs exploded by the right
side of the airplane. It felt like a kick in the pants."

The missile devastated the aircraft, wounding the gunner in
the leg and groin, causing severe structural damage and setting the
number seven and eight engines on fire. The aircraft commander,
Captain Jim Turner, shut down the number seven engine, pulled
number eight to idle and, with the right wing leaking fuel, headed
south. As the B-52 moved away from the target area Turner and
several of the air traffic controllers discussed landing at another
base, but Turner decided to return to U-Tapao.

Turner had an advantage handling the damaged B-52. On the seventh night of the operation one of his neighbors at U-Tapao, Captain John Mize, had brought a badly damaged B-52 back to the base and landed successfully, and had given Turner a through briefing on the problems he had encountered. One of the things that Mize told Turner was that, once committed to landing, there was no turning back. A badly damaged B-52 could not make a successful go around and come back around again.

Brent Diefenbach and his crew had already landed, and as Turner's plane approached, Diefenbach sat in the front of his crew bus filling out maintenance forms. Diefenbach was very pleased with how well the mission had gone when the bus suddenly stopped short of U-Tapao's single runway to allow Turner's damaged B-52 to land.

Colonel Bill Maxson, the commander of U-Tapao's consolidated maintenance wing, was in the command post when he was alerted about Ash 01's situation: "The tail gunner was wounded. The aircraft commander was experiencing flight control problems, but he intended to recover at U-Tapao rather than in South Vietnam at DaNang AFB, even though it was much closer to their present position. The gunner's wounds were not life threatening and the aircraft would be lighter when it got to U-Tapao because it would have burned off more fuel. This was approved and emergency recovery procedures started.

"The flight control problem involved battle damage to the hydraulic systems and was rather complicated, so maintenance experts were summoned to talk to the aircrew on how best to cope with what seemed to be a deteriorating situation. General Sullivan, Colonel Don Davis, and I, along with the team of experts, climbed into the Charlie tower to assist in the recovery of the bomber in any way we could. At least we had the top decision-makers there if a 'command decision' was needed, but the senior people let the experts call the shots."

The tension in the tower increased as the damaged bomber began its descent into the airfield and its navigation lights became visible. Radio chatter ceased. The airfield was cleared, crash crews waited with fire fighting equipment, and any unnecessary aircraft in the path of the landing bomber were moved as far away as possible.

"The aircrew was concentrating on wrestling this wounded beast to the ground," Maxson remembered, "but the flight control problem had worsened as they slowed their airspeed for landing. Now the bomber was on final, but even in the darkness we could sense the pilot was having difficulty keeping the wings level as he approached the runway."

Inside Ash 01, copilot Bob Hymel lowered the landing gear and felt the aircraft vibrate for a moment, then slowly begin to drift to the left. Watching from the Charlie tower, Bill Maxson saw the aircraft level off, then heard the engines begin to roar as Turner added power. Maxson was not an experienced B-52 pilot, but sensed that the bomber was going too slow to make a successful go around.

The bomber passed by the Charlie tower at eye-level, traveling so slowly that Maxson knew with a sinking feeling it was about to stall about 150 feet off the ground and with no runway left ahead of it. "I simply cannot describe the horror I felt as I saw the wing navigation lights starting to rotate as the aircraft stalled, rolled and crashed upside down just off the end of the runway. After hours of struggle on the part of the aircrew to bring this shot up 'bird' back home safely, after all of the efforts by those of us on the ground to save her, we had lost. I had seen B-52s and other aircraft crash before, but never have I felt such anguish and helplessness and despair for the valiant aircrew."

Sitting in the bus with his crew, Brent Diefenbach watched the B-52 float down the runway, then begin to drift. The engines began to roar, but as the stricken B-52 started to accelerate past the bus where Diefenbach and his crew were sitting it pitched nose up, stalled and crashed in a spectacular fireball and explosion about a mile away, outside the fence around the base.

After a moment, Diefenbach got up and walked off the bus, furious that the mission which had gone so well ended in this disaster. As he walked, he was drawn towards the crash scene, even though it was obvious no one was alive. He walked out the gate of the base and saw a Thai on a motorbike watching the fire, but when he tried to take the motorbike the Thai roared off.

Diefenbach then turned and waved down a "baht bus," a small, open pickup truck used as a taxi. The driver—perhaps persuaded by Diefenbach's .38 survival pistol—stopped, picked him up and took him close to the huge fire that marked the crash site. The aircraft was burning just beyond a field of waist-high grass. Diefenbach saw a path and moved towards the fire as he heard a rescue helicopter and fire trucks coming from the base. As he approached he called out "Is anybody there?" not expecting to find anyone alive. But inside the burning B-52 the copilot, Lieutenant Bob Hymel, was trapped in the wrecked cockpit, crammed against his seat and wedged against the instrument panel. He began to yell for help, and Diefenbach heard him.

There were no fire trucks or helicopters on the scene yet and Diefenbach thought, "Oh great, I'm gonna die." He zipped up his fire-resistant nomex flight suit, rolled down the sleeves to protect himself from the fire as much as possible, then ran through the fire to where the cockpit section had broken off the aircraft. He leaned in through the hatch, and saw Hymel alive but badly injured. Diefenbach tried to pull him out but found that Hymel was stuck in the wreckage. As Diefenbach worked to free him, the smoke and fire were closing in and the area around the cockpit was getting hotter and hotter, then suddenly there were a series of explosions as the oxygen bottles and tires exploded. With each explosion Diefenbach jumped a little bit higher, and he realized he had no idea if there were still bombs on the aircraft. Struggling desperately, Diefenbach worked the seat belt open but found Hymel's leg was pinned under the rudder pedals.

Hymel seemed to be dying on the spot, drifting in and out of consciousness, and Diefenbach had to hurry. He always carried a large knife with him, a carryover from his days as a forward air controller, and he realized he was going to have to use it to cut off Hymel's leg if they were to have any chance to escape. Then Hymel suddenly stirred and began to help pull, and the leg came free. Diefenbach dragged him clear of the fire, then put him down and tried to get the attention of the rescue crews. Finally a fire truck pulled up and took them to a helicopter that flew them to the hospital.

After the helicopter landed, Diefenbach went directly to the wing headquarters. Covered with blood and physically spent, he made his way to the command post, where he told a mesmerized audience what happened. When he finished he excused himself and said he had to go to maintenance debriefing. He was walking down the hall when one of the stunned colonels came running after him and took him to the hospital.

Ironically, the only other survivor of the crash was the tail gunner, whose wounds had been the reason the crew had passed up several alternate landing sites. The tail broke off in the crash, and the gunner unstrapped his safety harness and walked out of the broken fuselage to safety.

EVEN WITH THE TWO LOSSES, Night Eight's raid was a tremendous success. In a little over twenty minutes the B-52s dropped more than two thousand tons of bombs and all indications were that the attack from different directions had befuddled the North Vietnamese defenses. The two B-52s lost had been in two-ship cells that had proven to be terribly vulnerable, but the small post-target turn appeared to be effective, keeping the B-52s from blanking their own jamming antennas while changing the B-52s' flight path enough to make it difficult for the SA-2 guidance officers to manually track the aircraft.

In addition to the changes in the routes and post-target turns, a good deal of the credit for the low loss rate must be given to the large, dense chaff clouds that protected most of the flights. That night 85 percent of the bombers were inside the chaff cloud when they opened their bomb doors and made their post-target turn, as opposed to 5 percent on earlier missions, and the North Vietnamese noted the enormous increase in "fake B-52s."

SAC's fear of collisions, which had led it to choose the original single-file routes, was shown to be wrong. Simple altitude separation kept the bombers apart, and even though many cells missed their time over target badly (two were at least three minutes off their time and twenty miles off course) no near misses between B-52s were reported. "It proved the 'Big Sky' theory," one crewmember said. "The sky is big, and airplanes are little."

Kinh No had been attacked a total of six times, at the cost of four B-52s hit and three lost, and Night Eight was the last time it was bombed. Because it showed up well on the B-52s' radar it was bombed "direct," that is, without using offsets, and post-war photography showed that the bombing accuracy was "terrific." But the same pictures of the warehouses showed they contained railroad components like boiler rings and track, items that were basically indestructible. The North Vietnamese simply picked them up and used them again.

Unfortunately, there was also some serious collateral damage that night. An errant string of bombs fell on Kham Thien Street, a civilian shopping district, and killed over 250 civilians. This accident was significantly different from the damage to the Bach Mai hospital (caused when a B-52 was hit by a SAM as it dropped its bombs) and Gia Lam (which had been bombed in deliberate violation of orders). The bombing of Kham Thien Street became a *cause célèbre* in the international press, but it also had a profound effect on some of the civilian population. One survivor, Nguyen Van Phuong, was ten at the time and remembers, "Kham Thien Street was a major street in a densely populated and very poor area. There were no factories or anything else nearby, it was purely residential. Many people from Kham Thien Street didn't evacuate when there were bombing raids because there was nothing on the street that was any use to the Americans, so when the street was bombed it took everyone by surprise and many died. By killing so many people on Kham Thien Street the Americans united everyone behind the government. People perceived that the government was right in its claims that they would be killed if the Americans gained control of Vietnam."

DESPITE THE SUCCESS of the Eighth Night's missions, the tension between Seventh Air Force and SAC did not abate. General Meyer took a deliberate post-mission slam at General Vogt by ignoring the contribution of the Seventh Air Force support package while sending the Navy task force commander a congratulatory message: "So far we have been successful in striking the Haiphong area without loss ... at least in part to SAM suppression by Navy all weather aircraft. ... I am sure the [Navy attacks on SAM sites] assisted significantly the success of our strike force ... please extend my appreciation ... to all your planners and crews for their efforts in this outstanding achievement."

In fact, there was no justification for Meyer's comments. Navy air strikes did not hit a single SAM site, and after the war an internal Navy report freely admitted that Navy electronic jamming could not be distinguished from the total support package jamming in reducing B-52 losses.

TWELVE

The Last Nights
of Christmas

The successful bombing and low losses on Night Eight apparently had the effect on North Vietnamese political calculations that Nixon had hoped for. The next day, December 27, they sent a message to the United States offering to start negotiations again on January 8. Nixon replied that Kissinger would arrive on January 8 but he wanted preliminary negotiations to begin on January 2. To reinforce his message to both the North Vietnamese and the South Vietnamese, he let the B-52s continue bombing.

At this point Nixon had an extraordinary bit of public relations luck. President Harry Truman, Franklin Roosevelt's successor, died on December 26, and there were numerous news articles, editorials and television specials about his life and death. While the continuing bombing campaign was mentioned, the pressure on Nixon eased for several days as the country went through the ceremonies and eulogies for Truman, ironically the first president to stand up to "Communist aggression" in a limited war.

In the combat zone, neither the crews nor the staffs had any hint of the impending agreement. On Night Nine, December 27, just after Nixon sent his message to Hanoi, sixty B-52s and their support aircraft attacked North Vietnam again. Most of the bombers were sent to the new favorite target, Lang Dang, far from Hanoi's defenses, but there were also several targets in the Hanoi area. Four cells were assigned to attack the Trung Quang railroad yard, less than a mile from the Yen Vien rail yards that had cost so many B-52s, and in a new wrinkle, for the first time the B-52s were set to bomb SAM sites.

At U-Tapao the prospect of getting some revenge appealed to Captain John Mize, who had already been hit twice by the North

Vietnamese defenses. His cell, Ash, was scheduled to bomb one of the SAM sites, VN-243. Another cell was assigned to bomb SAM site VN-549, the "killer site" that U.S. intelligence had wrongly credited with having shot down six B-52s. The B-52s would use essentially the same tactics they had used on Night Eight—multiple entry headings, a chaff blanket, moderate and varied post-target turns, and large altitude separations.

On the ground in North Vietnam, Captain Pham Tuan, who had had such a difficult time with F-4s the first night, was also looking for revenge as he took off from his base at Noi Bai in a MiG-21. Chat Pham, commander of the 72nd missile battalion, was another anxious for retribution. His battalion had been sent from Haiphong to Hanoi before Christmas to shore up the defenses, but so far its only contribution had been firing at—and missing—an F-4 on December 26. After committing the sin of wasting missiles on a fighter, when the B-52s did attack, Pham's battalion missed with all their missiles. Now, as the B-52s moved in, Pham and his crew were given the first cell of B-52s attacking Trung Quang as a target. As the B-52s approached, the 72nd fired two missiles.

Steve Kovich was the aircraft commander in Cobalt 02, the second B-52 over Trung Quang. "We were coming in on the bomb run and multiple SAMs were in the air. I saw our leader, Cobalt 01, start to drift off course. If everybody was lined up on the right target we should have been in trail of each other, and I thought maybe we were off course, but our bomb nav team said no, we were on the target and our gunner said that Cobalt 03 was right behind us. Then I saw a group of seven SAMs come out of the clouds in front of us. I said to my copilot, Jim Lawton, 'Look, lead is turning and that's giving the SAMs a better angle.'"

PHAM TUAN JETTISONED his fuel tanks and, dodging F-4s, climbed to 30,000 feet. He located a cell of B-52s and called to his controller: "I have the target in sight, request order for the attack."

The response came back quickly. "You have permission to fire twice, then escape quickly."

Tuan checked his missiles, then pushed the fire bottom on the control stick and launched two heat-seeking missiles from about a mile. He reported "big flames were visible around the second B-52 when I broke sharply to left and descended to 2000 meters before landing at Yen Bai. The remaining B-52's immediately dropped their bombs and returned to base."

STEVE KOVICH CONTINUES. "Cobalt 03 radioed lead and asked where he was going and then, about two minutes from the target I saw SAMs explode into the lead aircraft. The fireball covered the dark sky; maybe it was just the warheads exploding, maybe it was the bombs and fuel too, then I heard the parachute emergency beacons sounding on Guard."

Frank Lewis, the aircraft commander of Cobalt 01, felt his bomber stop in mid-air, like a "car hitting a telephone pole," and the B-52's controls went limp as the windshield in front of him disappeared "like sugar glass in a movie." Shrapnel had hit every member of the crew and the navigator, Lt. Bennie Frywer, was killed instantly. Cobalt 01 began to burn and the four surviving crewmembers in the forward compartment bailed out as the bomber turned into a flaming torch.

In the rear of the aircraft, the tail gunner, Master Sergeant James Gough, waited for an intercom call or for the red Emergency Bailout Light to come on as flames roared past his turret and stretched well behind the aircraft. He was not aware that the fire and the loss of electrical power had cut out the intercom and burned through the wires of the battery-operated Emergency Bailout Light, and now he was alone in the burning bomber as it continued its flaming but gentle, wings-level descent. Gough tried frantically to call the rest of the crew, but there was no response as the dying B-52 approached the undercast. He realized he had to get out now or never, so he jettisoned his turret and pulled himself out into the night. As he cleared the aircraft, the B-52 began to disintegrate and he was surrounded by flaming debris while he fell. Fortunately his chute was not damaged; he landed safely, but was quickly captured.

Post-war analysis indicates that the MiG-21 flown by Tuan attacked Ivory cell, the last cell in the group of four, but his two ATOLL missiles missed. Distances are difficult to judge at night and Tuan broke off his attack as soon as he fired, so when he saw Cobalt 01 explode and catch fire after being hit by a SAM, Tuan quite reasonably thought his missiles had scored the kill.

MEANWHILE, TED DANIEL in Ash 01 was attacking SAM site VN-243 with John Mize and his crew in Ash 02 behind them. Daniel remembers, "It got really interesting about four minutes from the target. We started to see SAMs visually, coming mostly from the front, some pretty close but passing off to the right behind us. We made our bomb release and beat feet out to the west with a real nice tail wind." Daniel's tail gunner called out that a SAM was coming up behind them, then Daniel heard "something garbled about 'detonation ... number 2....'"

Mize was in his post-target turn when he saw the SAMs coming directly for him and steepened his bank so the B-52 was almost standing on its wing as the missiles passed by, all except the last one. Mize and his crew felt the tremendous concussion that marked a solid hit, and the aircraft continued to fall with the left wing on fire. All the systems on the left side of the aircraft were blown out and Mize's instrument panel was nothing but a mass of red emergency lights, but as he began to pull on the stick he realized that he still had hydraulic power and could control the aircraft. Mize slowly pulled the aircraft out of its shallow dive and turned towards Thailand.

A quick check told Mize that the aircraft had all four engines on the left wing out and two were on fire. He could control the aircraft but with only four engines functioning, he could not get it in level flight. Mize began to let the B-52 descend to build up speed, then pull it back up again, losing altitude with each maneuver but steadily getting closer to Thailand. He estimated that at the rate he was descending he could make it to Thailand with enough altitude to bail out—if the fire in the left wing didn't get worse.

Ted Daniel in Ash 01 had turned back towards Mize and notified the Search and Rescue forces, and soon a C-130 pulled close to the dying B-52. It was clear to Mize that they were not going to make the border, so he planned to bail out at 15,000 feet. As they descended through that altitude, the C-130 told them that they were still over no man's land. As if to punctuate the warning, a moment later several flares exploded on the ground below them and tracers began to crisscross the jungle as a major firefight erupted.

Slowly the B-52 edged west and closer and closer to safety. Mize had been battling the aircraft for almost an hour when suddenly the B-52 gave a sickening lurch as the bomb bay doors fell open, and one of the landing gear began to cycle, lowering then retracting. The hydraulic system was going and the B-52's descent steepened with the sudden increase in drag.

Mize could see the lights of the American base at Nakon Phanom when he felt the aircraft shudder in what was clearly its death throes. He told the crew to eject while he held the airplane steady, then heard the ejection seat booms and felt the draft of three seats blasting out of the aircraft, but not the fourth.

Below Mize, navigator Bill Robinson's ejection seat had failed. After several tries he frantically called Mize on the intercom and told him the situation. Mize, desperately struggling to hold the aircraft, told Robinson to unstrap from his seat and bail out of the hole where the radar navigator's seat had been—and to hurry. Mize fought to hold the doomed bomber level as long as he could then, at the last possible second, he ejected. Mize was picked up a few minutes later by rescue helicopters from NKP and found to his relief that Robinson had also been picked up.

Even though only two B-52s had been lost, the ferocity of the North Vietnamese defenses surprised and disturbed the American commanders and dispelled any feeling that they had turned the tide. The U.S. crews reported that the North Vietnamese had fired about 90 missiles that night, more missiles per sortie than they had fired on any other raid, and at least one crew reported they could not turn after they dropped their bombs because missiles were coming from both sides. Some of the crews said it was the worst night they had experienced.

There was much speculation about how long the North Vietnamese could fire SAMs in such large numbers. U.S. intelligence had been regularly promising that the North Vietnamese would run out of missiles, but the predictions were now looking impossibly optimistic. The number of SAMs fired and the two losses on December 27th raised questions about the advisability of continuing the B-52 attacks, and General Lucius Clay, the Air Force general who was Admiral Gayler's deputy in the Pacific, sent a cable to Washington saying, "It seems to me that there are few if any targets remaining in NVN which are worth the continuing [B-52] losses we are experiencing." This message, coming after Gayler's message on Day Three, was not received kindly in Washington, where the White House believed that the military was being affected by the negative publicity the raids were generating. Now that the respite after Truman's death had ended, Nixon's critics were in high dudgeon. The *New York Times* published a front-page account of the destruction on Kham Thien Street and another front-page story from a reporter on Guam noting that the B-52 crews, several of whom he knew personally, were "shaken." He also noted reports of B-52 crews sabotaging their aircraft so they did not have to fly.

More seriously, Republicans were joining the chorus. Republican Senator William Saxbe of Ohio said that, "The bombing raids are bringing the U.S. punishing losses. I have followed President Nixon through his convolutions and specious arguments but he appears to have left his senses on this issue. I can't go along with him on this one." Another Republican, Senator Clifford Case, said that if the bombing continued Congress would have to stop American involvement by cutting off funds immediately.

But while the criticisms and the strength of the SAM response were causing considerable angst among the Americans, in fact the North Vietnamese were in deep trouble. During the four-day period around Christmas when Hanoi had not been bombed the technical battalions had been able to assemble over a hundred SAMs, and these newly assembled missiles had been used the last two nights. But now the game was up. Though there were still a large number of missiles in containers, the North Vietnamese simply could not assemble them fast enough, and the new American tactics and the massive chaff blankets were overwhelming the defenses. By dawn on December 28th, though neither side realized it, the battle was effectively over. Mize and his crew were the last B-52 shot down in Linebacker II.

MEANWHILE, PETE CAMEROTA was still on the ground but reconsidering his options.

"I decided to climb further up to the top of the hill, but this was considerably harder than I expected because I hadn't had anything to eat or much to drink since I had been shot down. I had made a little paper hat out of a piece of my waterproof map and managed to catch a little water that ran down the rocky hillside, and scraped off a little dew from the sparse foliage in the mornings. Anyway, it was hardly enough to sustain a robust Air Force steely-eyed killer—or me, for that matter, as my climb made me realize. So there I was, at the top of my little hill, with a commanding view of the countryside where I could see farmers on the other side. As I looked around, it appeared that I was nowhere near where I should be. I thought I was somewhere southeast of Hanoi between it and the Gulf of Tonkin, but everything indicates to me that I'm SOUTHWEST of Hanoi, maybe 22 miles or so. I doubted my 'fixes' for a while, but I came to suspect I was correct. It was apparent that there was nowhere to go, and help was unlikely. Everything to the east and south was rice paddies, and the rest of the area was karst ridges. I was beginning to realize that I was probably not going to get rescued. I hadn't heard anything on the radio. I was getting a lot weaker, hallucinating, and wasn't sure when I was asleep or awake, and in my more lucid moments started to think that I was going to end up a dead hero if something did not change, and shortly."

WHILE THE B-52S POUNDED away at night, the Air Force and the Navy tried to keep the pressure on the North Vietnamese defenses with daily tactical strikes, but bad weather frustrated most of their efforts. Early in the operation Seventh Air Force scheduled laser-guided "smart" bomb missions every day, but heavy clouds had prevented most of these strikes, as well as other missions that would helped the B-52s, such as hunter-killer strikes on SAM sites.

General Vogt, the Commander of Seventh Air Force, was concerned about the White House response if it was discovered that he was not launching day strikes because of the weather, so he insisted on launching strikes with an all-weather bombing system known as LORAN.

LORAN involved triangulation between three stations that gave extremely precise navigation and position data when the system functioned properly. It had been in combat use since 1970, but had major problems with range and reliability. The system rarely worked over the Hanoi area because of the distance from the LORAN stations in Thailand, and to make matters worse LORAN was very sensitive to thunderstorms, common over Southeast Asia during periods of bad weather. The upshot was that the days when LORAN was needed most were the days when it was least likely to work, as General Vogt had been told numerous times by LORAN experts. But Vogt insisted on sending missions of LORAN-equipped aircraft over Hanoi leading a large group of fighter-bombers to drop bombs into the clouds.

Not surprisingly LORAN missions, which involved flying in tight formation for twenty miles straight and level at a fixed altitude and airspeed, were considered very dangerous and despised by the fighter-bomber crews that had to fly them. Flying above an overcast (always the case since, if the weather was good the fighters would be bombing visually) made the aircraft especially vulnerable to SAMs, and similar attacks in 1967 had brought brutal losses, including four F-105s on one mission. The aircrews and the wing commanders constantly complained to Seventh Air Force about the dangerous missions and how the entire LORAN system was unreliable around Hanoi, but General Vogt ignored the complaints and insisted that LORAN bombing missions be flown until the end of the operation. After the war he said proudly: "I was assured that it was not possible to develop the accuracy needed, at that distance from the ground stations. But I wouldn't take no for an answer, and said 'Damnit, we're going to do it!'"

In fact, post-war analysis showed that General Vogt was wrong and the experts were right. During Linebacker II more than two-thirds of the LORAN missions in the Hanoi area failed when LORAN broke lock on the ground stations, making it useless and forcing the fighters to drop on information furnished by the inaccurate F-4 radar or inertial navigation system. Even when it worked, post-war reports showed, LORAN missed its targets, even large area targets, by a wide margin and that "LORAN made no significant contribution to the damage level during Linebacker II."

If the North Vietnamese had fired SAMs at the LORAN flights, they would have certainly caused heavy losses, but because of the orders to concentrate on the B-52s—and perhaps because of the inaccuracy of the LORAN bombing—the North Vietnamese missile crews ignored them.

Ironically, General Vogt's inaccurate statements about LORAN bombing were responsible for one of the greatest successes of the

Linebacker II daylight bombing campaign. The Joint Chiefs had finally decided to attack the Quinh Loi SAM storage facility in Hanoi, but B-52s could not to be used because the facility was close to populated areas and there were concerns about civilian casualties. Seduced by General Vogt's inaccurate claims about the accuracy of LORAN bombing, the JCS gave Seventh Air Force permission to hit Quinh Loi with a LORAN strike of forty-two fighter-bombers. Given the inaccuracies of LORAN and the location of the target, the strike could have caused a large number of civilian casualties, but fortunately as the U.S. aircraft approached the Hanoi the clouds parted and most of the flights bombed visually and accurately. The next day another large tactical strike bombed the Trai Ca SAM storage area using LORAN and missed badly, but Trai Ca was thirty miles north of Hanoi in a relatively uninhabited area.

On the few days when the weather was good the tactical strikes were deadly. The day after the heavy B-52 losses on Night Three, F-4s with laser-guided bombs extracted some revenge by knocking out the Hanoi thermal power plant, a target that had been off limits for all of Linebacker I, but one that Nixon insisted be hit during Linebacker II. On December 27 four F-4s with laser-guided bombs hit the Hanoi International Radio transmitter without loss after 36 B-52s dropping over two thousand bombs had missed, at a cost of two B-52s damaged and one shot down.

ON NIGHT TEN, sixty more B-52s were sent to North Vietnam, but even at SAC Headquarters there was the feeling that the B-52s were running out of targets. A SAC planner described one target attacked that night. "We had a picture of a single railroad siding. There was a shack in the middle of the siding and the photography enabled us to see everything very clearly, and it was obvious that it was not being used. There was a clothesline and a little garden in the siding, and there were also a couple of pigs in a pen. I joked about this and then was told that it was a serious target. Three B-52's went after it and the bombing was very accurate."

Night Ten marked the "tipping point." The North Vietnamese began to show signs that their defenses were deteriorating and only a few SAMs were reported. The B-52 crews returned full of confidence, and one summed up their feelings: "We went four miles from Hanoi and it was a piece of cake.... We were sure that the North Vietnamese were running out of SAMs."

As a sign of their desperation, the North Vietnamese further increased their MiG activity. A MiG-21 flown by Vu Xuan Thieu pressed an attack the B-52s, but before he was able to get close Thieu was shot down by two prowling F-4s. The North Vietnamese later claimed Thieu's MiG collided with the B-52 and both crashed, but no B-52s were lost that night.

ON DECEMBER 29TH, Night Eleven, the B-52s moved away from the center of the still heavily defended capital city. Sixty B-52s attacked SAM storage areas, including Trai Ca ten miles northwest of Hanoi (which had been missed badly by a LORAN strike earlier in the day) and the Lang Dang railroad yard.

But the North Vietnamese defenses were not finished. Dwight Moore was the aircraft commander of Maple 03, one of the cells assigned to bomb the Trai Ca, and as they approached the target, Moore saw "six or eight" SAMs coming towards the aircraft. The gunner called out one that missed the aircraft by only about 300 feet, and Moore remembered that "when it went off it was so bright you could read a newspaper in the cockpit." The aircraft was not damaged, and except for Moore's close call, few SAMs were reported. After two straight nights of bombing without a loss, one B-52 crewmember said, "It was easy pickings."

While the B-52s were airborne and heading for their targets on Night Eleven, the order was flashed to all the U.S. bases that Linebacker II was to end at 6:59 A.M., December 30, Hanoi time. About two hours after Eighth Air Force received the orders, at 11:45 P.M., Grey 03, the last B-52 in the last wave, dropped is bomb load on Trai Ca and returned safely to base. Linebacker II was over— except for Pete Camerota.

"I was getting steadily weaker at the top of my hill. On the ninth day, I finally contacted an airplane. It was a Navy dude, off the Enterprise, I think .... I figured it was salvation at last, that my pleas on the radio had been answered. I said 'DeSoto Flight, this is Scarlet zero three echo', which meant I was Scarlet Three, and the fifth crewmember, the EW.

"He answered back, 'Standby, Scarlet!'"

"I thought to myself, 'I've been out here nine days and he tells me to standby!'

"When he came back on, I told him who I was and where I was to the best of my ability, which wasn't much, at that point. He said 'Goodbye and good luck.'

"About three hours later, I talked to ANOTHER Navy flight, Cadillac Flight. I thought maybe he had been sent, but no, it was just another chance encounter. And he said the same, 'Goodbye and good luck.' I was quite a bit higher in spirits at that point, and thought that maybe this would come out well.

"The next day, I waited for more contact. None, and to make matters worse, the weather had come down. My little hill was now covered in clouds and with the dampness I was pretty cold at times. I still was in and out of consciousness, day or night, so I'm not really sure when I made the decision, but I decided that I was going to 'submit to capture' before I died alone and unknown. I had told Joy that they would never get me alive, but now I had decided that it was far better to be a live coward than a dead hero.

"Tomorrow had to be the day, since I could barely move. I had come down off this small ledge to relieve myself, and it took all my strength to get back onto it. The ledge was only about waist high and, my urine, meager as it was, was black. I knew this was not a good thing.

"I figured it would be wiser to surrender in the evening to the farmers as they returned from working their fields. I figured that one of two things would happen: they would kill me or they wouldn't. Still, if they were going to kill me, I wouldn't let them do it with my own gun, so as they approached my position I took out all my bullets of my little Smith and Wesson and then tossed it, all 22 ounces, as far as I could. It landed about ten feet away. I couldn't believe it.

"So now I stand up to my full 5'6" and yell at the passing figures below. There was no reaction to this action—because I hadn't made a sound. I had no voice. When I tried again, I had the barest noise of a whisper. I figured I was going to die up there. I had once considered firing my S&W to attract their attention. I had rejected that as not too bright, really, since some of them carried rifles, and perhaps would not understand the difference between a signal and an aggressor. My pistol was out of reach anyway. Rats!! It sounded like a lot better idea now.

"I got out my flare gun from one of my survival vest pockets, opened the little holster, and tried to load it, but I was too weak. One has to pull down on this lever against some serious spring pressure to load the flare, but I couldn't move the lever down further than about half way. I finally placed the lever against a part of the rock outcropping, and pushed against the barrel with my hands, with the weight of my body behind it. After a couple of attempts, I got it depressed, loaded the flare, and looked back. The villagers were almost out of sight.

"I fired off the flare, and it got their attention. I could hear them yelling, and saw them looking around. I began waving at them. A few of them pointed at me, and then . . . they started SHOOTING AT ME!!! I thought, this is really stupid! I guess they are going to kill me. I curled up in a ball on the ground, right where I was (of course it was right where I was, because I couldn't go anywhere else!), and fell asleep. . . .

"The next thing I remembered was being rudely awakened by five or six pairs of hands pulling me to my feet. I couldn't walk, and after much consultation amongst themselves they fashioned a net truss under a pole, put me in it and off we went. I fell asleep intermittently— I was really close to being dead, I guess. We stopped somewhere once it got dark, and they gave me some water. Sometime later we stopped at what appeared to be a brick barn or building and somebody in uniform showed up and started asking me questions. It didn't go too well. He asked me when I got shot down. I told him. He called me a liar. He asked what kind of airplane I flew. I told him. He said I lied. He asked how many pilots were on board my airplane. I told him 'Two.' He called me a liar. He asked what position I flew. I told him. He didn't call me a liar.

"I had seriously considered lying about being an EW. There had been rumors that the Vietnamese really wanted EWs to find out about the magic they worked to defeat the Soviet SAMs. (Actually that may have been a bit of USAF urban legend started by some EWs who wanted more status, but the rumor persisted through much of the time I was there, and it went on to say that some captured EWs had been spirited directly to the Soviet Union.) Still, I had decided that I didn't know enough about the duties of the other positions to be able to bluff my way through as a nav or a pilot."

By the time he was captured, Camerota had been on the ground almost two weeks.

THE AFTERNOON OF DECEMBER 31 General Sullivan received a message at U-Tapao.

"How happy we were to hear the news of a bombing halt. You and your men can take a well deserved bow for your great contribution to any peace we get. May you have the biggest 73 ever, and that goes for all in your command. Bob Hope."

THIRTEEN

Dénouement

hile still publicly defiant, the North Vietnamese seemed to feel their political options were gone. Even though the U.S. Congress had taken the first steps towards cutting off funds to prosecute the war before the two sides had returned to Paris, the North Vietnamese had seen their Soviet and Chinese allies issue *pro forma* denunciations of the bombings but take no substantive actions. Without their support there was little prospect of the North Vietnamese continuing to resist, and on January 2 low-level meetings resumed in Paris. To keep the pressure on the North Vietnamese Nixon continued heavy bombing with B-52s below the 20th parallel, while telling Soviet Ambassador Anatoly Dobrynin that it was essential for both Moscow and the United States to control their clients and not permit them to sour the progress that had been made in improving relations.

On January 4, before Kissinger left for Paris, Nixon appointed General Haig to be the new Army Vice Chief of Staff, then he and Kissinger met with Laird, Moorer, and Secretary of State William Rodgers to review the situation and to insure that there would be no leaks of information while the delicate negotiations were still under way. Nixon said that the bombings had showed the North Vietnamese that "they can't play with us in Paris and prolong the war with immunity from retaliation." He also noted that the United States had weakened the North Vietnamese military and demonstrated to the South Vietnamese that the U.S. was ready to enforce the settlement. At the same time, Nixon emphasized to the group that "there must be no suggestion that our bombing has forced Hanoi back to the table." Kissinger also warned the military not to claim victory or anything else that might keep the North Vietnamese from signing the agreement, and the Defense Department sent a world-wide message to all military commanders: "There must be no, repeat no, comment of any sort whatsoever from any DOD personnel, civilian or military, of whatever rank. There is to be no comment, no speculation, no elaboration, and no discussion on the subject of the White House announcement of the suspension of the bombing and resumption of negotiations."

Ironically, the biggest problems in this area were expected to be from the Joint Chiefs of Staff—who had opposed the bombing—and SAC, whose poor tactics had almost made the operation fail. SAC leaders had already talked to several newspapers, including the *New York Times,* touting how successful the B-52s had been. To squelch this, Admiral Moorer followed up the meeting with a message to his commanders, including General Meyer, telling them to "stonewall any questions ... [in order to] prevent queries and speculation until forthcoming events unfold."

Publicly, the negotiations did not look promising. Le Duc Tho arrived in Paris on January 6 and presented the waiting reporters with a five-page statement of Hanoi's position and called the U.S. raids "demented," while a subdued Kissinger arrived the next day and only spoke briefly.

But the public atmosphere was not matched in the private meetings. Kissinger remembered his initial Paris meeting with Tho on January 8 was "frosty at the outset but thawed during the course of the meeting." He was pleased to find the North Vietnamese protests about the bombing were "brief and relatively mild," but he left the meeting without a real feel for the situation. In a message to Nixon, Kissinger noted that it would be difficult for the North Vietnamese to give in on the issues in the first meeting after the intense bombing, and cautioned that "they [may] plan to stonewall us again."

Then, the next day, Kissinger sent Nixon a message that began, "We celebrated the President's birthday today by making a major breakthrough on the negotiations...." While cautioning, "the Vietnamese have broken our hearts before," Kissinger said he was upbeat at the "mood and businesslike approach." As real progress began to be made, Kissinger insisted that this information be confined to the president alone: "There must not be the slightest hint of the present status to the bureaucracy, cabinet members, the Congress, or anyone else [lest] the North Vietnamese ... revert to their natural beastliness. ... If [the] State [Department] ever gets wind of the status of the talks ... we will never be able to keep things under control."

Kissinger ended the message: "What has brought us to this point is the President's firmness and the North Vietnamese belief that he will not be affected by either Congressional or public pressure. Le Duc Tho has repeatedly made these points to me, so it is essential that we keep our fierce posture during the coming days. The slightest hint of eagerness could prove suicidal...."

Things now moved swiftly. By January 11 the negotiations were far enough along that Kissinger was as worried about Saigon and Washington as the North Vietnamese. He was very concerned with avoiding a repeat of Thieu's performance in late October, telling Nixon, "It must be clearly understood that when we conclude here we must proceed to an initialing *whatever Thieu's answer is.* Under no circumstances will Hanoi hold still for a repetition of October or a renegotiation without blowing the whole agreement. We cannot get any more concessions...."

Nixon understood, and on January 14 he sent Haig to Saigon to make the point to Thieu. On January 16, Haig relayed Nixon's message: the United States would guarantee South Vietnam's security if Thieu would sign the peace agreement, but the U.S. was going to sign under any circumstances. If South Vietnam refused to sign it would mean almost certain cutoff of funds. On January 20, Thieu agreed to sign.

After considerable technical haggling, on January 23 Kissinger and Tho initialed the agreement and, on January 27, it was signed by the United States, North Vietnam, South Vietnam, and the Viet Cong.

AFTER THE END OF LINEBACKER II, the Bullet Shot crews who had been sent over "temporarily" in the spring expected to begin a rotation home. Most of them had been in the combat theater for nine months and had gone through the most difficult bombing campaign of the war, and many had family problems at home. The crews were heartened when they heard that General Meyer and some of the

SAC staff were coming to visit Andersen. This was Meyer's second visit to Guam but the first one, a few months after Bullet Shot began, had not gone well. Even though some of the crewmembers had been away from their families for two and a half of the last three years, Meyer had been insensitive enough to bring his family with him. Later, in a question and answer session, one of the rankled crewmembers pointed out the stress that the extended Bullet Shot tours were having on marriages. Meyer's answer reportedly boiled down to "some marriages weren't meant to last." Some say that Meyer was booed at this meeting, but others say there was simply an undercurrent of muttering. Nevertheless, after Linebacker II and with the end of the war in sight, the crews were optimistic and ready to give him another chance.

General Meyer disappointed them again. He elected to meet only with the aircraft commanders, ignoring the rest of the crewmembers, and he started the meeting by awarding the Air Force Cross to Colonel James R. McCarthy, the commander of Andersen's B-52D wing. The award stunned most of the assembly, because McCarthy had only flown two Linebacker missions—one on the second night when no B-52s were lost, and one on the eighth night. Many crewmembers were appalled that such a limited role resulted in America's second highest award for heroism, while others still resented his threat to court-martial any aircrew that maneuvered going into the target.

Meyer and the SAC staff also infuriated the crewmembers by describing how "the SAC staff had won the war" and calling the raids "SAC's finest hour." The crews viewed this as a double insult because they felt the SAC staff's initial rigidity and poor planning had caused the deaths of many of their friends, and it was only the suggestions—or demands—from the combat zone that forced SAC to change the tactics. As a final blow, Meyer made no mention of sending the Bullet Shot crews home.

The meetings went even worse at U-Tapao, though they started well enough when General Meyer presented the second Air Force Cross of the operation to Captain John Mize. Mize was a generally acknowledged hero who had flown six missions, been hit three times, shot down once, and stayed with his damaged aircraft so his navigator could bail out. But when the SAC staff explained again how "the staff won the war," the mood among the U-Tapao crews turned "distinctly frosty," one participant remembered.

The SAC staff noticed the change in mood and were not pleased with their reception at U-Tapao. The generals complained about it all the way back to Omaha, and there would be repercussions. A short time later the B-52 crews at U-Tapao were accused by Eighth Air Force of performing "wild maneuvers" during their bomb runs, and Eighth hinted that perhaps this breach of discipline had been encouraged by their commanders. There was talk of an investigation, but the matter was eventually dropped. There is some evidence that the accusation was made by B-52 commanders at Andersen.

By March 29, 1973, a total of 591 American prisoners of war, 566 military and 25 civilians, had been returned to U.S. custody. Peter Camerota, Red Wilson, John Yuill, Bill Mayall, Bill Buckley, Terry Geloneck, Bob Hudson, gunner Jim Cook, and 25 other B-52 crewmembers made up over 6 percent of those released, but they all were shot down in 11 days of the 3,000-day war and they spent the shortest time as prisoners. Cook was one of the first to be released, on February 11, because of the injuries to his legs and an infection that had dropped his weight from 175 to 90 pounds in the few weeks of his captivity. Both of his legs later had to be amputated below the knee.

As Norb Gotner, one of the few U.S. prisoners captured in Laos, was taken to the airport at Gia Lam to be released, he passed the Gia Lam rail yard, one the main B-52 targets. He noted with satisfaction: "Whoever put those bomb strings on the railroad yards only put a few out of the yard onto the village. The railroad yard was a twisted, broken pile of steel. There were no tracks that could be used for a long time. Damn good aim."

THERE WAS TREMENDOUS congressional interest in the bombing, and the Senate Armed Services Committee had early hearings on the subject. One of the main witnesses was the Chairman of the Joint Chiefs of Staff, Admiral Moorer. Moorer was seriously concerned because he knew the "party line" and he did not want to say anything that would conflict with SAC's glowing assessments of the operation. Certainly, he did not want to admit the operation had almost failed.

To make sure that he said the right thing, Moorer asked SAC to write a summary of the B-52s' operations for him to present to the committee. SAC, not surprisingly, gave him a presentation pointing out that the operation had been brilliantly and effectively executed and that losses were much less than the 3 percent forecast (without mentioning that General Meyer had been the one who had made this now very useful prediction). SAC also provided Moorer with pictures of targets wrecked by B-52 bombing, which the Admiral used during his presentation to show how accurate the bombing had been.

Admiral Moorer proudly showed one picture of the bomb damage to the international airport at Gia Lam International Airport—five runway cuts, the passenger terminal wrecked, five buildings, one Il-28 bomber, one An-24 transport, two helicopters and five trucks destroyed. What Admiral Moorer did *not* tell the senators (and may not have known himself) was that Gia Lam had been off limits during the bombing, a prohibition that had been reiterated by Secretary of Defense Laird at least twice during the campaign. Moorer also showed the committee pictures of the badly damaged Hanoi Fabrication Plant, another target that was never on the target list and had been bombed by accident. Fortunately for Moorer, the senators were impressed by the pictures and took him at his word that the pictures were of real targets.

For its part in the operation, Eighth Air Force received the Collier Trophy for the most significant aviation accomplishment of the year. The award was enthusiastically supported by the released POWs, who gave the credit to the B-52 crews for their release. One B-52 crewmember remembered that for years afterwards, "if there were ever POWs around, we could never buy a drink."

AFTER THE WAR, SAC ordered selected members of the SAC staff to develop a highly classified, internal analysis of the B-52 bombing. For the next three months, fifteen photo interpreters looked at every frame of film—satellite, SR-71, and drone—taken since the bombing, and were able to account for virtually every bomb dropped by the B-52s. Under strict secrecy, a two-hour briefing on the results was prepared, complete with target photographs, and given to General Meyer and key members of the SAC Headquarters staff.

The results were appalling. The overall circular error (CEP) was 2700 feet instead of the 800 feet that had been predicted, and thus the damage was less than a quarter of what had been predicted. The senior officers sat silently through the briefing, except for the SAC Director of Operations, General Sianis, who suggested the North Vietnamese might have been so badly intimidated by the apparently haphazard bombing that they rushed to the negotiating table.

The briefing was shown to fewer than twenty people, all very senior generals, including General Johnson at Eighth Air Force (who made a comment similar to Sianis's). Shortly after the briefing was presented all the copies were destroyed. A few months later a congressional staffer asked for the specific results of the bombing but, as a member of the SAC staff remembered, "we managed to muddle the issue so much that we never had to give an answer."

In spring of 1973, members of the SAC staff also did an analysis of SAC's tactics during Linebacker II, much of it based on meetings held with crewmembers just after the operation. Again, the report was scathing. One source document said "The repetitiousness [of the mission profile] allowed the North Vietnamese to anticipate our strike patterns ... the use of such patterns was a costly mistake" and continued by saying that the North Vietnamese lack of missiles was not the cause of the declining B-52 losses but rather the change in U.S. tactics after the third night. The report noted that certain SAC tactics the first three nights played right into the hands of the North Vietnamese defenders—the straight-line approach using of the same entry points, the same course to the targets, the same post-target maneuvers, and the four-hour break between raids.

The report was critical not only of the tactics, but also of SAC procedures for developing tactics, noting: "The present method of having tactics conferences above the unit level is bad. TAC learned this the hard way. Each level between the operator and the policy maker is one more chance for a loss of communication." The report on the tactical failures also pointed out that there were still no answers for basic questions about the B-52s' ability to penetrate a high-threat environment, especially now that the North Vietnamese had received the SA-3 missile from the Soviets, a major improvement over the SA-2.

A member of the SAC staff who listened to the presentation said, "The Headquarters staff concurred with the crews and briefed the same to the senior staff in no uncertain terms. This after action report was, strangely, accepted. Nobody got upset or pointed fingers."

WITH THE END OF THE VIETNAM WAR, SAC and the Air Force Chief of Staff (and former SAC commander), General John Ryan, breathed a sigh of relief and said, "At last we [can get] rid of the warlords." Brigadier General Glenn Sullivan, whose message to General Meyer turned the battle around, apparently fit Ryan's description. Sullivan's direct approach to SAC apparently did not sit well with General Johnson at Eighth Air Force, and the cool reception of the U-Tapao crews to the SAC staff's "victory tour" ended General Sullivan's career. He received one more assignment from U-Tapao, was not promoted, and then he retired.

SAC's internal analysis of its tactical mistakes was never distributed outside of SAC and, like the bombing accuracy report, was eventually destroyed. By 1974 SAC's conventional capability, developed at such a high cost over Hanoi, had all but disappeared. The stories of how the SAC mistakes almost caused Linebacker II to fail were told many times, but never in public. It all seemed to be destined to be gradually forgotten and become "bar talk," part of Air Force folklore.

It was not to be. In July 1977 the Air Force received a rude shock when an article titled "The Tragedy of Linebacker II," by Dana A. Drenkowski, appeared in the *Armed Forces Journal* and charged that SAC's mistakes had caused most of the losses in the early days of Linebacker II. This was followed by a two-part series titled "Linebacker II," in the September and November 1977 issues of *Soldier of Fortune* magazine where Drenkowski expanded on the charges. But it was the article in the well-respected *Armed Forces Journal,* a magazine widely read by the Washington defense *cognoscenti,* which was of the most concern to the Air Force.

Drenkowski's credentials put the Air Force in a difficult position. He was a former Air Force officer, an Air Force Academy graduate with over two hundred combat missions in Southeast Asia in both B-52s and F-4s. Drenkowski had flown F-4s during the Linebacker II strikes and had been a member of the fighter wing staff at

Udorn, so he had seen Linebacker II from both from the staff and the combat cockpit perspective. After the operation Drenkowski visited Andersen and U-Tapao where he said he was told the full story of the raids, the losses, and SAC's tactical and strategic mistakes. He said these visits, along with his contacts in SAC and in the fighter community acquired from his flying experience and from his classmates at the Air Force Academy, put him in a unique position to tell "the whole story."

In the articles Drenkowski made a number of charges, among them:

- Many crewmembers refused to fly, and the term "mutiny" was used by flight surgeons at U-Tapao and Andersen.
- After Brent Diefenbach pulled the copilot out of the burning B-52 on the night of December 26, SAC wanted to court-martial him for "leaving the base without permission."
- The losses were caused by piecemeal attacks, repetitive routes, poor tactics, and an unwillingness to listen to the crews even after losses mounted.
- The failures of the bombing campaign were caused because the SAC staff was full of "yes men" who were unwilling to tell the senior generals they were wrong.

The general thrust of Drenkowski's article—that SAC had bungled the operation and that poor tactics had caused many unnecessary losses—had been acknowledged by everyone from General Meyer to the B-52 crews as being true, but the mistakes had not been made public—in fact, quite the opposite. Linebacker II had acquired mythical status in the Air Force's history of Vietnam as "the operation that won the war."

Unbeknownst to Drenkowski and others, the post-Vietnam U.S. Air Force had a great deal of experience in covering its mistakes. Less than a year before, in mid-1976, the Air Force had testified to Congress and the families of a number of Air Force personnel killed in Laos during a secret operation in a way a professor at the Air War College called "imprecise, misleading, or simply fraudulent." Now they used this experience on Drenkowski, whose works threatened the Linebacker II myth. The Air Force Staff, with help from the SAC staff, moved quickly to destroy his credibility.

Numerous senior military officers, including Admiral Moorer, carried out *ad hominem* attacks on Drenkowski, and the former Eighth Air Force Commander, General Gerald Johnson, suggested he was mentally ill. There was also an official response. The August issue of *Armed Forces Journal* carried a quickly compiled but comprehensive Air Force response to the piece that began: "The Drenkowski [articles were] at best inaccurate, at worst gross distortions. . . . SAC planners continuously reviewed tactics and changed them throughout the operation . . . any suggestion of gross error or ineptness on the part of the operational planners is incorrect . . . [B-52] crew morale was high for the entire operation."

To Drenkowski's charge that "SAC's stereotyped tactics resulted in an unnecessarily large number of B-52s being shot down," the Air Force repeated the mantra "losses were well below the 3 percent predicted," not mentioning where the 3 percent prediction came from. The Air Force response added: "more than 6000 missions [to North Vietnam] were flown by B-52s prior to Linebacker II, 3600 of those in 1972 alone. . . . Only one plane was lost and one plane damaged by enemy anti-aircraft defensive fire. . . ." Unmentioned was the fact that most of these 6000 missions over North Vietnam turned back at the first sign of a SAM, and that many of the others were in areas of North Vietnam where there was no threat of missiles.

The Air Force counterattack was initially successful. *Armed Forces Journal* editor Benjamin Schemmer, who had taken Drenkowski's article at face value, completely accepted the Air Force's argument, published the Air Force response and criticized himself for "not checking Drenkowski's story out."

But immediately after the Air Force response was published in the *Armed Forces Journal,* Schemmer was inundated with calls from Air Force officers who had flown in Linebacker II and disputed the published official Air Force response. These officers provided Schemmer with numerous classified messages showing the mistakes SAC had made. After reviewing the messages Schemmer realized that the main points in Drenkowski's article—that SAC had brought on unnecessary losses by poor planning, inflexible tactics and an unwillingness to listen to the crews—were true. Schemmer also realized that he had been duped and said that the Air Force response published in *Armed Forces Journal* was "at best disingenuous, and probably dishonest."

According to Schemmer, when he realized this he went to "an Air Force general at the highest level" with the messages and demanded to know the truth. The general admitted that the messages were correct and the Air Force response to the article was "inaccurate." After some discussion, he asked Schemmer not to publish anything more about the story, and Schemmer reluctantly agreed. Schemmer told the author that he views this as the "biggest mistake he made as the editor of *Armed Forces Journal*."

A later internal Air Force memorandum noted with satisfaction that Drenkowski's story had dropped away and there was "little expectation for extensive media coverage.... Recent developments in other areas ... have removed the story from any significant news media interest."

THE AIR FORCE RESPONSE in the *Armed Forces Journal* destroyed Drenkowski's credibility, but his articles had seriously rankled some of the SAC senior officers who had been a part of Linebacker II. They felt the need to write—or rewrite—the formal history of the operation to make the same point the SAC staff had made to the crews at Andersen and U-Tapao immediately after the war—that the SAC staff was responsible for Linebacker II's success. The rewriting of the history of the Vietnam War to enhance general officers' reputations already had a strong history in the Air Force. General William Momyer, a former commander of Seventh Air Force, had almost completed a work whose Vietnam portion was described later by an Air University professor as partially "self-serving revisionism" and "a false history of [certain] events [by] seeking to maintain top-secret classification of source documents."

Momyer's approach might have been a template for the officer given the task of rewriting the Linebacker II history, Brigadier General James R. McCarthy, who as a Colonel had been the commander of the Andersen B-52D wing during Linebacker II. While McCarthy had a reputation as something of a "yes man" and had not argued for changes in the tactics until after General Sullivan's message, he seemed at first to be an odd choice to write such a work for SAC. He had been quite critical of SAC's tactics, saying in classified documents:

- "The inbound heading to the target and the post-target turn remained relatively unchanged for the first three days of LINE-BACKER II. This, in my opinion, caused the high B-52 losses sustained on the second and third days...."
- "We thought that [coming in on the same heading] stereotyped our attack pattern [and] our tactics ... we in the field violently disagreed with the [post-target turn] and events later proved us out...."
- "We thought that [the tactics] were too stereotyped and General Meyer agreed ... and after the third day's losses then we saw a change in tactics...."
- "All the raids used the same inbound heading, roughly the same post-target turn and the same withdrawal pattern.... We protested to Eighth Air Force who protested to SAC that we shouldn't do this every night.... This accounted in part for our significant losses on the third day...."
- "If there was one thing [SAC] is guilty of, it is not giving us the flexibility to vary tactics day by day. Had we done this ... we might have avoided the third day's losses."
- "[The enemy's] success in bringing down B-52s was at least partially dependent on the repetitive attack pattern the bombers employed ... it would be absurd ... not to admit that stereotyped operations allowed the NVA to predict our bomber tactics."

McCarthy had also chaired a conference at Andersen two weeks after the raids where the crews listed four single-spaced pages of tactical mistakes, which had been forwarded to the Eighth Air Force Director of Operations and then on to SAC.

But all that was forgotten as McCarthy focused on writing a monograph about Linebacker II that the SAC staff would approve, that could burnish his reputation, and that would officially bury Dana Drenkowski's articles. McCarthy made this latter point to a potential contributor: "I hope to offset in the monograph the bad publicity we [SAC] received in that 'Soldier of Fortune' magazine article. I believe that I have enough facts to refute the allegations of poor tactics."

Lt. Col. George B. Allison, a navigator who also flew Line-backer II missions from Andersen and was working for McCarthy at Blytheville Air Force base, accepted the opportunity to be the co-author. The two were given access to classified Air Force documents and had the complete cooperation of SAC and the Air Force. There was a minor difficulty because an Air Force monograph on Linebacker II written by three members of the Air War College, "Eleven Days in December: Linebacker II," was almost complete, and even the cover had been designed. This did not deter McCarthy, who asked the lead author, Colonel Billy Shackelford, and the other two authors to join him so he could use their material. Shackelford and the others demurred, later saying it was clear that "the general wanted to make SAC look good, whereas we wanted to tell the truth." The Air Force dropped their monograph, and turned the task of writing the "official" story over to McCarthy and Allison.

By selectively choosing source materials (specifically omitting the many critical comments by B-52 crewmembers for the original monograph), by cutting and editing letters from participants who had been asked to contribute to the monograph, and by controlling the people who were interviewed, McCarthy and Allison created an *apologia* for the SAC leadership's actions. McCarthy and Allison vigorously defended SAC's procedures that delayed changes in tactics, as well as supporting the idea that the SAC staff was a better judge of what worked in combat than the crews that flew the missions.

Typical of the author's approach were quotes from General Glenn Martin, the SAC Vice-Commander during the operation: "The timeliness of [SAC's] changes in tactics ... was impressive," Martin wrote. "That we [in SAC] were able modify and improvise our actions as quickly as we did is a positive testimony to the imagination, ingenuity, and resourcefulness of planner and aviator alike.... There was some real time criticism expressed, with spillovers of criticism continuing to the present, that SAC used stereotyped thinking and was slow to change tactics used in Linebacker II. These criticisms were based mostly on limited insight.... The opposite is true."

McCarthy himself said, in sharp contrast to his many earlier statements: "Some criticism has been expressed concerning the time lag between when a suggestion was made [and when] SAC actually approved the recommendation [3 to 5 days]. This criticism does not appear to be valid. . . ."

For information about what went on at SAC Headquarters, the authors relied on interviews with a few of the senior SAC staff, though General Sianis (who was responsible for the B-52 tactics the first four days) and many other principals did not contribute.

As their final argument, McCarthy and Allison repeated the mantra that SAC planned the missions properly because "losses were less than the 3 percent predicted" (ignoring that this loss prediction was based on General Meyer's "political English").

What McCarthy and Allison did not include is telling. They received an especially illuminating letter from the SAC Chief of Intelligence during Linebacker II, Brigadier General Harry Cordes, offering many insights into SAC Headquarters during the operation, including a lengthy and uncomplimentary description of General Meyer's dithering and delaying. But Allison considered part of his charter not to expose "the soft underbelly of the MAJCOMS [Major Commands, SAC and Eighth Air Force] . . . and high ranking flag officers by sharing their temper tantrums with the whole world," so this and many other examples of conflict within SAC were expunged. Significantly, neither the U-Tapao crews' contributions to the changes in tactics nor General Sullivan's message was ever mentioned, and the impression was left that the tactical changes finally implemented were conceived by McCarthy and the staff on Guam.

Before it was published, the McCarthy/Allison work, *Linebacker II: A View from the Rock* was carefully vetted all the way to the top of the Air Force chain of command to make sure that it reflected the "party line," and the monograph provided the story both McCarthy and SAC wanted—an excellent description of many of the operations at Guam, but one that relentlessly pressed the idea that the SAC staff had wisely planned the missions and quickly and imaginatively changed tactics when problems arose. It was published by Air University Press as part of its Southeast Asia Monograph series and widely distributed within that service, especially in the Air Force service schools. Since it was published by the Air Force, it is now considered the "official, approved" account of the battle. *View from the Rock* is still used by the Air University as *the* Linebacker II reference book. The picture the book paints—an efficient SAC staff's overcoming adversity to produce lower-than-predicted B-52 losses, and Andersen carrying the bulk of the bombing operation under the leadership of Colonel McCarthy—remains the accepted Air Force view of the last U.S. battle of the Vietnam War.

FOURTEEN

Retrospective

Vietnam is our great national myth ... what makes it so
terrible a tragedy and so fine a myth is its impenetrability.
—Paul Hendrickson

The North Vietnamese—now the Vietnamese—have a simple view of Linebacker II, best summed up by the name they have given the battle—"Dien Bien Phu in the skies." It has a hallowed place in Vietnamese history as the victory that drove the Americans out and as a major step on the road to unifying their country. As a memorial to this victory, the Vietnamese have built a museum in Hanoi known as "The B-52 Museum." The museum courtyard displays include two SA-2 missiles on launchers, one from the 77th battalion and one from the 59th, a radar van, and a huge pile of B-52 parts. Inside are more artifacts from the raid, and a theater that regularly plays a video with the Vietnamese story of the battle. The video begins: "Since time immemorial Hanoi, the capital of Vietnam, has always been the heart of the country ..." then moves on with martial music to the bombing raids, missiles blasting off into the night skies, B-52s falling in flames, sounds of bombs exploding and anti-aircraft fire, along with flashing lights on the terrain map signifying B-52s crashing, all interspersed with pictures of North Vietnamese leaders touring bombed-out buildings and giving encouragement to anti-aircraft crews. The video ends: "The Dien Bien Phu in the skies, the twelve days and nights' victory over the B-52s, is always the pride and spiritual strength of the good-willed and wise Vietnamese people."

The North Vietnamese missile battalions have not forgotten the battle either. All of the missile battalions have "Tradition Houses" that contain exhibits and diaries of the battalion's actions during the "Dien Bien Phu in the skies." Documents from the battle are also a core of the study curricula for both soldiers and officers.

There is something to be said for the Vietnamese view that

they won a victory that December. After Linebacker II, the sides signed a peace agreement and the United States left Vietnam, much as the French left after their defeat at Dien Bien Phu. With the Americans gone, the North Vietnamese were able use the troops left in South Vietnam as a framework for building up their forces. In April 1975, these North Vietnamese forces swept through South Vietnam and completed their goal of unifying the country. It was a short step to claim that the December 1972 victory over the Americans led to this unification.

Beyond its real significance and the parallels to the land battle of Dien Bien Phu, there are also psychological reasons that the "Dien Bien Phu in the skies" has a unique place in the ranks of historic Vietnamese victories. The B-52s were a legendary force, a symbol of the technological might of the United States, a technology the Vietnamese could not hope to match. The B-52s were defeated, not because of superior weapons, but because of the cleverness and bravery of the Vietnamese soldiers. It is the ultimate modern "David and Goliath" story, their Battle of Britain.

But there is an even more important psychological reason the "Dien Bien Phu in the skies" holds such an important place in Vietnamese history. The bombing served to unify a population that was beginning to chafe under years of unending war, because this battle was not fought on some distant battlefield but in the heart of the country. It has become a unifying moment in Vietnamese history, a moment that allowed the citizenry to share in both the hardships of the battle and the victory. The B-52 raids impacted virtually every person in North Vietnam at the time, and each of them has their own story that they still share with their families.

On the other hand the battle itself changed little for the North Vietnamese. The United States' withdrawal was inevitable, and the administration had long conceded that the North Vietnamese forces were going to stay in South Vietnam. The ultimate fall of South Vietnam was linked to Nixon's fall, which removed the possibility of further U.S. assistance to South Vietnam. It had nothing to do with the "aerial Dien Bien Phu."

THE AMERICAN SIDE can also make a convincing argument that Linebacker II was a victory. Linebacker II changed things. After the bombing, the North Vietnamese agreed to sign a peace agreement they had rejected in December, an agreement that obtained the release of the American POWs and got the best deal possible for South Vietnam given U.S. domestic realities. It is also a reasonable counterfactual to say that if Watergate had not forced Nixon from office, Linebacker II might have succeeded in its aim of preserving South Vietnam. There seems to be no question that the B-52 bombing of Hanoi and the terrific casualties North Vietnamese military forces suffered from U.S. air attacks in 1972 intimidated the North Vietnamese leadership. Had Nixon remained in power and the United States kept a significant B-52 presence in Asia, it is at least questionable if the North Vietnamese would have again risked a conventional invasion of South Vietnam. It was only after the fall of Nixon that the fall of South Vietnam became inevitable.

IF LINEBACKER II HAS a strong symbolic and ideological significance for the Vietnamese as the "Dien Bien Phu in the skies," it has an equally strong symbolic position in parts of the American population as to "what might have been." It is an article of faith among many former U.S. military officers that the Vietnam War was lost because the U.S. political leadership used half measures until late in 1972. When America finally unleashed its full military capability—symbolized by Linebacker II—the North Vietnamese quickly signed a peace agreement. The question that regularly arises when discussing Linebacker II is, "Why didn't the U.S. do this sooner?" More often, it arises as the declarative statement, "If the U.S. had used the B-52s on Hanoi sooner, the U.S. could have won the war."

But could the U.S. have used massive force—specifically, the B-52s—earlier to force the North Vietnamese to give up their aim of uniting the country?

The answer is not a simple one. Throughout the war, while most senior military officers believed that a heavy bombing campaign would dramatically shorten the war and cut American casualties, *none thought it was critical to winning. The U.S. military believed that the U.S. was already winning the war,* albeit slowly. The thought that the United States might eventually lose the war was ludicrous.

It should be noted that for the Americans to win, the North Vietnamese would have had to lose. While Ho Chi Minh was alive (he died in September 1969, though he was in poor health for much of the 60s), the power of his beliefs and revolutionary faith would almost certainly have prevented the North Vietnamese from giving up their ambition of uniting the country, no matter how much damage the U.S. inflicted on North Vietnam. As World War II demonstrated, populations and leaders are remarkably resilient to bombing, and there is no reason to believe that the North Vietnamese were different. That, combined with the fact that the North Vietnamese had relatively little infrastructure to destroy, argues that massive bombing would not have broken the North Vietnamese will while Ho was alive.

There is little to suggest that the situation changed significantly after his death in 1969. Nixon was to say later that not conducting a Linebacker II–type bombing of North Vietnam just after he took office was one of his "biggest mistakes," but this was almost certainly "Monday morning quarterbacking," to use a phrase Nixon would have appreciated. The facts are that after Ho's death in 1969 the American military still believed that the United States was winning the war, so it would have been difficult—perhaps impossible—to justify a bombing campaign on the scale of Linebacker II in support of a war the United States was winning. Nixon's judgment also ignores the burgeoning and increasingly aggressive anti-war movement.

Additionally, not long after Nixon was elected for the first time in 1968, the possibility of effective Soviet intervention in the event of a massive air campaign had significantly increased. Prior to 1969 the main Soviet export surface-to-air missile system was the SA-2, but by 1969 the Soviets had shown a willingness to provide a new surface-to-air missile system, the SA-3 Goa, to their allies. In March of 1970 the Soviets supplied SA-3s to the Egyptians, locked in the War of Attrition with the Israelis, and the new missile proved to be extremely effective against Israeli F-4s using American electronic countermeasures. As long as the Soviets and the United States were at odds, a Linebacker II–type bombing campaign might have encouraged the Soviets to supply SA-3s to the North Vietnamese, and SA-3s would have exponentially increased B-52 losses.

IT IS IMPORTANT TO ACKNOWLEDGE that the United States came close to suffering a major defeat in Linebacker II. SAC's planning failures, leading to the losses of the third and fourth nights, and the failure of nerve in Omaha that shifted the bombing away from Hanoi when the North Vietnamese were out of missiles gave their leadership the confidence they needed to hold out long enough for Congress cut off funds for the war. Had SAC—prodded by Haig, Sullivan and Moorer—not acknowledged its mistakes and turned most of the mission planning over to Eighth Air Force, or had the U.S. suffered a large number of B-52 losses the night of December 26, it is difficult to see how B-52 attacks on Hanoi could have continued. There seems to be little doubt that the United States Congress would have cut off all funding for the war at that point.

The results of such a cutoff would have been catastrophic: the pell-mell withdrawal of American forces followed by the almost certain quick loss of South Vietnam, and the North Vietnamese keeping almost six hundred American prisoners of war to use as negotiating pawns and to generate further humiliation. For those who think that the United States lost the war, this alternate scenario is worth pondering. It would have been a REAL defeat. It should be noted that this defeat would have taken place close to the time Nixon was resigning. The possible effects of two such events in a short time on the American psyche are interesting to contemplate.

DURING THE 1980S the failure of the American ground operation in Lebanon and clumsy efforts in Grenada and Panama stood in sharp contrast to the success of the April 1986 "El Dorado Canyon" Libyan bombing operation, a sudden, heavy air attack using the latest weaponry intended to influence political behavior. Because Libyan President Muammar el-Qaddafi appeared to stop his terrorist activities after the El Dorado Canyon bombing, some said it showed air power offered the best chance for low casualties and heavy damage. Gradually the idea that air power could be used for coercion—as it was perceived to have done in Linebacker II—began to resurface and became a part, if not the centerpiece, of the new Weinberger/Powell doctrine.

Thus, when Iraq invaded Kuwait in 1990, the perceived success of Linebacker II and subsequent intense air operations strongly influenced American military and civilian planners. Politically, President Bush's attitude was basically the same as Nixon's, and the campaign began with an attempt to force the Iraqis out of Kuwait with a large-scale, relatively unrestricted bombing campaign. While the bombing campaign failed to achieve that objective, the following quick land victory with its small number of casualities made it clear that a massive air operation, even if it failed as a coercive force, made any ground operation much easier.

But the tantalizing idea that air power could, in and of itself, act as a coercive force was not dead, primarily because it offered a possibility of success with very few casualties. Thus, in 1999, when the situation in Kosovo deteriorated to the point where President Clinton decided that American intervention was required, he (and the NATO allies) opted for a purely air campaign. Though the campaign was similar to Linebacker II—it involved heavy air strikes with the most powerful U.S. weapons and was aimed at achieving a political solution—it was highly controversial in the military and among military pundits because many of the "lessons of Vietnam" were seemingly forgotten. The bombing campaign was gradual, not striking immediately into the heart of Yugoslavia, and political considerations—such as avoiding casualties, both friendly military and civilian—were considered vital. The *commenteria* were sharply critical of the air attacks, repeating again and again that "air power alone has never won a war," and former military officers were even more scathing in their comments.

Then, to the surprise and consternation of the critics, the gradual-escalation bombing campaign, combined with diplomacy, was successful. There were no allied casualties, and by mid-2001 the Yugoslav leader, Slobodan Milosevic, had been overthrown and was awaiting trial in the West as a war criminal. It was an outcome that had to be considered a stunning success, even by the most bitter critic of how the campaign was conducted.

After Kosovo, the possibility of winning political concessions by the coercive power of massive air strikes seems a realistic possibility to American political leaders, and the attractiveness of military campaign with few or no casualties has set a standard for future operations. In retrospect Linebacker II was the first example of such an operation and, ironically, an operation that was almost a disastrous failure instead became a model for U.S. military operations in the '90s and into the next millennium.

IN 1992, THE STRATEGIC AIR COMMAND was disbanded, and its B-52s were absorbed into the Tactical Air Command. The new command was named the Air Combat Command

APPENDIX ONE

Analysis

Fifteen B-52s were shot down (9 Ds and 6 Gs), three were seriously damaged (two Ds and one G) and six had minor damage. Overall, the B-52s flew 795 sorties with a loss rate of 1.89 percent. Only about half of the total sorties—372—went to Hanoi, but all of the 15 B-52s lost were hit within a thirteen-mile radius of the capital and the loss rate there was over 4.3 percent. Of the 15 B-52s shot down, 10 crashed "on the spot" in North Vietnam and 5 were able to move out of the Hanoi area and into Laos or Thailand before they crashed.

Ninety-two crewmembers were involved in the 15 losses, and 61 of the 92 were in the 10 aircraft that crashed in North Vietnam. Of the 61 crewmembers involved in aircraft that crashed in North Vietnam, 28 died (the bodies of 7 of these have not been recovered) and 34 were captured. (One of those captured died from his wounds and is included as killed in action).

The 5 B-52s that crashed in Thailand and Laos carried 31 crewmembers. Of these, 26 were rescued, 4 were killed in the crash at U-Tapao, and 1 remains missing.

Over 1300 individual B-52 crewmembers flew one or more missions. The 307th SW U-Tapao had less that one-third of the B-52 crews but carried the bulk of the load. Supplemented for the last half of the operation by crews from Guam, the 307th flew 340 of the 729 missions, over 46 percent, and dropped over half the bombs. Not only did the 307th crews fly many more missions, they suffered heavier aircraft losses (7 lost and 4 damaged) and went to North Vietnam every day of the operation. Still, despite flying most of the most difficult missions, the U-Tapao wing had the lowest loss/ damage per sortie ratio of the three wings.

The Andersen D wing, the 43rd SW, flew 170 missions (exactly half as many sorties as the 307th), lost 2 B-52s and had 5 damaged. The Andersen G model wing, the 72nd SW, flew 219 missions, lost 6 aircraft and had 1 damaged, the highest loss rate of all (about 2.7 percent) even though they did not go to Hanoi after the third night. Unmodified Gs (without the ALT-22) suffered a loss rate of over 10 percent over Hanoi.

Most of the U-Tapao crewmembers flew five or more missions; the highest number was apparently nine. Because of the length of the missions and the two days when they flew no missions into North Vietnam, the Andersen crews flew fewer missions. Only 44 crewmembers (and 7 pilots out of 222) from Andersen flew four or more missions, which was a low *average* number of missions for crewmembers at U-Tapao.

SEVEN HUNDRED TWENTY-NINE B-52s made it to their targets, but only 703 were considered "effective" (releasing at least 50 percent of their bombs). They dropped about 15,000 tons of bombs on 34 targets. Railroad yards and supply depots were the best B-52 targets but unfortunately the most important rail yard was in downtown Hanoi, and was not attacked by B-52s to avoid civilian casualties. F-4s bombed it with laser-guided bombs, but the yard was too big for these to inflict serious damage. Post-strike analysis showed that, while the B-52 strikes crippled the North Vietnamese rail transport system, this had little effect on the North Vietnamese transportation network because most supplies were moved into North Vietnam by trucks from China. (Only one truck park was bombed by B-52s.)

While there was a great deal of collateral damage, North Vietnamese casualties were light—about 1600 in Hanoi and 300 in Haiphong. This was a combination of several factors—the U.S. policy of not attacking the populated centers of the two cities, the continuous (if somewhat belated) evacuation of the civilian populations, and a very efficient North Vietnamese civil defense and shelter system.

SAM sites were considered a difficult target for B-52s, yet of the twelve SAM sites attacked by B-52s one was hit and destroyed, indicating they might have been better targets than SAC thought.

The chances of damaging the SAM sites would have been vastly increased if the B-52s had used cluster bombs (which had been used before and were available at Andersen) on the SAM sites but SAC never ordered their use, even after the B-52s began to attack the sites. The cluster bombs were very effective and much feared by the North Vietnamese, and since most of the sites were well away from populated areas the attacks could have devastated the North Vietnamese defenses. Some crews at Andersen asked their commanders to use them, but were told that "SAC selected the weapons, and they knew best."

THROUGHOUT LINEBACKER II, the lack of bomb-damage assessment (BDA) photographs was a significant problem, and was to give a foreshadowing of problems later in the Gulf War and the conflict over Kosovo. Weather problems hampered tactical reconnaissance aircraft, the Air Force's RF-4Cs and the Navy's RA-5s. The highly touted SR-71 "Black Bird" flew missions over Hanoi and North Vietnam every day but its systems at this time were fairly primitive, and bad weather made the SR-71 almost useless. They brought back good pictures only on two missions, December 21 and December 27.

The much less sophisticated AQM-34L drones, launched from specially modified C-130 carrier ships and recovered by HH-3 helicopters, collected by far the best and largest number of the photographs. The drones could fly as low as low as 500 feet and under the clouds. While their routes were not always precise (fewer than half flew their assigned route), the quality of their coverage was excellent. Forty-one AQM-34s were launched; 4 were lost (all due to maintenance problems) and 37 drones recovered. Thirty-four had photographs of 338 targets and got bonus photos of 366 targets taken when the drone deviated from its route.

Two complete sorties were wasted on a JCS directed mission to look at the Bac Mai hospital after it was accidentally bombed, but the missions failed, apparently because the Defense Intelligence Agency had given the drone squadron the wrong address of the hospital.

Had the aim of Linebacker II been a military one, the lack of bomb-damage photographs would have had a major impact on the operation. Without photographs, bomb damage had to be estimated using SAC's predictions, but the first bomb-damage photographs made it clear that the damage to the targets was much less than SAC had claimed. Fortunately target damage was not the issue; Linebacker II was a political campaign that used physical damage to send a message. The BDA photograph problem was disconcerting but not critical, so it went uncorrected only to come back to haunt the U.S. forces in the Persian Gulf War, where lack of BDA photographs became a major issue.

PSYCHOLOGICALLY, THE F-111S were the *bêtes noires* of the North Vietnamese who put an inordinate amount of effort into trying to shoot them down. Despite this, only two were lost, one attacking a transmitter site and one attacking dock facilities on the Red River. The cause of the first aircraft's loss has never been determined. It probably crashed in the Gulf of Tonkin, perhaps because of an aircraft malfunction. The crew of the second aircraft bailed out and was taken prisoner after a small caliber AAA hit knocked out the F-111's hydraulics, a victory that occasioned a great celebration among the North Vietnamese defenders.

Linebacker II
"Urban Legends"

Thesere are a number of "urban legends" surrounding Linebacker II, legends that have taken root because of incorrect or incomplete information from earlier accounts. Some are trivial, but some—such as the belief that many crewmembers refused to fly—are important.

1. *The North Vietnamese were not firing on the early cells so they could "go to school" on them and see if the B-52s were using the same tactics as the previous nights.*

In fact, the opposite was true; the highest losses were in first cell, and the most dangerous spot to be in a cell was the number one, or lead, position. The lead position in the cell suffered 9 of the 15 losses (3.6 percent loss rate) and 13 of the 24 hits (a 5.3 percent hit rate), three times the rate of other positions.

Moreover, attrition rates showed no real pattern based on the B-52s' actions. Some waves flew very close to SA-2 sites and survived, while others further away were hit; some did not maneuver and were hit, while others maneuvered and were also hit. This variation seemed to be caused by the skill of the SAM crew assigned to engage the B-52. Some SAM battalions were very effective, others were not. As usual in air combat, a small number of sites were responsible for the majority of the kills, and a B-52 crew under attack by one of these sites was in for a difficult time.

2. *Several B-52s were lost because they went to Hanoi with jammers out under SAC's "press on" criteria.*

SAC's "press on" criteria for Hanoi missions came in for some criticism from the crews after the operation. Post-war analysis showed that eight of the 107 cells that flew over Hanoi contained one aircraft that would have aborted on a normal "no sweat" mission including bad electronic countermeasures systems. Of these, only one was lost while following the "press on" criteria, Ebony 02 on Night Eight.

3. *There was a "killer SAM site," usually identified as site number VN-549, that was using special radars to guide its missiles and that shot down six B-52s. A few assert it was actually an SA-3 site.*

North Vietnamese records show there was no such site. The 77th Battalion of the 257th Regiment shot down three or possibly four B-52s—Rose 01 on Night One, Orange 03 and Olive 01 on Night Three, and possibly Cobalt 01 on Night Nine. The 57th Battalion of the 261st Regiment shot down three B-52s, Brick 01 and Tan 03 on Night Three, and Scarlet 03 on Night Four. The 93rd Battalion of the 261st Regiment had one kill and might have been involved in hitting—but not downing—two other B-52s. No other battalion had more than one.

There is also no evidence that the North Vietnamese used special radar to guide the SA-2s, though they did use a variety of radars to track the B-52s and some may have been more effective than others. There were no SA-3s in North Vietnam during Linebacker II.

4. *MiGs were used to pass information to North Vietnamese SAM sites about the B-52s' course and altitude.*

North Vietnamese sources said there were only twenty-seven MiG reactions against the B-52s, and that is consistent with American records (and a tribute to the Americans' ability to track the MiGs at night). The B-52 crews reported a much larger number of MiGs in the air while the fighter crews, with much more experience in high-threat areas, reported considerably fewer.

Accounts of Linebacker II from the North Vietnamese histories indicate that the MiG pilots had a great deal of difficulty locating the B-52 flights. The histories do give a few vague references to MiGs providing "information," but in general North Vietnamese histories try to share as much credit as possible so this is far from conclusive. In fact, when the author told several North Vietnamese officers about MiGs flying next to B-52s they were somewhat amazed, and one—after being assured several times that U.S crews had reported it—asked, "If our MiG had been that close, why wouldn't he have shot the B-52 down?"

5. *Many B-52 crewmembers refused to fly and/or 'mutinied' over the poor tactics.*

One of the most serious enduring "urban legends" of Linebacker II concerns crewmembers' refusal to fly on the missions and/or mutinying in protest to the SAC tactics. Drenkowski asserts this in his article "The Tragedy of Linebacker II," but he is certainly not alone in this assertion. At least seven of the crewmembers the author interviewed mentioned one or both of these crew behaviors. The Air Force, on the other hand, asserts that only one crewmember refused to fly and that "crewmembers were actually trying to get off DNIF to fly."

This is an important question and deserves closer examination. It actually has two separate parts: (1) did crewmembers refuse to fly because of fear or moral objections and (2) did they threaten to refuse to fly because SAC would not change tactics and a belief that the missions were suicide missions.

Refusal to fly because of fear or moral objections

While a number of B-52 crewmembers report that other crewmembers refused to fly on the operation, the Air Force confirms only one case of a B-52 crewmember who refused to fly because he was afraid, Captain Michael Heck from Barksdale AFB, Louisiana, who was stationed at U-Tapao. Interestingly, many did not condemn Heck for his position. Brigadier General Glenn Sullivan, the 17th Air Division Commander about U-Tapao, said about Heck: "he was a captain and a co-pilot, a great little guy, he was afraid, he was just flat afraid to do it. He handled himself very well, he to this day never said anything derogatory about the United States Air Force, about what we were doing, he had nothing to say about it being immoral. " In addition to Heck, readers can make their own judgments about the conduct of Gunner John Schell, who left his aircraft just before takeoff on Night Eight, described on pages 190–93.

The author pursued the rumors of others refusing to fly by asking many of the crewmembers who flew the missions "could you identify by *name* a crewmember besides Heck that refused to fly?" Only one crewmember was able to come close to meeting this criterion, a copilot from McCoy who said he had a friend and fellow copilot who refused to fly, but he could not remember his name, though another said, "several crewmembers refused to fly and just hung around, because the leadership did not seem to know what to do with them. It was awkward."

At this point in the war, neither the Air Force nor SAC was interested in admitting that B-52 crewmembers—who had been through a special "Human Reliability" testing program to insure they were stable enough to be around nuclear weapons—would not fly missions to North Vietnam. It also would have been fairly easy to go "DNIF," duty not involving flying, by feigning illness to the flight surgeon. This would certainly have been an easy way not to fly without the public stigma. Nevertheless, while DNIF rates at Andersen did rise during Linebacker II, DNIF rates were actually higher in August, 1972, when 4 percent of D and G crews were out.

Based on the evidence, the author is prepared to conclude that a few—probably less than five—B-52 crewmembers refused to fly Linebacker II missions out of fear. This has to be considered a very small number, especially given the psychological shock the crews must have suffered when the losses began to mount and the unpopularity of the war. It is also below the number that the Eighth Air Force experienced in World War II flying out of England.

There is also substantial evidence to suggest that several—perhaps many—crewmembers tried to get the flight surgeons to *remove* them from DNIF status to fly the missions. General Sullivan, General McCarthy and General Johnson, as well as many crewmembers, assert this point. While this might seem incongruous in the light of the number of crewmembers who hesitated, it simply reflects individual differences. Many crewmembers, for personal reasons, wanted badly to fly the missions. The alternative—not flying on the biggest missions of the war, not being able to stand with your contemporaries and tell the same stories and share the same experiences, was simply intolerable. It had little to do with wing leadership, morale, or other factors—just how a person lived with himself.

"Mutiny"

The second "refusal to fly" question concerns the reported "mutiny" of crews when they were forced to fly to Hanoi again and again using the same tactics and bombing the same targets. While this also widely reported by crewmembers, it seems to have been couched in vague threats with no names mentioned. It also seems to have been more associated with U-Tapao than Guam.

After many discussions with crewmembers, the author believes that the "mutiny" stories have two sources. The first source was individual crewmembers who were very outspoken in their complaints about the tactics and saying "I'm not going to fly if this keeps up." This was almost certainly rhetorical. The second source for the stories was almost certainly General Sullivan's message, which the Andersen crews heard about third or fourth hand. It would have been easy for these Andersen crews to interpret the story as "the U-T crews were going to refuse to fly unless the tactics were changed." The author found no evidence that there was a real mutiny.

Number of
SAMs Fired

The figures of how many missiles the North Vietnamese fired are considerably different on each side. U.S. sources generally settle between 800 and 1000. The North Vietnamese, on the other hand, say they fired a *total* of 239 missiles during the operation, or something less than a third to a quarter of the number of missiles the U.S. reported.

While there is no way to determine the precise number of missile fired, there are a few hints. The American reports had two ways to determine the number, by crew reports or electronic indications. The B-52 crew reports, while sincere, cannot be considered reliable, because lights are very difficult to interpret at night and because the crews were under considerable stress and maneuvering, which may have affected their count. Additionally, there was the problem of double counting. For example, if the #1 aircraft in a cell reported 15 missiles, the #2 reported 8, and the #3 reported 11, how many were reported? 34 (the total)? 11 (the numerical average)? Obviously, the room for error in the crew reports is large.

The second method, U.S. electronic intelligence, is highly suspect. While the precise method of counting the missiles fired remains classified, their information simply had to come from emissions of various launch and/or control signals from the North Vietnamese missile sites, and the North Vietnamese were expert at using these signals to deceive. Nevertheless, it is these figures—called *COMFY COAT*—that would have had to have been used to get the numbers of missiles fired. At best, one *might* be able to say that the North Vietnamese activated somewhere over 1000 launch *signals* during the operation.

The North Vietnamese claim they engaged the B-52s 134 times with 239 missiles. This would indicate that almost all of the B-52 cells were engaged once, but in fact several were engaged more than once and others not at all. This also shows that often the North Vietnamese fired less than two missiles per engagement, too low a number for consistent kills, according to Soviet tactical doctrine against jamming targets (the Soviets recommended using three missiles against a jamming target). This probably reflects the shortage of missiles, though throughout the war the Soviets noted the North Vietnamese were reluctant to fire three missiles at one target no matter what the situation.

The ten Hanoi missile battalions probably had a full load of missiles when the operation began, about 120. The technical battalions assembled about 300, which meant that the 361st Air Defense Division had access to about 420 missile for the operation. This would make the North Vietnamese claim of firing 239 missiles from the Hanoi area seem too low. In a desperate battle one would have not expected them to ration their missiles.

There are several possible explanations. The North Vietnamese may not have counted missiles that malfunctioned, or perhaps the technical battalions did not assemble 300 missiles. There is also the possibility that their number is low for propaganda purposes, to show that they were shooting down a large number of B-52s with a few missiles.

Interestingly, crews from U.S. U-2 and RC-135 crews flying over the Gulf of Tonkin, watching the raids, tend to support the North Vietnamese numbers. From static platforms, not under pressure, and tasked with the responsibility for counting missile firings, they are probably the best American source, but only a few of their numbers have been declassified. Overall, the evidence suggests that the North Vietnamese fired many fewer missiles than the U.S. thought.

Key Organizations and Personnel for Linebacker II

United States

Admiral James Moorer,
Chairman of the Joint Chiefs of Staff

General John Meyer, Commander,
Strategic Air Command

ANDERSEN AIR FORCE BASE, GUAM

Lt. General Gerald Johnson, Commander,
Eighth Air Force

Colonel James R. McCarthy, Commander,
43rd Strategic Wing (B-52D), Andersen AFB

Colonel Thomas Rew, Commander,
72nd Strategic Wing (B-52G), Andersen AFB

U-TAPAO ROYAL THAI NAVY BASE, THAILAND

Brigadier General Glenn R. Sullivan, Commander,
Seventeenth Air Division

Colonel Donald Davis, Commander,
307th Strategic Wing (B-52D)

Colonel Bill V. Brown, Vice Commander,
307th Strategic Wing (B-52D)

Colonel Bill Maxson, Commander,
340th Consolidated Maintenance Wing

Democratic Republic of Vietnam

Premier: Pham Van Dong

Chief of the General Staff: Vo Nguyen Giap

Commander of Air Defense: Le Van Tri

257TH MISSILE REGIMENT

Commander: Nguyen Dien

77TH MISSILE BATTALION

Commander: Dinh The Van

Fire Control: Nguyen Van Duc

Range Tracking: Pham Hong Ha

Elevation Tracking: Luu Van Moc

Direction (Azimuth) Tracking: Do Dinh Tan

78TH MISSILE BATTALION

Commander: Nguyen Chen

261ST MISSILE REGIMENT

Commander: Tran Huu

57TH MISSILE BATTALION

Commander: Nguyen Van Phiet

Fire Control Officer: Nguyen Thu Tan

59TH MISSILE BATTALION

Commander: Nguyen Thang

Fire Control: Duong Van Thuan

Range Tracking: Ngo Van Tu

Elevation Tracking: Xuan Linh Le

Direction (Azimuth) Tracking: Nguyen Van Do

93RD MISSILE BATTALION

Commander: Nguyen Manh Hung

Fire Control Officer: Ho Duc Vinh

Operators:
Tran Thanh Houng
Nguyen Kim Con

Staff Assistant: Nguyen Xuan Minh

94TH MISSILE BATTALION

Commander: Tran Minh Thang

363RD AIR DEFENSE DIVISION (HAIPHONG)
72ND MISSILE BATTALION
(TRANSFERRED TO HANOI FROM HAIPHONG
24 DECEMBER)

Commander: Chat Pham

Glossary

A-6   An extremely effective two-seat, two-engine, all-weather attack aircraft used by the United States Navy.

AAA   Automatic anti-aircraft; the normal term for anti-aircraft gunfire. Also called flak.

AC-119   The gunship conversion of the large, twin-boom, twin-engine C-119 transport aircraft.

ADVON   Advanced Organization.

Air War College   Part of the Air Force's advanced professional education system, the Air University.

ALT-22   An advanced jammer on the B-52Ds and some B-52Gs; replacement for the ALT-6B.

ALT-6B   Predecessor of the ALT-22; mounted on about half the B-52Gs during Linebacker II.

APR-20   One of the B-52 electronic warfare officer's scopes that displayed radar signals.

APR-25   Another of the B-52 electronic warfare officer's scopes that displayed radar signals.

Arc Light   Name given to all B-52 strikes during the Vietnam War.

ARM   Anti-radiation missile (also see Shrike, Standard ARM).

Automatic tracking (SA-2)   Also known as auto-track, the mode of the SA-2 guidance system that guided the missile automatically rather than by crew inputs.

B-29   A large, four-engine World War II and Korean War bomber. Very advanced for its time.

Bag drag   The term given by the B-52 crews to a rapid movement from one aircraft to the spare aircraft.

Beeper   A device placed in parachutes and in ejection seats designed to be activated automatically when an ejection took place. It broadcast a cycling wail on Guard frequency.

BUFF   Big Ugly Fat Fucker, the slang name for the B-52. The official Air Force translation was Big Ugly Fat Fellow.

Bullet Shot   Program that sent a large force of B-52Ds and Gs in several stages to Southeast Asia in 1972.

Bullseye   Hanoi. Distances were often given using this as a center point, e.g., "Bandit, Bullseye 240 [bearing] for twenty [range in miles]."

Burn through   The distance a radar can overpower or "burn through" electronic jamming.

C-123   Twin engine tactical cargo aircraft used in the Vietnam War for a variety of missions.

C-141   Large, four engine jet transport/cargo aircraft.

Cell   The standard B-52 formation, three aircraft in trail in an offset "V."

CEP   Circular Error Probable. The standard measure of bombing effectiveness.

Chaff   Small pieces of tinfoil-like metal strips cut to a specified length to jam enemy radars.

Charlie   A highly qualified B-52 pilot who made all decisions while the aircraft were on the ground or taxiing.

CINC (as in CINCPAC and CINCSAC)   Commander in Chief.

CJCS   Chairman, Joint Chiefs of Staff.

Combat Tree   A highly classified radar attachment to some F-4 radars which allowed them to separate MiG radar returns from American aircraft.

DMZ   Demilitarized Zone, the dividing line between North and South Vietnam.

EB-66   A twin jet bomber used by the USAF as a jamming aircraft.

ECM   Generic name for electronic countermeasures. Usually applied to systems carried by an aircraft.

Eighth (8th) Air Force   The local controlling organization for B-52 operations over Vietnam, based at Andersen AFB, Guam.

EW (EWO)   Electronic warfare officer, the officer who operates jamming systems.

F-105   A single-engine attack aircraft used extensively during the Vietnam War. During Linebacker II the two-seat version, the F-105G, was used extensively as a "Wild Weasel" SAM-suppression aircraft.

F-111   A twin jet USAF all-weather attack aircraft with a crew of two seated side by side and "swing" wings. Capable of very high speed at low level.

F-4   Twin engine, two-seat multipurpose fighter used by the USAF and the U.S. Navy.

Fan Song   The radar used to control the SA-2 missile and guide it to its target.

Flak   *See* AAA.

Frag   The entire mission plan for a bombing operation. Each unit takes the section, or "fragment," that applies to its aircraft.

Guard   A UHF radio frequency (243.0) reserved by the Americans for emergency transmissions. All U.S. aircraft had one transmitter and two receivers, one of them that received only Guard channel. This receiver could be switched off manually.

HQ   Headquarters.

Jump seat   A fixed seat between and immediately behind the B-52 pilot and copilot.

KC-135   The four-engine military version of the Boeing 707, used mainly as an air refueling tanker.

Laser-guided bomb (LBGs)   A highly accurate conventional bomb with a kit attached that allowed it to follow a laser beam to a ground target.

Linebacker   The name given to the two major American bombing campaigns against North Vietnam in 1972.

Linebacker I   Mainly tactical bombing attacks from May to the end of October 1972.

Linebacker II   Mainly B-52 attacks from Dec 18–Dec 29, 1972.

MiG-21   Small, single-seat, single-engine Soviet interceptor with high performance, but with limited radar and air-to-air missile capability.

MiGCAP   MiG Combat Air Patrol.

Nav   Slang term for B-52 navigator.

Offset aim point   A ground point at a known bearing distance from a target that shows up on radar; used to bomb targets that do not show up on radar.

P-12   A Soviet long-range radar to locate airborne targets.

PACAF   Pacific Air Forces, the air component of the Pacific Command (PACOM).

PACOM   Pacific Command. Controlled virtually all U.S. forces in the Pacific.

PCS   Permanent Change of Station; a transfer.

PDI   Pilot direction indicator. A pointer followed by the B-52 pilot on the bomb run.

Pilot   Slang term for a B-52 aircraft commander.

Post-target turn (PTT)   A steep turn of forty-five degrees angle of bank used by B-52s immediately after bomb release.

POW   Prisoner of war.

PTT   *See* Post-target turn.

Radar offsets   *See* Offset aim point.

RF-4   The reconnaissance version of the F-4.

RHAW   Radar Homing and Warning; carried by U.S. fighter and attack aircraft to display enemy radar signals.

RN   Slang term for Radar Navigator, the bombardier of the B-52. AKA "Radar."

Rolling Thunder   First bombing campaign against the Hanoi area. Ended in early 1968.

Route Package VI (RP VI)   The area around Hanoi (RPVIA) and Haiphong (RPVIB).

SA-2 battalion. A full firing unit which manned a site.

SA-2 site. A collection of pre-prepared launch positions designed to accommodate a SA-2 battalion.

SA-3   An advanced Soviet missile system supplied to North Vietnam immediately after Linebacker II.

SAC   Strategic Air Command.

SAM   Surface-to-air missile. Usually applied to the SA-2 during Linebacker II.

SEA   Southeast Asia. A slang term for the combat zone of the Vietnam War.

Seventh (7th) Air Force   Controlling organization for most USAF tactical operations in Southeast Asia.

Shrike   A small anti-radiation missile carried by Wild Weasels.

Smart bombs   Generally applied to laser-guided bombs, but also applicable to other types of guided bombs.

Spoon Rest   A Soviet radar located in a SA-2 battalion used to locate targets for the missile (but not to guide the missile).

Standard ARM   A large, long-range anti-radiation missile carried by Wild Weasels.

Strobe   A point or strip of light, usually applied to a return on a radarscope.

TAC   Tactical Air Command. Generally (but inaccurately) used to refer to fighter forces as opposed to the bomber forces (SAC).

Target folder   A number of papers, usually including predictions of radar offset aim points, supplied to a crew before bombing mission.

TDY   Temporary duty. A temporary assignment, usually no more that six months.

Thud Ridge   Name given to the Tam Dao mountain range northwest of Hanoi.

Tiny Tim   The name given to B-52 support forces prior to Linebacker II.

TOT   Time over Target. The time a bomber force is planned to arrive over the target.

UT   Slang name for U-Tapao Royal Thai Navy Base.

Wild Weasel   Any of a number of types of specialized fighter-type aircraft used to attack SAM sites.

Acknowledgments

There were a large number of people who provided me with assistance and encouragement with this project. I would like to especially acknowledge former Louisiana Congressman Bob Livingston, his assistant (and my former classmate) Stephanie Newell, and Ambassador Pete Peterson in Hanoi. Jim Rotramel read two of the drafts and made many useful corrections. I was fortunate to spend a year as the Verville Fellow in the Aeronautics Department of the National Air and Space Museum in Washington, and the members of the department—the Chairman, Dom Pisano, Dorothy Cochrane, Tom Crouch, R.E.G. Davies, Tom Diets, Von Hardesty. Peter Jakeb, Russ Lee, Alex Spencer, as well as Tim Cronen and Michael Neufield were all helpful. Special thanks to Collette Williams, who persevered in forwarding some vital documents from Hanoi to me after I left the museum. I also owe much to the regular encouragement I received from my friends from the "Greatest Generation"—Robert Monsted, Douglas McIlhenny, Laurance Eustis, Dr. George Schneider, Paul Westervelt, as well as my agent, Tony Outhwaite and my publisher at Encounter Books, Peter Collier.

Reference Notes*

Prologue: Peace Is Our Profession

1 *Strategic Air Command:* In fact, SAC was not technically part of the Air Force. It was a "specified command" officially reporting to the Joint Chiefs of Staff, but was manned entirely by members the newly independent United States Air Force.

2 *caricature of the military man:* The most obvious example was the Air Force general Jack D. Ripper, in Stanley Kubrick's *Dr. Strangelove: Or How I Learned to Stop Worrying and Love the Bomb.*

2 *Air Force becoming a separate service:* Worden, *Rise of the Fighter Generals,* p. 22.

2 *modern tactical weapons systems:* Ibid., p. 50. The USAF did have a modern fighter, the F-86, but it had been designed as a bomber interceptor. Most USAF fighter development for the next decade was in bomber interceptors or nuclear capable fighter-bombers.

3 *worst B-29 units to Korea: Strategic Air Warfare: An Interview with Generals Curtis LeMay, [et al.],* p. 55

3 *outside of SAC's direct control:* Ibid., p. 90; see also Worden, *Rise of the Fighter Generals,* p. 190

3 *46 percent of the total defense budget:* Worden, *Rise of the Fighter Generals,* p. 67.

3 *"... insistent on SAC being 'it.'...":* Ibid., p. 101.

3 *"has to have fighters":* Ibid., p. 100.

4 *A Gathering of Eagles:* In the 1960s movies like *Dr. Strangelove* and *Failsafe* mirrored SAC's decline.

4 *for using SAC's forces: Strategic Air Warfare,* p. 50.

5 *"... never utter a syllable": U.S. News & World Report,* 16 March 1998, p 28.

6 *ready for immediate launch:* This was to make sure the bombers would not be destroyed by a surprise attack. Tankers also sat on alert to insure they would be airborne to refuel the bombers. As the Soviet

---

*Numbers in left-hand column indicate page numbers.

nuclear force grew the response time for the alert force steadily decreased until the crews were on fifteen minute alert, which required that these crews remain very close to the alert building.

6   *counterparts in other Air Force units:* SAC crews flew 10- to 12-hour missions a few times a month, but generally made only one landing per flight. It was not unusual for a copilot to log just a few landings *a year.* The limited flying time meant the general level of SAC flying proficiency was considered quite low. Interview with Brig. General J. B. Cobb, USAFR, 3 November 2000.

6   *Ellsworth AFB, South Dakota:* The B-52s had to be based in the northern part of the United States to reach their targets in the Soviet Union via the polar route.

6   *new pilot training graduates:* Worden, *Rise of the Fighter Generals,* p. 143.

7   *LeMay quickly fired him:* For a detailed account of this purge, see Worden, *Rise of the Fighter Generals,* pp. 104–6.

7   *total disaster for SAC:* General John Ryan interview, 20 May 1972; Worden, *Rise of the Fighter Generals,* p. 51 *et passim.*

7   *force them to falsify reports:* Ibid., p. 153. Many officers blame the SAC system of false reporting for the false or exaggerated reports filed by the Air Force during the Vietnam War. After the "bomber generals" left the highest levels of the Air Force the Air university published a series of studies on "Ethics in the Air Force" which focuses on these complaints. Falsifying reports was listed as the number one problem. *Ethics in the U.S. Air Force, 1988* (Maxwell AFB: Air University Press, 1990), p. 65.

8   *air-to-air combat:* For a full account, see Michel, *Clashes: Air Combat over North Vietnam, 1965–1972,* p. 43 *et passim.*

8   *"doomsday scenario":* The staple of this SAC briefing was that the Soviet Union and China could—and would—attack the U.S. without warning in a coordinated nuclear attack. The only forces that could counter such an attack were SAC's manned bombers on alert, which would devastate the enemy. The fact that the Soviets and Chinese had not attacked was "proof that SAC's deterrence worked."

8   *didn't support the Air Force positions:* Worden, *Rise of the Fighter Generals,* p. 112.

8   *"nervous" with military power:* Oral History Interview of Lt. General Glenn W. Martin, 6–10 February 1978.

8   *"... or its capabilities":* Strategic Air Warfare, p. 110.

8   *Attorney General Robert Kennedy:* Ryan interview, pp. 72–74. Ryan spoke disparagingly of the Kennedy administration as a "bunch of liberals."

9 *"... how new it was":* Worden, *Rise of the Fighter Generals,* p. 110.

9 *"... they can learn in SAC":* Ibid., p. 42. There is a great deal of anecdotal evidence to support this. One former SAC pilot (and later Air
Force general) described to the author how five of the highly coveted
AFIT assignments were sent to his SAC base to be filled. One was filled
by a ground officer, one by an officer who had just had strong disci-
plinary action taken against him, and the other three were turned back.
The SAC crewmembers on the base were never even told the assignments were available. Interview with J. B. Cobb, 3 November 2000.

10 *"none of them":* "The Right Man," *Military History Quarterly,* Spring
1966, p. 63.

10 *Soviets to back down:* One of LeMay's SAC cohorts was later to say
that "was totally missed by the Kennedy administration, by both the
executive leadership and by McNamara." *Strategic Air Warfare,*
p. 113. LeMay was also sharply critical of the fact that the administration had made any concessions at all to the Soviets.

10 *top of the list:* A SAC program, the ICBM, was actually first, but at
McNamara's insistence. The SAC generals—mostly bomber pilots—
were wary of missiles, but not completely opposed.

One: War Is Our Hobby

11 *now the president:* Mark Perry, *Four Stars* (Houghton Mifflin, 1989),
pp. 130–31.

11 *Air Force had selected:* The 94-target list known as the Rolling Thunder Target List (RTTL, pronounced "rattle") was a constant feature
of Air Force planning throughout the war.

11 *Chinese nuclear weapons program: LeMay Oral History,* January
1965, p. 73.

12 *flying 433 sorties:* Shackelford, et al., "Eleven Days in December:
Linebacker II," Air University monograph (unpublished, 1977), p. 49.

12 *"... dropping conventional bombs":* Worden, *Rise of the Fighter Generals,* p. 173.

12 *"... screaming into SEA":* Letter, Brigadier General McCarthy to Zentner, 4 April 2000.

12 *Westmoreland's Air Force deputy:* The title of the Air Deputy in Vietnam was the Commander of the Second Air Division, later to become
Seventh Air Force.

13 *ADVON:* Advance Organization.

13 *thirty B-52Fs:* U.S. production military aircraft have letters behind
their numbers to indicate changes, e.g. B-52A, B-52B, B-52C, etc. The
B-52 series ended with the B-52H.

13 *almost twenty tons:* Dorr and Lindsey, *B-52 Stratofortress: Boeing's Cold Warrior, p.* 126.

13 *Arc Light One:* Ibid., p. 129.

14 *totaling 60,000 pounds:* Ethell and Christy, *B-52 Stratofortress,* p. 59. The B-52s could carry either 84 Mk82 500-pound or 42 M117 750-pound bombs internally and 24 of either size on the two external wing racks.

14 *political turbulence and tension:* Charles K. Hopkins, *SAC Bomber Operations in the Southeast Asia War,* vol. 4, p. 31; and *History of the 307th Strategic Wing,* vol. 1, p. 119. The Thai military government had public executions close to U-Tapao in December 1971, and there was a North Vietnamese sapper attack on the base in January 1972.

15 *"... their outmoded methods":* Broughton, *Thud Ridge,* p. 75.

15 *"... a lot of vegetation":* Nalty, *Air Power and the Fight for Khe Sanh,* p. 102.

15 *and a half-mile wide:* This was known as a target box, or simply "box." The boxes would vary in size from 1km x 1km to 2km x 5km, but a mile long and half a mile wide is a reasonable average.

15 *"... orders to get out":* Truong Nhu Tang, *A Viet Cong Memoir* (New York: Vintage, 1985), p. 168.

15 *black camouflage scheme:* The D model's anti-reflective black camouflage was designed to absorb the beam of searchlights. The bomber had green/dark brown/tan upper surfaces, and the camouflage was very similar to the scheme of British night bombers in World War II. The B-52G models that were rushed to Guam retained their white undersurfaces.

15 *"... won by the [B-52s]":* Nalty, *Air Power and the Fight for Khe Sanh,* p. 68.

16 *Demilitarized Zone (DMZ):* The border between North and South Vietnam.

16 *SA-2 Guideline:* SA-2 (Surface-to-Air Number 2) Guideline was the NATO number/name given to this missile and was used in all U.S. accounts of the missile. The Soviet designation for the missile was the V-75 Dvina. Zaloga, *Soviet Air Defense Missiles: Design, Development, Tactics,* p. 36.

16 *beam of the radar:* The SA-2 was a "beam rider" as opposed to other types of guidance, i.e. "heat seeker," which homed in on the heat from the engine or other parts of an aircraft.

16 *The entire system was moveable:* The SA-2 has often been incorrectly described as a "mobile" system. A mobile system is one that is mounted on vehicles and can fire from the vehicles. The SA-2 has to be moved, taken off the trucks and set up before it can be fired.

16   *"... similar western systems":* Patrick K. Barker, Captain, USAF, *The SA-2 and the Wild Weasel: The Nature of Technological Change in Military Systems,* pp. 12–13.

17   *the system almost useless:* For the Soviet view, see *Military Parade JS,* 1998, p. 4.

17   *no chance of a hit:* See draft, Alexy Vassiliev, *Missile under the Lotus Blossoms* (unpublished ms.), pp. 240–43.

17   *courage of the B-52 crews:* The feelings were certainly understandable. During Rolling Thunder (1965–1968) fighter crews, especially the fighter crews in the F-4 and F-105, took great risks and suffered heavily; for example the F-105s, which flew most of the missions in Rolling Thunder, had a loss rate of 3.32 per 1000 sorties and the F-4s had 2.84 losses per 1000 sorties. The B-52 operations were entirely different; they were in no danger flying over South Vietnam and from 1965 until the end of October 1972, B-52s flew about 5000 sorties over all of North Vietnam and did not suffer a single combat loss.

18   *"... and things like that":* Broughton, *Thud Ridge,* p. 27.

18   *fighter pilot/bomber pilot conflict:* Even today (March 2001) *Thud Ridge* remains on the Air Force Chief of Staff's reading list. The tactical crews were more charitable to the crews of SAC's KC-135 tankers, because the fighters and tankers worked together every day and a tanker was a sweet sight to a fighter coming out of North Vietnam low on gas and perhaps battle damaged. Not only that, but from time to time a KC-135 crew—in violation of SAC regulations—would fly deep into North Vietnam to meet fighters who were so low on fuel they could not reach the approved tanker orbits in Laos.

18   *"... principle of surprise ...":* Broughton, *Going Downtown: The War against Hanoi and Washington,* p. 106.

18   *(... in the lower ranks):* Worden, *Rise of the Fighter Generals,* pp. 223–25.

19   *B-52 Arc Light tours:* Until early 1968, one hundred missions over North Vietnam constituted a tour, and the hundred missions could be accomplished in about six months.

19   *six-month Arc Light tour:* Some crews from G models were trained in Ds and sent over to fly Arc Light tours, but H model crews were sent very rarely. Gradually Arc Light tours were flown by the crews of other B-52 models, the G and H models, but the D crews still bore the brunt of the operation and the family separation. Letter, McCarthy to Zetner, 4 April 2000.

19   *"... a morale problem":* Ibid.

20   *"... was ruining SAC":* Worden, *Rise of the Fighter Generals,* p. 195.

Two: Getting Serious

21 *negotiations with the North Vietnamese:* Kissinger had actually done some negotiating with the North Vietnamese as early as 1967, and after Nixon's appointment he carried on secret negotiations with them from August 1969 through November 1971. Thompson, *To Hanoi and Back,* pp. 158–59.

22 *take hold of their country:* By the end of 1971 the government in Saigon had about 97 percent of the country under their control, up from 23 percent in 1968. Robert A. Pape, *Bombing to Win: Air Power and Coercion in War,* p. 197.

22 *couldn't—or wouldn't—fight:* Ibid., p. 198.

23 *B-52s already at U-Tapao:* The bombers were sent to Andersen because U-Tapao had no more ramp space. General Gerald W. Johnson, End of Tour Report, p. 22.

23 *before action became necessary:* It is not totally clear that Nixon did not try to have it both ways. In late 1971 and early 1972 the Commander of Seventh Air Force, General John D. Lavelle, instructed U.S. air forces to execute strikes against targets in the North Vietnamese buildup in southern North Vietnam. General Lavelle was eventually fired and court-martialed, but many in the Air Force are convinced to this day that he was following orders from Washington—either from General Ryan or the president—in making the attacks. Given Nixon's willingness to use military force and his penchant for secrecy and plots—Watergate is just one example—in the author's judgement this cannot be discounted.

23 *Operation Nguyen Hue:* Nguyen Hue was a Vietnamese emperor who launched a pre-emptive strike to stop a Chinese invasion in 1789.

23 *unhappy ... with the air campaign:* Clodfelter, "Nixon and the Air Weapon," p. 169.

24 *reactions to the situation "wild":* Zumwalt, *On Watch,* p. 401.

24 *Rolling Thunder campaign:* Clodfelter, "Nixon and the Air Weapon," p. 170.

24 *central panhandle:* While the magnitude of the strike may have surprised the North Vietnamese, they could not have been impressed with the bombing. It was accepted that even under the best circumstances B-52s did not bomb with pin-point accuracy and there were many errors that could creep into a normal bomb run that could result in bombs hitting outside the "box." Still, the bombing of April 9 was exceptionally bad. Four days later, on April 13, the B-52s returned to North Vietnam for an early morning raid on the Bai Thong airfield in the center of the North Vietnamese panhandle, but this time the bombing was very accurate. This raid alleviated the anxiety about the B-52's accuracy.

24   *Route Package VI:* Following a formula begun in the Korean War, the USAF and USN divided up North Vietnam into six separate areas called Route Packages, and then divided them between the services. *USAF Operations against North Vietnam, 1 July 1971–30 June 1972,* pp. 67–68.

24   *". . . certainly got their attention":* Message, Kissinger to Haig, 21 April 1972.

25   *". . . a more helpful role":* Message, Nixon to Kissinger, 231945Z, April 1972.

25   *". . . with conventional weapons":* Panel Discussion on Linebacker II at Maxwell AFB, November 1995, with Generals Sullivan, Maxson and Beck.

25   *insisted that the B-52s use it:* The reasons why SAC insisted are unclear. See Corona Harvest Report V, *Special Missions, 1 July 1971–30 June 1972,* p. 33–34.

26   *would be lost in South Vietnam:* Abrams said, "I can think of no diversion of assets from the battle for SVN that would be as damaging [as the withdrawal of the B-52s]." MACV Message to Admiral McCain, CINCPAC, 180305Z, May 1972.

26   *". . . no one really believed them":* E-mail from Nguyen Van Phuong, Hanoi resident in 1972, now living in Melbourne, Australia.

26   *so close to victory:* Pape, *Bombing to Win,* p. 198.

26   *adamantly refused to do:* This operation was called "Pocket Money."

26   *operation known as Linebacker:* Later known as Linebacker I, to distinguish it from the December 1972 B-52 bombing, Linebacker II.

27   *mainly using normal bombs:* The Navy had a very limited supply of guided bombs at this point, though they did have—and used—a few · TV-guided bombs.

27   *". . . when it was given":* Message Nixon/Haig to Kissinger, 19 May 1972.

27   *almost 300 crews:* The actual numbers were 207 B-52s and 286 crews.

28   *". . . shape up or get out . . .":* New York Times, 30 April 2000, p. 16.

28   *forces in South Vietnam:* Kissinger, *White House Years,* p. 1189.

28   *U.S. proposals since 1970:* Ibid., p. 1347.

29   *initial American attacks:* Haig, *"Inner Circles,"* p. 283.

29   *equipment not be sent:* U.S. intelligence first saw the SA-3s on January 13, 1973. Also, the author interviewed Mr. Nguyen Hung, one of the SA-3 missile crew, who was trained in the Soviet Union in mid-1972. He confirmed that the missiles did not arrive until mid-January 1973 "because the Russians wanted to end the war."

29   *fighter ace in World War II:* Ironically, by a fluke in the bomber-dominated SAC Air Force, not only was Meyer a former fighter ace but so was the Eighth Air Force commander, Lieutenant Gerald W.

Johnson, and the new commander of Seventh Air Force, Lieutenant General James Vogt.

30 *north of the capital: Annex to the History of Eighth Air Force, 1 July 1972–30 June 1973,* ch. 5, p. 2.

30 *squelched the idea:* Ibid., p. 3.

30 *commander of the Pacific Air Forces:* Broughton, *Going Downtown,* p. 52. While PACAF commander, Ryan had ordered an ill-fated night-bombing campaign by poorly equipped F-105s, which suffered heavy losses, and many believed he ordered the campaign simply to keep up with the Navy sortie rate. In 1972 Ryan had also failed to support General Lavelle, the commander of Seventh Air Force, when he was accused of bombing North Vietnam without permission. Many Air Force officers believed that Lavelle was following Ryan's unwritten orders and that Ryan refused to support him to protect his own career.

30 *Admiral John S. McCain Jr.:* The admiral was the father of Senator John McCain III of Arizona.

30 *escalating the war:* These discussions are covered in detail in the *Annex to the History of Eighth Air Force, 1 July 1972–30 June 1973,* ch. 5, pp. 8–12.

30 *a single bathroom in between:* Their conditions were still much better than those of the maintenance personnel, who lived in tents and open-bay metal buildings with no air conditioning to ward off the tropical heat. Geloneck, "At the Hands of the Enemy: A Bomber Pilot's View," p. 7.

30 *occasional problems:* Ibid., p. 13.

30 *only twice a week:* This was because of the relatively small numbers of missions flown from Guam and the need for crew rest.

31 *"... understanding of this letter":* Letter of Admonition to Major Arthur C. Mizner, 15 April 1973.

31 *question why they were there:* Geloneck, "At the Hands of the Enemy," p. 13.

32 *keep them under control:* Pat Hruby e-mail.

32 *as Bullet Shot continued:* See, for example, Stocker to Zentner, response to survey questionnaire, undated, 2000.

32 *"... over this holiday season":* History of Eighth Air Force, 1 July 1972–30 June 1973, vol. 1, pp. 257–58.

32 *during a bomb run:* The B-52G used spoilers in the wings to maneuver instead of ailerons.

33 *prevented the bombs from dropping:* McCarthy and Allison, *Linebacker II: A View from the Rock,* p. 70.

33 *countermeasures and jamming equipment:* Four ALT-28 ECM transmitters and three ALT-22s or three ALT-6Bs. Johnson, End of Tour Report, p. 89.

33 *refused to fund the upgrade:* Ibid., p. 56.

33 *". . . in the Air Force inventory":* Panel Discussion on Linebacker II at Maxwell AFB; also Bruce Smith interview.

33 *". . . equal to an EB-66 . . .":* "Fighting the B-52s," *Vietnam Magazine,* April 1996, p. 28.

35 *". . . lucky to have them at that time . . .":* Ted Daniel e-mail.

35 *bombing the right target:* The author is grateful for this explanation of offset aim points from Bill Beavers and Bob Mayall.

35 *to SAC for approval:* Greg Crosby letter, quoted in McCarthy and Allison, *View from the Rock,* p. 26.

36 *jamming on their radarscopes:* "Taking Aim at the B-52s," p. 29; *Historical Notes of the North Vietnamese Air Defense Command.*

37 *turn on their jammers:* Hopkins, *SAC Bomber Operations,* vol, 4, pp. 59–60.

38 *two methods of guiding the SA-2:* The author is grateful to Bodo Siefert and Tony Zlinsky for this explanation.

38 *"September Plan": Historical Notes of the North Vietnamese Air Defense Command.*

38 *North Vietnamese army suffered:* North Vietnamese accounts show that the bombing was hurting badly and their negotiators in Paris knew this. *Historical Notes of the North Vietnamese Air Defense Command.* Interestingly, U.S. intelligence did not agree. An assessment on September 29, 1972, said that while 78 percent of North Vietnam's POL storage had been struck and 25 percent destroyed, the U.S. could not close North Vietnam's major highways and that the "near term effects [of Linebacker I bombing] were minimal." *Linebacker Operations, September–December 1972,* p. 117.

39 *Nixon sensed an opportunity:* Haig, *"Inner Circles,"* p. 293.

39 *". . . our international responsibilities":* Kissinger, *White House Years,* pp. 1345–46.

39 *targets deeper in North Vietnam:* Corona Harvest Report, *USAF Air Operations in Southeast Asia, 1 July 1972–15 August 1973,* vol. 2, p. IV–24.

39 *". . . threat became severe":* McCarthy and Allison, *View from the Rock,* pp. 30–32. As incongruous as it seems, these orders were issued while SAC Headquarters was planning to send B-52s to the most heavily defended areas of North Vietnam to penetrate areas defended by North Vietnamese SAMs.

40 *refused to reconsider:* Hopkins, *SAC Bomber Operations,* vol. 4, p. 72.

Three: "Attacks must be brutal ..."

41 *"... an agreement is near":* Message HAKTO 41, 221306Z, October 1972.

41 *southern part of the country: Linebacker Study,* MACV, unpublished draft (20 January 1973), p. 164.

42 *"... as if it has lost":* Message HAKTO 31, 22 October 1972.

42 *"... highly emotional state":* Message from Bunker to White House, 221152Z, October 1972.

42 *"... committing suicide": New York Times,* 30 April 2000, p. 16.

42 *"... [of his refusal]":* Message HAKTO 41, 221306Z, October 1972.

42 *agreement needed "clarifications":* Elizabeth A. Hartsook, *Air Power Helps Stop the Invasion and End the War,* p. 166.

42 *mainly cosmetic—changes:* Pape, *Bombing to Win,* p. 203. Ibid., p. 165.

42 *felt betrayed:* Nixon, *R.N.: The Memoirs of Richard Nixon,* p. 717.

43 *forces decimated them:* Pape, *Bombing to Win,* p. 177.

44 *"TTR maneuver":* Target Tracking Radar maneuver, designed to disrupt a SAM's target-tracking radar.

44 *have to be broken off:* Message HAKTO 13/051435, November 1972.

45 *without being attacked: Historical Notes of the Hanoi Air Defense Command.*

45 *a B-52 with an SA-2:* The big bomber was able to land safely at U-Tapao. Corona Harvest Report, *USAF Air Operations in Southeast Asia, 1 July 1972–15 August 1973,* vol. 2, p. IV–47.

45 *"... just a SAM indication":* Ibid., p. IV–48.

46 *"... a suspected truck park":* Jim Farmer e-mail, January 2001.

46 *112,000 missions:* Corona Harvest Report, *USAF Air Operations in Southeast Asia, 1 July 1972–15 August 1973,* vol. 2, p. IV–54.

47 *formations—since 1967:* Johnson, End of Tour Report, p. 47.

47 *radars available in the United States:* SAC did not test the B-52 tactics against the SA-2 systems until five days *after* Linebacker II started.

47 *not "on the spot":* The North Vietnamese method of claiming kills is confusing and is connected with Communist ideology and propaganda, but only peripherally with the western concept of shooting down an aircraft. Often a "kill" is claimed when no U.S. aircraft was hit, and other times a "kill" is claimed when a U.S. aircraft was hit but not downed. Additionally, "kill" appears to have been applied on a sliding scale depending in the sophistication of the weapon, i.e. kills claimed small-caliber weapons fired by militia members were more likely to be granted than those of more heavier weapons. A kill "on the spot" was an entirely different matter. "On the spot" meant that the carcass of the aircraft was on the ground

and could be identified. The North Vietnamese understood the difference and clearly attached much significance to kills "on the spot." At the same time, an aircraft that came down in two (or more) parts might be classified as more than one kill "on the spot."

47   *"... the enemy's electronic warfare":* Historical Notes of the Hanoi Air Defense Command.

48   *prior to any large operation:* Johnson, End of Tour Report, p. 46.

48   *"... advantage in firing [SAMs]":* Colonel Theodore Hanna, SAC ADVON Commander, Saigon, End of Tour Report, p. 13.

48   *"... have loyally supported us ...":* Back-channel message, Nixon to Kissinger, 24 November 1972.

48   *second thoughts about the agreement:* On November 24, Le Duc Tho told Kissinger, "the election is over, and from our point of view the war can indeed continue."

49   *"for maximum psychological impact":* Linebacker Study, MACV, p. 138.

49   *existed only on paper:* This unit was apparently the first one scheduled to receive the SA-3, which had not arrived.

50   *preparations to move:* Historical Notes of the Hanoi Air Defense Command.

51   *"... high priority targets":* Linebacker Study, MACV, pp. 139–40.

52   *American POWs:* Malcolm McConnell, *Inside Hanoi's Secret Archives: Solving the MIA Mystery,* p. 201.

Four: "Maximum effort, repeat, maximum effort ..."

53   *in seventy-two hours:* Hartsook, *Air Power Helps Stop the Invasion and End the War,* p. 143.

53   *used B-52s or fighters:* Haig, "Inner Circles," pp. 308–9.

53   *a quick resolution:* Pape, *Bombing to Win,* p. 199.

53   *wait for good weather:* Haig interview.

53   *accepted the plan:* Haig, "Inner Circles," p. 306.

54   *on domestic political grounds:* Laird's opposition to military action was so strong that Kissinger had to set up a special channel to Admiral Moorer so he could work with him without Laird's knowledge. Ibid., pp. 308–9.

54   *signed and then violated:* Zumwalt, *On Watch,* p. 415.

54   *using B-52s over Hanoi:* Linebacker Study, MACV, p. 144.

54   *electronic warfare equipment:* Haig, "Inner Circles," pp. 308–9.

54   *his loneliest decision:* Nixon, *In the Arena,* p. 393.

54   *not reluctant to do so:* Clodfelter, "Nixon and the Air Weapon," p. 167. Nixon later said he regretted not starting the bombing in 1969 after

he first came into office. NBC, *Meet the Press*, April 1988; and Haig 2000 interview.

54 *with nuclear weapons:* Clodfelter, "Nixon and the Air Weapon," pp. 168–69.

55 *returned in January:* Haig, *"Inner Circles,"* p. 300.

55 *protect South Vietnam:* Clodfelter, *Limits of Air Power,* p. 178.

55 *as well as military effect:* Ibid., p. 182.

55 *extend the campaign indefinitely:* The weather would hamper the fighter-bombers with laser-guided bombs that could hit targets in populated areas where B-52s could not bomb. *Joint Chiefs of Staff History, 1972,* p. 668.

56 *"... this target or that one":* Clodfelter, *Limits of Air Power,* p. 190.

56 *until Congress returned:* Corona Harvest Report, *USAF Operations in SEA, 1 July 1972–1 August 1973,* vol. 5, p. 3.

57 *not a military, decision:* Joint Chiefs of Staff History, 1972, p. 668.

57 *SAC Headquarters in Omaha:* Thompson, *To Hanoi and Back,* 264–65 *et passim.*

58 *CEP [circular area probable]:* The definition of an 800-foot CEP: take the center point and draw a circle with a radius of 800 feet; 50 percent of the bombs will hit within that circle.

58 *bombing on a Sunday:* Corona Harvest Report, *USAF Operations in SEA, 1 July 1972–1 August 1973,* vol. 5, p. 13.

58 *in time to support the operations:* After reinforcement, the Air Force began the Linebacker II operation with a total of 135 tankers in the area, which could fly about 131 sorties a day. Ibid., p.16.

59 *2 percent loss rate:* AFGOAS Study, "B-52 Attrition," Section: "High Altitude Penetration Problem," 26 September 1968, p. 7.

59 *"... estimates he passed out":* Most SAC estimates were based on a one-time, low-level nuclear attack, and were never meant to be used for conventional operations. Cordes letter.

59 *notified about the raids:* Johnson Oral History, p. 1.

59 *"... in terms of recommendations":* Ibid., p. 7.

60 *a large number of B-52s:* Even at Andersen the experience with attacks against heavily defended targets in NVN was sparse. McCarthy and Allison, *View from the Rock,* p. 34. Apparently one Andersen aircraft commander had flown a tour in F-4s as a GIB ("guy in back" or back-seater) during Rolling Thunder and he was consulted, but if this is true it was very foolish. His experience would have been useless—indeed perhaps worse than useless, since anti-SAM tactics had changed so much.

60 *"... large amounts of red tape":* Nixon, *R.N.: The Memoirs of Richard Nixon,* p. 390.

60 *Yen Bai and Phuc Yen:* Hopkins, *SAC Bomber Operations,* vol. 4, p. 778.

61 *suited for B-52 attack: Linebacker II Briefing,* undated, probably presented early 1973 at Andersen, p. 32.

61 *MiG airfields were targeted:* Airfields, while they seem to be good targets, are very difficult to knock out. They are spread over a wide area but only a few parts of the airfield are vulnerable—the runways (which are hard), structures and aircraft.

61 *B-5D and G models:* Letter, Grosshuesch, DCS Ops/Plains PACAF, Summary and Analysis of LBII, 9 January 1973.

61 *visiting their families:* General Tran Nhan Memoir, FBIS EAS-88-006, 11 January 1988, p. 55.

62 *airport at Gia Lam:* Baez, *And a Voice to Sing With,* p. 195.

62 *wasted their money:* McCarthy and Allison, *View from the Rock,* p. 11.

64 *not going home:* Ibid., pp. 40–41.

65 *North Vietnamese defenses:* Cordes interview.

65 *"Basketweave" flight paths:* McDonald e-mail, 17 March 2001; also see Thompson, *To Hanoi and Back,* 271–72.

66 *B-52s available for the operation:* 53 Ds and 99 Gs on Andersen and 54 Ds at U-Tapao. McCarthy and Allison, *View from the Rock,* p. 151.

67 *clearance to even see them:* Military personnel are given security clearances based on an assessment of the classification of the types of material they will be handling; for example, if an officer's job requires only a SECRET clearance, he will not be allowed to use or even see TOP SECRET material. In this case, SAC classified the mission planning details at such a high level most of the planners, at least initially, could not view the materials. Even after the operations began, some orders were so highly classified the planners could not see them. Letter, Grosshuesch DCS Ops/Plains PACAAF, Summary and Analysis of LBII, 9 January 1973.

67 *jet stream wind:* Corona Harvest Report, *USAF Operations in SEA, 1 July 1972–1 August 1973,* vol. 5, p. 43.

67 *North Vietnamese defenses: Linebacker II Briefing,* undated, p. 4.

68 *would not be effective:* Corona Harvest Report, *USAF Operations in SEA, 1 July 1972–1 August 1973,* vol. 5, p. 36.

68 *a few degrees in a heading: History of Eighth Air Force, 1 July 1972–30 June 1973,* vol. 1, pp. 15–16 *et passim.*

68 *taking longer to receive:* Cordes to McCarthy letter.

68 *further and further behind:* Ibid.; also, Letter, Grosshuesch DCS Ops/Plains PACAF, Summary and Analysis of LBII, 9 January 1973.

69   *"... beyond three days, if necessary":* Hopkins, *SAC Bomber Operations,* vol. 4, p. 17.

69   *tell their crews any specifics:* Clement, "A Fourth of July in December," p. 26.

70   *"... conduct of this crucial operation":* Corona Harvest Report, *USAF Operations in SEA, 1 July 1972–1 August 1973,* vol. 5, pp. 42–43.

70   *"... more than 3 percent":* Clodfelter, *Limits of Air Power,* p. 188.

Five: "Downtown, where all the lights are bright ..."

72   *crews even more tense:* Clement, "A Fourth of July in December," p. 26.

73   *"... sitting next to you":* Clodfelter, *Limits of Air Power,* p. 186.

73   *not maneuver on the bomb run: History of the 43rd Strategic Wing, July 1972–31 December 1972: Bullet Shot, Part 2, With Emphasis on Linebacker II,* p. 69.

73   *flying into SAM areas:* Corona Harvest Report, *USAF Operations in SEA, 1 July 1972–1 August 1973,* vol. 5, p. 79.

74   *"... the bombs will hit":* Linebacker II Panel Discussion, Maxwell AFB, November 1995.

74   *target study officers:* George B. Allison, "The Bombers Go to Bullseye," p. 234.

74   *just before takeoff:* Ibid., p. 235.

75   *prepare for an attack:* General Tran Nhan Memoir, FBIS EAS-88-006, 11 January 1988, p. 51.

75   *"... taken off from Andersen Airport":* Historical Notes of the Hanoi Air Defense Division. This information was almost certainly from the Soviet trawler off Guam and passed through the Soviet embassy in Hanoi. While American crews were sure that the trawler always passed such information on, it seems this was erratic. Many raids—specifically the eighth night—apparently surprised the North Vietnamese with their timing.

75   *Kep and Hoa Luc:* Torperczer e-mail.

76   *"... credibility at home was concerned":* Baez, *And a Voice to Sing With,* p. 199.

76   *"... tolerances were extremely critical":* Colonel James McCarthy, *43rd Commanders Summary,* p. 3.

76   *"... break to the gunner's left":* Mark Anich, B-52 gunner, e-mail.

77   *all of their flight bags:* B-52 crews' flight bags were large and heavy because they had to carry all of their manuals and a variety of personal equipment with them on each flight.

78   *first of the 28 B-52s:* Only 27 were scheduled to attack. The extra was an airborne spare.

78   *one onlooker remembered:* Pat Hruby e-mail; also see Clement, "A Fourth of July in December," p. 27.

78   *water injection system:* Water injection was used to boost takeoff thrust for heavily loaded bombers and tankers. The water thickened the air in the engine and made it denser and more powerful.

80   *not cause any undue alarm: History of the 307th Strategic Wing, October–December 1972, U-Tapao, Thailand,* p. 52.

84   *device called "Combat Tree":* See Michel, *Clashes,* p. 181 *et passim.*

Six: The Night of the Fan Songs

88   *Dinh repeated the message:* "Fighting the B-52s," *Vietnam Magazine,* April 1996, p. 29.

88   *progress of the raid:* General Tran Nhan Memoir, p. 54.

88   *center of North Vietnam, Hanoi:* The proper transliteration used by the Vietnamese is actually Ha Noi, but since common Western usage is Hanoi, the author will use the single word.

88   *". . . Tran Quoc pagoda":* General Tran Nhan Memoir, p. 51.

89   *air defense staff on the other side:* Ibid., p. 54.

89   *two battalions ready for combat: Historical Notes of the Hanoi Air Defense Division.*

89   *had been in 1967:* Ibid.

89   *electronic emissions:* Lt. Colonel Anton Zlinksy e-mail.

90   *supply them with missions: Historical Notes of the Hanoi Air Defense Division.*

90   *watch the action:* Baez, *And a Voice to Sing With,* p. 204.

91   *intercept the B-52s: Historical Notes of the Hanoi Air Defense Division;* and Torperczer e-mail.

92   *the B-52s' inbound course:* The winds were predicted to be 290 degrees at 85 knots but were actually 280 degrees at 71 knots.

92   *". . . no protection at all":* Craig Mizner e-mail.

93   *virtually windowless:* The EW's station had a very small window that wags called the "day/night indicator."

93   *". . . targets of downtown Hanoi":* Broughton, *Thud Ridge,* p. 21.

95   *confusion as the battle began:* General Tran Nhan Memoir, p. 52.

95   *". . . across the sky by F-4s?":* "Fighting the B-52s"; also, *Historical Notes of the Hanoi Air Defense Division,* December 1972.

96   *"Why haven't they opened fire?":* General Tran Nhan Memoir, p. 54.

96   *4,000th U.S. airplane:* This was by North Vietnamese count. The

actual number of U.S. aircraft losses was about one-fourth of the North Vietnamese claims.

96 *became increasingly tense:* General Tran Nhan Memoir, p. 56.

98 *"... between theory and practice":* Historical Notes of the Hanoi Air Defense Division.

100 *"... force our surrender":* General Tran Nhan Memoir, p. 54.

100 *"... never looked outside again":* Allison, "Bombers Go to Bullseye," p. 223.

102 *"... battalions are launching!":* "The Last Missile," *Nhan Dan,* undated.

103 *"'... we're going home'":* Mulligan, *The Hanoi Commitment,* p. 267.

103 *"... bright as daylight":* "White House Says Raiding in the North Will Go on until There Is an Accord," *New York Times,* 19 December 1972, p. 1.

105 *"... detonate in the air":* General Tran Nhan Memoir, p. 58.

108 *"... a B-52 on the spot":* Ibid., p. 57.

109 *"... carrying on the resistance":* Ibid., p. 59.

109 *"Is it really De Castries?":* Ibid.

111 *damaged the aircraft:* Torperczer e-mail.

111 *for a "MiG damaged":* Red Baron III, Event 11, 18 December 1972.

115 *exploded just off the left wing:* The missile was probably fired by either the 57th or the 93rd Battalion of the 261st Regiment. *History of the 361st Air Defense Division.*

115 *picked up all of the crewmembers:* Corona Harvest Report, *USAF Operations in SEA, 1 July 1972–1 August 1973,* vol. 5, p. 58.

118 *"... 'kill it like a lamb'":* General Tran Nhan Memoir, p. 60.

119 *"... two missiles in close succession":* Ibid., p. 61.

120 *400-pound warhead:* 280 pounds of the SA-2 warhead were high explosive.

122 *"... change the axis of attack":* Clodfelter, *Limits of Air Power,* p. 239.

Seven: The Second Day

123 *"... the people and the Army":* General Tran Nhan Memoir, p. 54.

123 *"... a bit of a joke":* E-mail from Ms. Nguyen Van Phuong, Melbourne, Australia, Hanoi resident in 1972.

124 *last for all of Linebacker II:* General Tran Nhan Memoir, p. 56; also *Historical Notes of the Hanoi Air Defense Division.* Necessity was part of the reason for this allotment of forces. There were only about eight night-qualified MiG-21 pilots.

125 *"... have to work together":* "The Last Missile," *Nhan Dan,* undated.

126   *hit in the post-target turn:* Nalty, *Tactics and Techniques in Electronic Warfare versus North Vietnam*, p. 104.

127   *time for bomb release:* Hopkins, *SAC Bomber Operations*, vol. 4, p. 783.

128   *close to the B-52 operations: Linebacker II Operational Reports*, J-35, Memo 0083-73, p. 8.

128   *made by their flares:* Ibid., p. 7.

128   *". . . cone of fire of the B-52s": History of the 43rd Strategic Wing*, p. 100.

128   *the control agency:* Stations that provided information to the F-4s on MiG locations. Control agencies were Navy radar ships off the coast, Air Force EC-121 surveillance aircraft and ground-based radar and listening posts. Michel, *Clashes*, p. 136 *et passim*.

129   *". . . with their knees knocking":* Haig interview, 19 September 2000.

129   *the anti-war activists:* Herz and Rider, *The Prestige Press and the Christmas Bombing, 1972*, p. 23.

131   *"I can't do anything":* McCarthy Oral History Interview, p. 9.

131   *". . . needling him about it":* Gabreski got 28 air-to-air kills, Meyer 24; additionally, Gabreski was an ace in Korea while Meyer scored just two MiG kills.

132   *". . . dangers of doubtful action":* Regan, *Great Military Disasters*, p. 32.

133   *not seen combat since then: Air Force Official Biographies*, Air Force Leaders website, http://www.af.mil/lib/bio.

134   *". . . a final firm decision":* Cordes to McCarthy letter.

134   *". . . in the planning room":* Ibid.

134   *". . . target and mission planning":* Ibid.

135   *"wall-to-wall SAMs":* Hopkins, *SAC Bomber Operations*, vol. 4, p. 786.

135   *B-52s' jamming systems:* Clement, "A Fourth of July in December," p. 31.

135   *would be court-martialed:* McCarthy and Allison, *View from the Rock*, p. 68.

136   *encouraged to maneuver:* There is no explanation for this change. SAC had not seen the picture of the strikes the night before, so they had no rationale for changing the criteria. One is tempted to say that, since they had no reasons to ban the maneuvering in the first place, they simply came to their senses. *History of the 43rd Strategic Wing, July 1972–31 December 1972: Bullet Shot, Part 2, With Emphasis on Linebacker II*, p. 105.

136   *SAMs seemed heaviest: History of the 307th Strategic Wing, October–December 1972, U-Tapao, Thailand*, p. 65.

137   *". . . hair on your arms":* Ibid., p. 65.

138 *a total of nine minutes: Historical Notes of the Hanoi Air Defense Division.* The White House assigned the Hanoi international radio transmitter at Me Tri, even though SAC's calculations showed that if nine cells (27 B-52s) attacked it they had only a 32 percent probability of damaging the transmitter. The same calculation showed that two flights (8 F-4s) that used laser-guided bombs had a 99.6 percent chance of hitting the target. Nevertheless, B-52s were assigned the target initially but when they missed it, F-4s attacked with laser-guided bombs and knocked it out. Corona Harvest Report, *USAF Operations in SEA, 1 July 1972–1 August 1973,* vol. 5, p. 90.

138 *no B-52s were hit:* Ibid., p. 101.

138 *"one of the greatest moments of my life":* History of the 307th Strategic Wing, p. 67.

Eight: The Slaughter of the Gs

139 *"... scrupulous manner at all levels":* General Tran Nhan Memoir, p. 55.

139 *a few hours' sleep:* Ibid.

140 *the south relatively unprotected: Historical Notes of the Hanoi Air Defense Division.*

141 *built-in target simulator:* General Tran Nhan Memoir, p. 56.

142 *"... been so short":* "The Last Missile," *Nhan Dan,* undated.

142 *"... missiles in a salvo": Historical Notes of the Hanoi Air Defense Division,* December 1972. Soviet doctrine called for firing three missiles at a jamming target, but the NVN often fired less. In this case, it seems that from December 19 to 20 they were firing only two missiles at a time, and occasionally only one. The Soviets had earlier noted this with some disgust. They had tried to explain to the North Vietnamese that firing three missiles at a jamming target not only increased the chances of a kill but was cost-effective, since there was virtually no chance of scoring a kill firing three missiles singly. The North Vietnamese, the Soviets noted, never understood the concept. Bodo Seifert e-mail.

143 *about forty missiles:* This computation is based on both interviews with SA-2 battalion commanders and North Vietnamese records, which indicate that the two technical battalions produced about 300 missiles during the Linebacker II operation. The North Vietnamese missile assemblers wrote messages on the side of the missiles, such as "Revenge for our Ha Noi compatriots," while at Andersen and U-Tapao, U.S. maintenance crews wrote messages on the sides of their bombs.

143   *technical battalion, the 80th:* The 261st's technical battalion was the 85th.

143   *as darkness approached:* General Tran Nhan Memoir, p. 55.

144   *"... seemed to be behind":* Cordes to McCarthy letter.

145   *"... bombing of the North":* Project CHECO: Johnson, *Linebacker Operations September–December, 1972,* p. 70.

145   *all but assured":* Clement, "A Fourth of July in December," p. 33.

145   *bomb-release problem:* McCarthy and Allison, *View from the Rock,* p. 70.

146   *"... gut reaction or impulse":* Ibid., p. 97.

146   *"... one point in the sky":* *Linebacker II Operational Report,* pp. 15–16.

146   *"... known SAM sites":* Clodfelter, *Limits of Air Power,* p. 237.

147   *bombed on its last mission:* Geloneck, "At the Hands of the Enemy," p. 21.

148   *far from the sites:* General Tran Nhan Memoir, p. 56.

148   *"... change their tactics":* Ibid., p. 57.

149   *closed on the target:* Ibid., p. 57.

149   *"... end of the war for me":* Geloneck, "At the Hands of the Enemy," p. 22.

150   *relaxed the headquarters staff:* General Tran Nhan Memoir, p. 58.

150   *"... —not SAC procedure, but ...":* Clement, "A Fourth of July in December," p. 35.

152   *continued on the bomb run:* Two MiG-21s had to land at about this time and all the missile sites ceased firing for a short period. *Historical Notes of the Hanoi Air Defense Division.*

153   *"... the previous two nights":* General Tran Nhan Memoir, p. 58.

154   *recall the second raid:* Johnson, *Called to Command,* p. 206.

157   *"... SAC could do the job":* Phone conversation with General Cordes, 24 May 2000, 12:30 EST.

157   *send the G models to attack:* McCarthy and Allison, *View from the Rock,* p. 85.

157   *"... loss of crewmembers and aircraft":* Initially the author questioned whether this conversation took place between Wave Two and Wave Three or at some later point. After two letters and three phone interviews with General Harry Cordes (30 and 31 October 2000) and numerous e-mail exchanges with George Allison, who had quoted Cordes in *View from the Rock,* the author has concluded this represents the discussion that did take place between the recall of Wave Two and the decision to send the Gs of Wave Three.

157   *"... turned back by an enemy action":* Letter, General Glenn Martin to McCarthy; and *View from the Rock,* p. 85.

157 *"... beepers on our guard channel":* UHF freq. 243.0 was monitored by all American aircrews for emergency messages. The "beepers" were emergency locators in the parachute that went off when an ejection seat was fired.

158 *in full auto-track:* General Tran Nhan Memoir, p. 59.

159 *mutual jamming coverage:* Corona Harvest Report, *USAF Operations in SEA, 1 July 1972–1 August 1973,* vol. 5, p. 121.

159 *only partially resupplied:* General Tran Nhan Memoir, pp. 58–59.

159 *missiles to down Olive 01:* Ibid., p. 59.

160 *roared off into the overcast:* "The Last Missile," *Nhan Dan,* undated.

161 *would have been decapitated:* Mize interview.

162 *"... instead of a narrow corridor":* Linebacker II Panel Discussion. Some crewmembers remember General Sullivan being at these sessions, though he does not mention it.

162 *"... not a very good thing to do ...":* Ibid. It was quite a serious breach of the chain of command to skip one's superior and send a message directly to the next level of the command.

162 *"... before he sent it to SAC":* Ibid. For further conformation, see Message, Sullivan to Johnson, SSO, 22/0806Z, December 1972; and Hopkins, *SAC Bomber Operations,* vol. 4, p. 151.

163 *out of the peace talks: New York Times,* 22 December 1972, p.1.

Nine: Dien Bien Phu of the Air

164 *only thirty-five missiles:* General Tran Nhan Memoir, p. 59.

165 *"... increase the number of missiles":* "The Last Missile," *Nhan Dan,* undated.

166 *"... our ECM wasn't effective":* McCarthy, *43rd SRW Commander's Oral History,* p. 10.

166 *go on indefinitely:* Hopkins, *SAC Bomber Operations,* vol. 4, p. 772.

167 *cutting back on its attacks:* The president was not notified either, but General Haig said that the White House would not have expected to be notified, "leaving these things to SAC." Nevertheless, the SAC staff complained regularly about "Washington" involvement. Haig and Cordes interviews; Allison e-mails.

167 *"... in some detail [why not]":* Message, Meyer to Vogt, SSO SAC to AFSSO 7AF, 210220Z December 1972.

167 *"... [Wild Weasels] are concerned":* Message, Vogt to Meyer, AFSSO 7AF to AFSSO SAC, 210540Z December 72.

167 *all to come from U-Tapao:* To rationalize this cut in the number of B-52s raiding the capital, SAC said later they had planned a maximum effort only for the first three nights, and they would have to

stand down for maintenance on the Guam-based B-52s for a longer operation. In fact, Andersen flew thirty B-52 sorties the fourth day, but all of Andersen's missions were sent to South Vietnam where there was no risk of loss.

168   *a "feet wet" exit:* Hopkins, *SAC Bomber Operations,* vol. 4, p. 133.

173   *not working and must be stopped:* In a phone interview on November 5, Admiral Gayler told the author, "General Haig was right, that was certainly my view ... and I not only thought it, I said so.... My feelings were that bombers were an inappropriate weapon.... I recall I recommended not once but several times that the bombing be stopped." A letter followed the interview, January 2001.

174   *"... certainly continue to bomb":* Haig interviews, August 1999 and September 2000.

174   *"... change their [tactics]:* Nixon, *R.N.: A Memoir,* p. 737.

174   *to Eglin Air Force Base:* McCarthy and Allison, *View from the Rock,* p. 83.

175   *with virtually no risk:* Thompson, *To Hanoi and Back,* p. 288; also Jane Geloneck e-mail.

175   *"fear shedding":* Steven Pressfield, *Gates of Fire* (1998), p. 129.

175   *"... all that fear out in the open":* Clodfelter, *Limits of Air Power,* p. 195.

175   *had been officially acknowledged:* McCarthy and Allison, *View from the Rock,* pp. 98–99.

175   *fly early in the operation:* Johnson, End of Tour Report, p, 46. This was below the August 1972 rate of DNIF, so it is difficult to draw conclusions. See also *History of the 307th Strategic Wing, October–December 1972,* p. 99; and see Appendix for a fuller discussion of this issue.

176   *"... asking for problems, etc.":* Moore, response to Zetner questionnaire.

177   *a complete absence of signals:* Project CHECO Report, *Linebacker Operations, September–December 1972,* p. 66.

177   *knock out site VN-549:* McCarthy and Allison, *View from the Rock;* also see Corona Harvest Report, *USAF Air Operations in Southeast Asia, 1 July 1972–15 August 1973,* vol. 2, pp. IV–282–4.

177   *77th battalion of the 257th regiment:* It is difficult to correlate U.S. locations for their numbered SAM (VN-xxx) sites with North Vietnamese battalion numbers because of the large scale and imprecise location of battalion sites on the NVN maps.

178   *some as far as ten miles:* U.S. fliers thought they pointed to the target, but the North Vietnamese accounts show the importance of chaff corridors. Even the narrow chaff corridors were distracting to their defenses and they never associated the corridors with targets, perhaps because

they just pointed to Hanoi. See *Chaff Effectiveness in Support of Line-backer II Operations,* Briefing for the SAC Director of Operations, undated (probably mid-1973), slides 6 and 7.

178   *". . . to the water and get rescued": History of the 307th Strategic Wing, October–December 1972, U-Tapao, Thailand,* p. 79.

179   *". . . you're going to do it right":* Ibid., pp. 80–81.

179   *the North Vietnamese off guard: Historical Notes of the Hanoi Air Defense Division.*

179   *get organized and fire its missiles:* The 363rd had also sent two battalions to reinforce Hanoi. *Historical Notes of the Hanoi Air Defense Division.*

180   *". . . 'Dien Bien Phu of the Air'":* Article, *Nhan Dan,* date unknown.

Ten: Holding On

181   *a classic "milk run": History of the 307th Strategic Wing, October–December 1972,* p. 81

181   *rather than one large one: Linebacker II Briefing,* undated (probably presented early 1973 at Andersen), p. 14.

182   *commanders returned to the party:* McCarthy and Allison, *View from the Rock,* p. 110.

182   *decorations into the pool:* Several crewmembers who were present have confirmed this story.

183   *load into the B-52: Linebacker II Briefing,* undated (probably presented early 1973 at Andersen), p. 16.

184   *crewmembers yelled "SAM, SAM": History of the 307th Strategic Wing, October–December 1972,* p. 84.

184   *focus to residential areas: Historical Notes of the Hanoi Air Defense Division.* There is some doubt that this assessment was made at the time. The official history was written many years after the campaign when the NVN had complete access to U.S. accounts of the battle, and it may be that the North Vietnamese predictions at the time were not as complete and accurate as they are portrayed in their history.

185   *with a remarkable voice:* Baez, *And a Voice to Sing With,* pp. 215–16; also see Taylor, "Hanoi Under the Bombing: Shelters, Rubble and Death," *New York Times,* 7 January 1973.

185   *unjammable for the past year:* The newer SA-2 radar, known as the Fan Song F (Mod 5) had a more powerful downlink and coded transponder. See Hopkins, *SAC Bomber Operations,* vol. 4, pp. 224–25.

186   *other parts of the SA-2 system:* Corona Harvest Report, *USAF Air Operations in Southeast Asia, 1 July 1972–15 August 1973,* vol. 2, p. IV–280; Hopkins, *SAC Bomber Operations,* vol. 4, pp. 169 and 224.

186 *"... support for your forces":* Hopkins, *SAC Bomber Operations,* vol. 4, p. 200.

187 *had been vastly exaggerated:* Corona Harvest Report, *USAF Operations in SEA, 1 July 1972–1 August 1973,* vol. 5, p. 176. There was originally some question as to whether JCS would support another series of strikes against Hanoi targets. Bad weather had prevented good photos over most of the targets until several days into the operation (for all the hype, the sophisticated SR-71 was useless in bad weather) and, without photos, SAC had made damage estimates based on their predictions of bombing accuracy. SAC's damage predictions were badly off, and the limited amount of damage made the Chiefs support a post-Christmas bombing of Hanoi and Haiphong. They also showed that there had been a great deal of collateral damage. The poor results were a combination of poor force allocation (too many Gs were assigned to targets that needed to be heavily bombed), grossly inaccurate estimates of bombing accuracy by the SAC staff, and normal bombing errors. Corona Harvest Report, *USAF Operations in SEA, 1 July 1972–1 August 1973,* vol. 5, p. 161; and Corona Harvest Report, *USAF Air Operations in Southeast Asia, 1 July 1972–15 August 1973,* vol. 2, p. IV–234.

188 *holding out a little longer:* What the North Vietnamese *politburo* was thinking at this time is unknown, but there are many hints. They almost certainly thought they had defeated the B-52s, for the time being at least. The heavy losses and failure of the Americans to return were ample evidence for North Vietnamese who might have been making this argument.

188 *planning was left to Eighth:* Hopkins, *SAC Bomber Operations,* vol. 4, p. 754.

189 *110 aircraft for the mission:* 52 escort/MiG CAP; for SAM suppression the Air Force supplied 10 hunter-killer teams of 10 F-105s and F-4Es and the Navy 8 A-7 Iron Hand aircraft; for jamming, the Air Force had 3 EB-66s, while the Navy had 2 EA-6Bs, 2 EA-6As, and 2 EK-3As over the Gulf of Tonkin. Corona Harvest Report, *USAF Operations in SEA, 1 July 1972–1 August 1973,* vol. 5, p. 205.

189 *F-111s would attack SAM sites:* SAM sites were considered unsuitable targets for F-111 because the F-111 bomb strings had long spaces between each bomb and it was difficult to get a concentration on the target. The F-111s were best suited for targets that were visible on radar (which SAM sites were not). Still, according to the North Vietnamese accounts, their harassment value was considerable, much greater than the U.S. knew.

189 *needed to be in the target area: Linebacker II Briefing,* undated (probably presented early 1973 at Andersen), p. 32.

189   *moved back by three hours:* Corona Harvest Report, *USAF Operations in SEA, 1 July 1972–1 August 1973,* vol. 5, p. 193.

190   *key to the North Vietnamese defenses:* Ibid., p. 195.

190   *in from different directions: History of the 307th Strategic Wing, October–December 1972,* p. 85.

190   *". . . in the lives of his children":* Hopkins, *SAC Bomber Operations,* vol. 4, p. 769.

192   *". . . Air Defense Headquarters quite tense": Historical Notes of the Hanoi Air Defense Division.*

192   *saved for the B-52s:* "Keeping the Promise," newspaper article.

192   *start of the campaign: Historical Notes of the Hanoi Air Defense Division.*

Eleven: The Eighth Night

193   *the same north of Haiphong:* The third target area, Thai Nguyen, had very limited defenses and did not get a chaff corridor.

194   *they turned northwest:* After the mission Craig Mizner received notification that he had been given an "in-flight violation" for flying too close to Hainan Island. When he checked further, he found that there was a highly classified map that the crews had not seen that had a "no fly zone" with a radius of fifteen miles around Hainan Island. The crews had not been told because they did not have a "need to know."

195   *three-point manual guidance: Historical Notes of the Hanoi Air Defense Division.*

195   *The second of the 76th's missiles: History of the 361st Air Defense Division.* American sources (Hopkins, *SAC Bomber Operations,* vol. 4, p. 815) state that Ebony 02 was hit by four SAMs from Site VN-271, and that the post-target turn put the cell in "an ideal position for VN 271 to hit it" because it was broadside to the site. Since a SAM site could fire no more than three missiles at any one time and North Vietnamese firing doctrine called for never firing more that two, their account is more persuasive.

196   *In the tail of the aircraft:* Notes on emergency escape from the gunner's compartment provided by Peter (Scotty) Burns, e-mail.

197   *devastated the aircraft:* There is some question as to which SAM battalion hit Ash 01. Both the 86th of the 274th and the 93rd of the 261st claimed hits on B-52s, but the time is off, by twenty minutes in the case of the 86th and about twelve minutes in the case of the 93rd. *History of the 361st Air Defense Division.* Alternately, is it possible (but unlikely) that a different battalion hit it.

201   *5 percent on earlier missions:* A post-war U.S. study said that: "the proper employment of chaff ... was probably the most important single factor in enhancing B-52 survivability. .... [N]ot one of the B-52s lost during Linebacker II operations was in the main portion of the chaff cloud when hit." *Chaff Effectiveness in Support of Linebacker II Operations,* Briefing for the SAC Director of Operations, undated (probably mid-1973).

201   *increase in "fake B-52s":* Historical Notes of the Hanoi Air Defense Division. Four B-52s hit and three lost: Corona Harvest Report, *USAF Operations in SEA, 1 July 1972–1 August 1973,* vol. 5, p. 219.

202   *used them again:* Borden interview.

203   *"... in this outstanding achievement":* Hopkins, *SAC Bomber Operations,* vol. 4, p. 228.

203   *reducing B-52 losses:* The support the Navy provided to the B-52 raids on Haiphong supplemented Air Force support but Haiphong's defenses had been reduced to sending missile battalions to Hanoi, and in the event Haiphong's missile battalions were much less efficient than Hanoi's. It should also be noted that when the Navy supported B-52 strikes in the Hanoi area, there was no difference in B-52 losses—in fact, the Navy supported the B-52 operations of the third wave on the third night, when the B-52s suffered their heaviest losses. *Navy ECM Support of B-52 Strikes during Linebacker II Operations,* Memorandum prepared by D. E. Muir, Scientific Analyst for Op-50, for the Director of Aviation Plans and Requirements, January 1973.

Twelve: The Last Nights of Christmas

205   *the 72nd fired two missiles:* "A Promise Kept," article, undated.

206   *"... returned to base":* Torperczer, *The Air War over North Vietnam,* p. 51; and later e-mails.

208   *90 missiles that night:* History of SAC Recce Operations, FY 1973, Historical Study no. 127, p. 44.

208   *worst night they had experienced:* "History of the 307th Strategic Wing, October–December 1972, p. 89.

208   *"... losses we are experiencing":* Corona Harvest Report, *USAF Air Operations in Southeast Asia, 1 July 1972–15 August 1973,* vol. 2, p. IV–246.

209   *Kham Thien Street:* "Newsman in Hanoi Visits Street of Ruins," *New York Times,* 29 December 1972, p. 1.

209   *did not have to fly:* "The War Is Suddenly Grim for B-52 Fliers," *New York Times,* 30 December 1972, p. 1.

209   *cutting off funds immediately: New York Times,* 4 January 1973, p. 1.

210   *known as LORAN:* Long Range Navigation. Aircraft with LORAN systems were recognizable by a white "towel bar" antenna along the spine of the aircraft. They were mounted on F-4s from several wings and the RF-4Cs of the 432nd TRW.

210   *LORAN stations in Thailand:* The Master LORAN Station was located in Satthip, Thailand, close to U-Tapao but almost six hundred miles from Hanoi. Corona Harvest Report, *USAF Air Operations in Southeast Asia, 1 July 1972–15 August 1973,* vol. 2, p. IV–10.

211   *flying in tight formation:* The tight formation was necessary for bombing accuracy.

211   *vulnerable to SAMs:* One can imagine the "bomb burst" effect when a SAM popped out of the clouds heading for a group of a dozen or more fighters in formation.

211   *four F-105s on one mission:* Thompson, *To Hanoi and Back,* pp. 103–4.

211   *about the dangerous missions:* For one of the combat wing commander's views of LORAN, see Scott Smith, 432nd TRW Commander, End of Tour Report, pp. 18–23. For post-war analysis, see *Linebacker Operations, September–December 1972,* pp. 43–44.

211   *"'. . . we're going to do it!'":* Project CHECO Report, *Linebacker Overview of the First 120 Days,* p. 64.

211   *inertial navigation system: Linebacker II Operational Report,* p. 19.

211   *". . . damage level during Linebacker II":* Project CHECO Report, *Linebacker Operations, September–December 1972,* p. 44.

212   *visually and accurately: Linebacker Study, January 20,* MACV, p. VI–12.

212   *and missed badly:* Corona Harvest Report, *USAF Air Operations in Southeast Asia, 1 July 1972–15 August 1973,* vol. 2, p. IV–244.

212   *and one shot down:* Even the LGB hits did not put the radio station out of business; the North Vietnamese had an alternate transmitter, and Hanoi Radio continued to function. Thompson, *To Hanoi and Back,* p. 310.

212   *a few SAMs were reported:* Only 23, according to *Linebacker II Briefing,* undated (probably presented early 1973 at Andersen), p. 25.

213   *". . . running out of SAMs": History of the 307th Strategic Wing, October–December 1972,* p. 96.

213   *two prowling F-4s: Project Red Baron III,* p. 303.

214   *would come out well:* In fact, U.S. intelligence said that Camerota's radio calls were a North Vietnamese trap. There was never an attempt to rescue him.

Thirteen: Dénouement

217   *had returned to Paris:* The House Democratic Caucus voted to cut off all funds to military operations in Southeast Asia, contingent on prisoner release and safe withdrawal of U.S. troops, and the Senate Democrats followed by a vote of 36 to 12. "Congress Critics of War Threaten to Fight Funding," *New York Times,* 3 January 1973, p. 1; and "Senate Democrats, 36–12, Back Action to End War," *New York Times,* 5 January 1973, p. 1.

217   *". . . forced Hanoi back to the table":* Kissinger, *Memo for the President, Meeting with Secretaries Rogers and Laird and Admiral Moorer,* 4 January 1973.

218   *". . . forthcoming events unfolded":* Linebacker Study, MACV, p. 156.

218   *". . . stonewall us again":* Message HAKTO 02, 082010Z January 1973.

219   *". . . could prove suicidal . . .":* Message HAKTO 05, 091620Z January 1973.

219   *". . . any more concessions . . .":* Memo, Kissinger to Nixon, 11 January 1973.

219   *Thieu agreed to sign:* Message, White House to Kissinger, 2223000Z January 1973.

220   *coming to visit Andersen:* History of Eighth Air Force, 1 July 1972–30 June 1973, vol. 1 (23 August 1974), p. 71.

220   *". . . weren't meant to last":* Meyer's exact comments at this meeting were remembered slightly differently by the crewmembers interviewed by the author, but they all agreed on the thrust of his remarks.

220   *undercurrent of muttering:* One crewmember said, "We did NOT actually 'Boo him off the stage.' He WAS a four star. But he got the message." The author considers this scenario much more likely. No matter how much the crewmembers disliked Meyer and his policies, he was still CINCSAC; it is most unlikely (but not impossible) that there would be any loud, overt show of disrespect.

220   *award for heroism:* To this day, the award sticks in the craw of virtually all of the LBII crewmembers the author interviewed. One said, "All McCarthy did was ride . . . across Hanoi and he got the Air Force Cross. The hundreds of the rest of us were there and were working and if we got the DFC, we were lucky."

220   *"SAC's finest hour":* General Johnson also said that the missions showed SAC's contingency planning was "the best in the world." *Tropic Topics* (Andersen AFB newspaper), 12 March 1973, p. 8.

220   *Bullet Shot crews home:* Hoortuchi e-mail.

221   *"distinctly frosty":* A maintenance enlisted man, Ron Shively, had a particularly poignant memory: "I ran into an old high school friend

who had been on a flight crew during Linebacker II. ... My friend told me that he and his group were expecting a 'well done' speech, but in fact they had gotten chewed out en masse, being told that the reason several of the BUFFs were lost was because they [the flight crews] weren't being professional." E-mail from Ron Shively.

221 *would be repercussions:* It appears that, despite what was said to the crews, both the SAC staff and General Meyer agreed that the tactics were bad. In his January visit, General Meyer apparently admitted to the senior staff on Guam that SAC's stereotyped tactics were partially responsible for the heavy losses, that SAC "had put too much dependence on ECM," and confirmed what he had told Haig: "the third day we had rather high losses *because of the planning process.*" General Meyer did not share these views with the crews, perhaps understandably. McCarthy Oral History, p. 10.

221 *B-52 commanders at Andersen: History of the 43rd Strategic Wing, July 1972–31 December 1972: Bullet Shot, Part 2, With Emphasis on Linebacker II,* pp. 140–41.

221 *returned to U.S. custody:* McConnell, *Inside Hanoi's Secret Archives,* p. 62.

221 *shortest time as prisoners:* There were several tactical crews shot down during Linebacker II who spent an equally short time as POWs. Indeed, several returned to the U.S. before they would have if they had served a normal tour and had not been shot down.

222 *bombed by accident:* At the time Admiral Moorer showed the senators the picture, the Air Force still did not know what the plan produced.

223 *four-hour break between raids: Crew Comments and Recommendations on Tactics Used on Compression Missions,* Andersen AFB, Guam, 7 January 1973, p. 3, 1.g. (1).

224 *"... rid of the warlords":* Worden, *Rise of the Fighter Generals,* p. 211.

224 *all but disappeared:* Ibid., p. 219.

224 *concern to the Air Force:* Lt. General Glenn Martin interview.

225 *"leaving the base without permission":* There is no evidence for this charge. Diefenbach, in an interview with the author, denied it happened.

225 *The Air Force staff:* Drenkowski says that the Air Force Chief of Staff, General David Jones, took a personal interest in the response. Given the "clout" of the *Armed Forces Journal* at this time, it is certainly plausible that Jones was involved.

226 *criticized himself:* Schemmer actually gave himself a "dart" for the story: *Armed Forces Journal* has a small section of "darts" and "laurels" for bad and good information.

227 *"... and probably dishonest":* Schemmer letter, 13 September 1999.

227 *"... at the highest level":* In one interview with the author Mr. Schemmer said he talked to the AF Chief of Staff, General Jones, but in a later interview he said he talked to the Air Force Vice Chief of Staff.

227 *"... classification of source documents":* Castle, *One Day Too Long,* p. 180.

228 *"... second and third days ...":* Col. James McCarthy, *43rd SRW Commander's Report.*

228 *"... later proved us out ...":* McCarthy Oral History, 11 April 1975, p. 8.

228 *"... change in tactics ...":* Ibid., pp. 10–11.

228 *"... losses on the third day ...":* History of the *43rd Strategic Wing, July 1972–31 December 1972: Bullet Shot, Part 2, With Emphasis on Linebacker II,* p. 137.

228 *"... third day's losses":* Ibid., p. 138.

228 *"... predict our bomber tactics":* Ibid., p. 139.

228 *then on to SAC: Crew Comments and Recommendations on Tactics Used on Compression Missions,* 7 January 1973.

228 *"... allegations of poor tactics":* Letter, McCarthy to Flynn, July 1977. Later McCarthy's co-author Allison denied that the *Soldier of Fortune* article had any impact on *View from the Rock,* telling the author, "Our writing goal was a done deal, long before the article burst on the scene." In fact, *View from the Rock* was published in 1979, two years *after* Drenkowski's article.

229 *Colonel Billy Shackelford:* Shackelford e-mail.

229 *"... planner and aviator alike ...":* McCarthy and Allison, *View from the Rock,* p. 97.

229 *"... The opposite is true":* Ibid., p. 158.

230 *"... not appear to be valid ...":* McCarthy also tried to give examples of SAC's willingness to delegate authority but had to settle for pointing out that the local commanders could authorize the B-52 tail gunners to flash a light at the bomber behind them to show their position.

230 *principals did not contribute:* Unfortunately, General Meyer died in 1977, apparently without leaving any written recollections of Linebacker II.

230 *within SAC were expunged:* Allison e-mail. Allison at first denied cutting or modifying any of his source documents until he learned that the author had copies of the originals, then admitted there had been changes.

230 *Air Force chain of command:* The Air Force Historical Research Agency at Maxwell has a large number of "vetting" letters from various Air Force generals commenting on the manuscript.

231   *"... last U.S. battle of the Vietnam War": View from the Rock* was followed by other Air Force apologias repeating that Linebacker II was "SAC's finest hour" and the mantra, "B-52 losses were far lower than had been anticipated." Occasional popular magazine articles written about Linebacker II are basically repackaging of *View from the Rock* and invariably repeat that the SAC staff did a superb job of planning and executing the operation.

Bibliographical Note

Facts are necessary—if not sufficient—for a book like this, and Maxwell Air Force Base in Alabama is the place to begin to find the facts of the American side of Linebacker II. At Maxwell, the Air Force Historical Record Agency—the AFHRA—and adjoining Air University Library have most of the American official military documents that have been written about Linebacker II. Both have a number of Air Force official histories that provide the details of the missions, targets, losses, etc. The AFHRA also has all of the wing histories, of varying usefulness. Sadly, the histories from the Andersen units—Eighth Air Force, the 43rd SW, and the 72nd SW—are in great measure propaganda, very similar to North Vietnamese histories, meant to extol the virtues of the leadership rather than to offer a real history of the operation. Fortunately, U-Tapao's 307th Strategic Wing History is exactly the opposite. It is certainly the finest wing history I have ever read, and the Wing Historian deserves a great deal of credit for this work. The AFHRA also has a large number of messages, reports, studies, official histories, and other paperwork generated by the United States Air Force during this period, as well as a few U.S. Navy reports and some photographs, mainly from Air Force reconnaissance aircraft. The Air University Library has a number of personal accounts of the operation as papers written by students who were Linebacker II veterans. At the AFHRA, Archie Defante and the rest of the staff were unfailingly helpful, as was Dr. Shirley Brooks Laseter and her staff at the Maxwell Library.

I should note that the Maxwell resources have already been heavily mined, and the researcher might find little new material.

However, more documents are being declassified, so there is always the potential for new information.

Another place that has some unique information about the American military part of Linebacker II is the Air Force History Office at Bolling Air Force Base in Washington, D.C. Dr. Wayne Thompson, author of the excellent book *To Hanoi and Back,* as well as numerous other works, and the librarians, Yvonne Kinkaid and Vicky Crone, were as always generous with their time. The National Archives in College Park, Maryland, were the source of most of the messages and memos between President Nixon, Henry Kissinger, Alexander Haig and others.

Several books proved especially useful. The section on Linebacker II in Mark Clodfelter's classic book, *The Limits of Air Power,* as well as several of his articles and a personal interview were very helpful. Colonel R. Michael Worden's excellent *The Rise of the Fighter Generals: The Problem of Air Force Leadership, 1945–1982* documented and quantified the bomber-fighter pilot rivalry that was the cause of many of the problems that arose in Linebacker II. Every Air Force officer knew that the rivalry and internecine conflict existed and was in many ways the central issue in the Air Force from its founding until well into the 1980s, but knowledge is different from proof. Prior to Colonel Worden's book virtually all of the evidence of this rivalry was anecdotal rather than scholarly, but *The Rise of the Fighter Generals* has put an end to all that. Anyone interested in the history of the United States Air Force as an organization and who wants to understand Air Force decision making from its founding is in Colonel Worden's debt.

Another book I must comment on is Joan Baez's book *And a Voice to Sing With.* Ms. Baez was very anti-war, but I found her long chapter describing her time in Hanoi during Linebacker II moving, amusing and profound.

I should note that in my judgment Herz and Rider's book, *The Christmas Bombing and the Prestige Press,* gives a mistaken impression of the press coverage of Linebacker II. I read this book before I read the newspaper articles from U.S. newspapers, especially the *New York Times* and *Washington Post,* and expected to find the reporting highly prejudiced. Instead, I found the news articles to be, on the whole, quite reasonable and factual. The editorial coverage, on the other hand, was quite scathing, but that is the nature of editorials. One should also note that Nixon and his staff eschewed any attempts to counter these editorials, feeling that it would be counterproductive.

The first-person accounts of the American and Vietnamese participants in the operation are the heart of this book. These first-person accounts come from letters, e-mails, and interviews, often a combination of both, and the participants range from high-ranking officials in Washington and generals in Omaha to the ordinary crewmen on both sides.

I was especially fortunate to have Brigadier General Glenn R. Sullivan's son, Ray Sullivan, and General Sullivan's wife, Nadine, give me full access to General Sullivan's pictures, letters, and tapes. If there was a single hero of the Linebacker II it was General Sullivan, a man who exhibited real moral courage—the willingness to express unpopular views and say what needs to be said. Many crewmembers probably owe him their lives, but General Sullivan, like Dowding and Park after the Battle of Britain, was not well treated. One of the most illuminating pieces of information in General Sullivan's estate was a tape of General Sullivan, General Bill Maxson and two other U-Tapao commanders discussing Linebacker II very frankly at a seminar at Maxwell Air Force Base in 1995. Hopefully a full transcript of this tape will be released in the near future. I have also used three excellent and as-yet-unpublished memoirs written by General Maxson and two B-52 crewmembers, Bob Certain and Bill Beavers. Certain's memoir is tentatively titled *Out of the Depths* and hopefully will be published soon.

I was able to correspond with about 50 B-52 crewmembers, including 30 from Andersen and 20 from U-Tapao. All of these were important and many are quoted directly, but I must give special thanks to Gerald Hortuchi, who provided many of the names of the people I contacted, as well as to Air Force Major John Zetner, who provided me with more names, as well as comments and survey results from a paper he was working on at the Air Command and Staff College. I would also like to thank Craig Mizner and his Linebacker II crew, E-57 from Carswell Air Force Base, who in their "electric BUFF" answered so many of my questions ranging from where the crews ate to the minutiae of radar offset aim points. Some of the B-52 aircrews' families became interested in the project and told their stories, as well as providing the names of other crewmembers. I am grateful for their help and cooperation in describing a period of time that was, for many, very painful.

I was fortunate to have many senior SAC officers who were willing to share their experiences. Here, for the first time, are accounts of the commanders at U-Tapao, then Colonels Bill V. Brown, Don Davis, and the aforementioned Bill Maxson. All were very frank and open with me in telling their stories and filling in many gaps. Their wing bore the brunt of the losses and, despite the risk to their careers, they, along with General Sullivan, tried and eventually did change things. I am happy to say that all were promoted to general after Linebacker II.

At SAC headquarters, Andy Borden was very helpful, as well as two other colonels on the staff who had access to the meetings and personalities, but who requested anonymity in exchange for their observations. I have respected that request.

Unfortunately, a very small number of the senior SAC senior officers withdrew their cooperation when they found that this book was not going to be more gilding of SAC's Linebacker II legends or their own personal reputations. Several became resentful, and their attitudes made it clear to me why the reaction to Dana Drenkowski's articles was so violent. I was also taken aback at how much these officers still resented the fighter forces. This clearly played a huge part in how Linebacker II was fought and made it possible, if not easier, for me to understand why SAC did not consult with Seventh Air Force on how to penetrate the North Vietnamese defenses around Hanoi. It was not a pleasant revelation.

Another unpleasant revelation was that several people, especially one low-ranking officer from the Air Force Staff at the Pentagon during the operation, have since tried to take credit for many of the tactical changes after Night Four. These self-aggrandizing individuals, despite their claims, had no influence on the changes.

Some of the oral accounts shed genuine new light on the operation. Among these are General Haig's account of the lack of support for the bombing within the Nixon administration and in the military, especially once the battle had started. Additionally, General Haig tells for the first time his story of the reactions in the White House during the period of the heaviest losses (Nights Three and Four). In my judgment, General Haig's perseverance was mainly responsible for what the bombing achieved.

The "end of tour" reports from General John Meyer, CINCSAC, and General Pete Sianis, whose SAC Operations Directorate was responsible for the planning of the first few nights of raids, remain classified. Either or both would shed considerable light on the planning and decision-making process at SAC. Some of the other participants—General Glenn W. Martin and General Gerald W. Johnson, to name two—did give Air Force Oral History Interviews, but the questioning was less than critical (since the interviews were voluntary and conducted by lower-ranking personnel, this is understandable). Unfortunately, these two and most of the other main military participants on the U.S side have died without having to face serious interviews with follow-up questions or to respond to legitimate criticisms—in short, to explain why they acted the way they did during the operation. For this reason I am especially grateful to those senior officials who allowed me to ask some hard questions and who responded to them—General Haig, Admiral Noel Gayler, Generals Brown, Davis, and Maxson, General Harry Cordes from SAC Headquarters, and others.

I am also indebted to Dana Drenkowski who told me the full story of how he wrote his articles and the Air Force reaction, and to Benjamin Schemmer, former editor of *Armed Forces Journal,* for sharing with me his vivid recollections of the Dana Drenkowski article and its aftermath.

FOR A FULL UNDERSTANDING of Linebacker II, a visit to Hanoi is essential, and I am grateful to Linda Shiner, the editor of the Smithsonian Institution's *Air and Space Magazine,* who encouraged me to go and published an article based on what I found there. At the time I went, no American writer had gone there to discuss the "aerial Dien Bien Phu," as the Vietnamese call it. The Defense Attaché at the U.S. Embassy in Hanoi, Lt. Colonel Frank Miller, USMC, took time from his busy schedule to talk to me and later to introduce me to Mr. Nguyen Ngoc Hung, Director of Studies at the Vietnamese Language Center in Hanoi. Mr. Hung is a veteran of the "American

War," speaks excellent English, and has become a regular speaker at American veterans' gatherings in the United States. He was very helpful to me in a variety of ways, especially in explaining the psyche of the North Vietnamese people under bombing attack. He was also kind enough to introduce me to Mr. Do Duy Truyen, deputy rector at Hanoi University, who was also very helpful. Ambassador Pete Petersen, U.S. ambassador to Hanoi and a former POW, was also generous with his time and shared his recollections of this period.

Gary Flannigan of the Joint Task Force-Full Accounting (JTF-FA) in Hanoi helped me immensely in my understanding the mentality of the Vietnamese, as well as in a variety of practical ways. The Defense POW/MIA Office in Washington, D.C. was also very helpful while I was preparing for my trip.

Dr. Istvan Toperczer, the author of several English-language books on the North Vietnamese Air Force, was kind enough to provide me with the accounts of the actions of MiG-21 pilots during the operation.

While in Hanoi I was able to talk to several missile crewmembers, but the conversations were not as useful as I had hoped. History is not the same in all cultures, and what is history in the United States is current events in Hanoi. The Vietnamese have their history of "the aerial Dien Bien Phu," and the battle still serves a purpose for the communist government that did not end just because the war was over. Because of this attitude, many Vietnamese are quite circumspect when discussing the details of military operations, even those that occurred almost thirty years ago. Adding to their concern is the fact that the SA-2 missile system remains a central part of the Vietnamese air defenses, and their former missile crews and other military officers are constrained from talking about it because of security concerns.

Offsetting this was the great amount of written material I found in Hanoi about the battle, including official histories and articles. There were significant differences in the approach the two took. The histories are accurate but are laced with propaganda and revolutionary clichés that make them very heavy going. The articles, on the other hand, generally featured personal accounts from missile crews as they struggled to shoot down the B-52s, and were generally quite lively and good. Interestingly, there was an outburst of articles in late 1987 and early 1988, on the fifteenth anniversary of the bombing. This was apparently because the government felt that the enthusiasm of the young conscripts for military service was falling and saw the need to reintroduce the new draftees to their military history of their country.

All the published Vietnamese accounts of the battle are in one sense "official" accounts because they are approved by the government, and some readers might be concerned that these Vietnamese histories are falsified propaganda. The author approached all Vietnamese writings with caution (as he did with all official U.S. information) and found that it was possible—indeed, quite easy—to separate fact from propaganda and, most importantly, to detect references to mistakes that were made by everyone from the General Staff to the missile crews themselves. The large number of articles and histories and the fact that many of them were written some time after the operation (the propaganda content diminished noticeably over the years) made it possible to cross-reference events for accuracy. Overall the official histories, supplemented by the personal accounts of the participants, present a relatively complete picture of the battle.

I was pleased to find that the North Vietnamese credits for the B-52 kills are meticulous and quite accurate, especially concerning the number of B-52s shot down "on the spot" and which units shot them down. There was apparently a great deal of effort spent making certain that SAM missile battalions that actually got the kills were given credit, because there was so much honor associated with shooting down a B-52 "on the spot."

All the Vietnamese material was in Vietnamese but some of the material had already been translated into English. For the articles that I needed translated I was lucky enough to find Ms. Nguyen Van Phuong of the University of New Orleans. Ms. Nguyen lived in Vietnam until 1995 and was familiar with many of the nuances of post-unification Vietnamese culture, and was especially helpful with meaning as well as the literal translation. Through Ms. Judith Henchy, the head of Southeast Asia Section, University of Washington Libraries, I was able to locate a translator for the North Vietnamese official histories, Mr. Stephen Collins of Melbourne,

Australia. Without the help of Mr. Collins and Ms. Nguyen, this book would not have been possible in its present form.

For the interested scholar there will be considerable frustration with some of the North Vietnamese material, especially with the *Historical Notes of the Hanoi Air Defense, December 1972.* The text was partially translated by Mr. Collins and edited by the author, but there is no English copy available at this time. Additionally, several of the North Vietnamese articles were taken from a collection published in one tabloid-sized paper titled "The Aerial Dien Bien Phu." These articles were without attribution or date, though most (if not all) were probably published in *Nhan Dan,* the official North Vietnamese newspaper. Within the next year the full text of the *Historical Notes of the Hanoi Air Defense, December 1972* will be published along with a translation of all the articles in a book which is tentatively titled *The Christmas Bombing: The View From Hanoi.*

IT IS IMPOSSIBLE TO WRITE about Linebacker II without some knowledge of the technology involved. I am grateful to Jerry Sowell, Eglin AFB, Florida, for explaining the workings of the SA-2 system, then reading the North Vietnamese documents and explaining to me how they were using the system. I am also very grateful to two former SA-2 battalion commanders, Bodo Siefert and Anton Zilinsky, for patiently taking me through the full scope of the SA-2 system, from assembling the missiles to the color of the buttons on the panels. The extensive information these three provided will be included with the full translations of the North Vietnamese documents in the upcoming *Christmas Bombing.*

Understanding the B-52's bombing and electronic warfare systems was also necessary, and for the information on the B-52 I am grateful to Bill Beavers and Bill Mayall for their descriptions of offset bombing, and to "Scotty" Burns for a description of the B-52D tail gunner's station, especially the cumbersome but vital task of jettisoning the turret for bail out. For the description of the B-52's electronic warfare systems, how they converted into the "beeps and squeaks" on the electronic warfare officers' scopes, and then for describing how the EWs worked with them, former EWs Frank Nicito and Ted Hughes were invaluable.

I should note that all of these people answered all my questions with more patience and in more detail than I had any right to expect, and any mistakes in the descriptions of these systems are mine and mine alone.

In the end the book is the sum of the stories of the participants, and I hope that those who participated and read this book will find it a satisfactory answer to the question, "What really happened?"

—Marshall Michel
New Orleans, Louisiana, 2001

Partial Bibliography

U.S. Military Official Documents

Analysis of Downed Aircraft. SAC DOXI. 22 March 1973 (with handwritten notes).

Area Bombing: A Discussion of Concepts. Operations Analysis Report. HQ SAC. August 1968.

Chaff Effectiveness in Support of Linebacker II Operations. Briefing for the SAC Director of Operations. Undated (probably mid-1973).

Corona Harvest Reports:

USAF Air Operations in Southeast Asia, 1 July 1972–15 August 1973. Vols. 1, 2, 5.

Air Force Operations over North Vietnam, PACAF, undated (approx. September 1972).

USAF Operations against North Vietnam, 1 July 1971–30 June 1972. HQ PACAF in cooperation with SAC, undated (probably late 1972).

Dell, Albert H. *Navy, Marine Corps, and Air Force Fixed Wing In-Flight Combat Losses to MiG Aircraft in Southeast Asia from 1965 through 1972.*

Eggers, General, Deputy Director for Operations (Strategic and General Operations), J-3, Joint Chiefs of Staff. *Employment of Missiles and Guided Weapons in Southeast Asia.* Briefing, undated (probably late 1972).

Gilster, Herman L., and Captain Robert E. M. Frady. *Linebacker II USAF Bombing Survey.* PACAF, 1973.

Greenwood, John T. *Chronology of SAC Participation in Linebacker II.* Offutt AFB, 1973.

History of Eighth Air Force, 1 July 1972–30 June 1973. Vol. 1. 23 August 1974.

History of Eighth Air Force, 1 July 1972–30 June 1973. Vol. 2.

Annex to the History of Eighth Air Force, 1 July 1972–30 June 1973. Ch. 5, "Linebacker II."

History of the 43rd Strategic Wing, July 1972–31 December 1972.

History of the 307th Strategic Wing, October–December 1972. Vol. 1. U-Tapao, Thailand.

History of Seventh Air Force, Summer–December 1972. Vol. 4.

History of Seventh Air Force, July 1972–19 March 1973. Vol. 1.

History of the 388th Tactical Fighter Wing, Korat RTAFB, October–December 1972. Vol. 1.

History of the 8th Tactical Fighter Wing, Ubon RTAFB, October–December 1972. Vol. 1.

History of the 544th Aerospace Reconnaissance Technical Wing, January–March 1973.

History of SAC Reconnaissance Operations, FY 1973. Historical Study No. 127. Prepared by the History Division, Strategic Air Command.

History of the Joint Chiefs of Staff. Office of the Joint Chiefs of Staff, Washington, D.C.: December 1972.

Hopkins, Charles K. *SAC Bomber Operations in the Southeast Asia War.* 5 vols. Strategic Air Command, Offutt AFB, 1983.

Linebacker Study. 20 January 1973. Military Assistance Command, Vietnam (MACV). Uncoordinated draft.

Linebacker II Briefing, 18–29 December 1972. Presented to General Momeyer, Commander of Tactical Air Command. Undated (probably early 1973).

Linebacker II Operational Reports. J35 Memo 0083-73. 2 July 1973.

Linebacker II Tactical Aircraft Attrition. Center for Naval Analysis memorandum. 15 February 1973.

Linebacker II USAF Bombing Survey. April 1973.

Navy ECM Support of B-52 Strikes during Linebacker II Operations. Memorandum prepared by D. E. Muir, Scientific Analyst for Op-50, for the Director of Aviation Plans and Requirements, January 1973.

Operations Analysis: Linebacker II, Air Operations Study. Briefing presented to CINCPACAF. 18 January 1973.

Peterson, Maxie J., Captain, USAF. *Linebacker II Air Operations Summary (18–29 December 1972).* Operations Analysis Office, Headquarters PACAF, March 1973.

Preliminary Study of Linebacker. Center for Naval Analysis Working Paper.

Project CHECO Southeast Asia Reports:

> Johnson, Calvin R. *Linebacker Operations, September–December 1972.* 31 December 1978.

> Picinich, A. A., *et al. The F-111 in Southeast Asia, September 1972–January 1973.* 21 February 1974.

> Porter, Melvin F. *Linebacker: Overview of the First 120 Days.* 1973.

> ———. *Proud Deep Alpha.* 1972.

> Pralle, James B. *Arc Light, June 1967–December 1968.*

> *Tactics of Electronic Warfare, July 1974.*

Project Red Baron III. Vol. 2, *Events Reconstructions,* part 2, *Events 59–127, 4 July 1972–12 January 1973.* USAF Tactical Weapons Center, Nellis AFB, June 1974.

SAC Operations in Linebacker II: Tactics and Analysis.

Tactical Air Command. *SEA Tactics Review Brochure.* Vol. 1. January 1973.

Tactical Air Command. *SEA Tactics Review Brochure.* Vol. 2. April 1973.

USAF Air Operations in Southeast Asia, 1 July 1972–15 August 1973. Vols. 1, 5. Headquarters PACAF, undated.

USAF Air Operations in Southeast Asia, Linebacker II Operations, 18–29 December 1972.

Miscellaneous Documents

Barker, Patrick K., Captain, USAF. *The SA-2 and Wild Weasel: The Nature of Technological Change in Military Systems.* Master's Thesis, Lehigh University, 1994.

Bombing of North Vietnam. Hearings of the Subcommittee on Appropriations, House of Representative, Tuesday, 9 January 1973.

Operation Desert Storm: Limits on the Role and Performance of B-52 Bombers in Conventional Conflicts. GAO Report, May 1993.

Scott, Maj. Roland A., B-52 crewmember. *Linebacker II Narrative.* 21 October 1977.

U.S. Military Messages

Arc Light Compression Tactics. Message sent from Gen. Sullivan to Gen. Johnson, 22/0806Z. December 1972.

Daily Wrap Up. Gen. Vogt (CO 7th AF) to Gen. Ryan, Gen. Meyer and Gen. Clay, 211045Z. December 1972.

Linebacker Missions, 18, 19 and 20 December 1972 (DTG280405Z). Seventh Air Force to PACAF. 28 December 1972.

Meyer to Vogt, 210220Z 72.

Vogt to Meyer, 210540Z 72.

Letters

Allen, Gen. James, USAF Chief of Staff, to B/Gen. James McCarthy. 27 December 1977.

Cordes, B/Gen. Harry, to B/Gen. James McCarthy. Undated.

Crosby, Maj. Greg, Eighth Air Force Navigation Division Planner, to B/Gen. James McCarthy. 18 November 1977.

Grosshuesch, L. V., Director, Operations Plans, DCS/Operations, PACAF. *Summary and Analysis of Linebacker I.* 9 January 1973.

———. *Summary and Analysis of Linebacker II.* 1 February 1973.

Martin, Glenn W. (retired USAF general officer and former member of the SAC Staff) to B/Gen. James McCathy. 15 August 1977.

McCarthy, B/Gen., to Lt. Gen. John Flynn, USAF Inspector General and former POW in Hanoi. 19 July 1977.

Preciado, Col., DCS/Operations PACAF. *Linebacker II, "Lessons Learned."* 2 February 1973.

Air University Reports

Clement, Robert A., Major, USAF. "A Fourth of July in December: A B-52 Navigator's Perspective of Linebacker II." Unpublished research paper. Air Command and Staff College, Maxwell AFB, Alabama, March 1984.

Geloneck, Terry M. "At the Hands of the Enemy: A Bomber Pilot's View." Research paper. Air University, Maxwell AFB, Alabama, May 1981.

Leonard, Raymond W. "Learning from History: Linebacker II and Air Force Doctrine."

Shackelford, Billy, *et al.* "Eleven Days in December: Linebacker II." Unpublished monograph. Air University, June 1977.

Articles and Papers

Allison, George B. "The Bombers Go to Bullseye." *Aerospace Historian,* December 1982, pp. 227–38.

Arkin, William. "Frustration with Expectations of a Perfect War: Analysis of the Persian Gulf Bombing of Baghdad, the Balkans War and the Air Force." *Washington Post,* 26 April 1999.

Boyne, Walter J. "Linebacker II: A Look Back." *Air Force Magazine,* November 1997, pp. 50–57.

Chief of Naval Analysis Working Paper. "Preliminary Survey of Linebacker Operations." 4 February 1973.

Clodfelter, Mark. "Nixon and the Air Weapon." Paper presented at the seminar *An American Dilemma: Vietnam 1964–1973.* Chicago: Imprint Publications, 1993.

Drenkowski, Dana. "Tragedy of Linebacker II." *Armed Forces Journal,* July 1977.

———. "Operation Linebacker II—Part 1." *Soldier of Fortune,* vol. 2, no. 3 (September 1977), pp. 32–37, 60–61.

———. "Operation Linebacker II—Part 2." *Soldier of Fortune,* vol. 2, no. 4 (November 1977), pp. 48–59.

Hanson, Victor D. "The Right Man." *Journal of Military History,* vol. 58 (April 1994), pp. 267–303.

Holt, Joan. "Richard Nixon, Vietnam, and the American Home Front." Paper presented at the seminar *An American Dilemma: Vietnam 1964–1973.* Chicago: Imprint Publications, 1993.

Hopkins, Charles K.. "Linebacker II: A Firsthand View." *Aerospace Historian,* September 1976.

Jameson, Theodore R. "General Curtis LeMay, the Strategic Air Command, and the Korean War, 1950–1953." *American Aviation Historical Journal,* vol. 41, no. 3 (Fall 1966), pp. 190–98.

Lewis, Ray. "Modeling the Soviet V-750VK Dvina Air Defense Missile," MARS Pathfinder, NARAM-37, vol. 10, no. 2, pp. 10–13.

"The Paris Agreement on Vietnam: Twenty-Five Years Later." Conference transcript. Washington, D.C.: The Nixon Center, April 1998.

Reynolds, Jon A., Lt. Col. USAF. "Linebacker II: The POW Perspective." *Air Force Magazine,* September 1979, pp. 93–94.

"Soviet Comments on SA-2 V. B-52s." *Military Parade JSC,* 1998.

Stephens, Rick. "The 'Earth Pig': The Complete Guide to the General Dynamics F-111." *World Air Power Journal,* vol. 14 (Summer/Fall 1993).

Teixeira, Leonard D. G., Lt. Col. USAF. "Linebacker II: A Strategic and Tactical Case Study." Air War College paper. Maxwell AFB, Alabama, April 1990.

"Tragedy of Linebacker II: The USAF Response." *Armed Forces Journal,* August 1977, pp. 24–25.

Wolff, Robert E., Capt., USAF. "Linebacker II." *Air Force Magazine,* September 1979, pp. 88–91.

New York Times Articles

"Kissinger Says Talks Have Not Reached an Agreement . . ." 17 December 1972, p. 1.

"White House Says Raids Will Go On . . ." 19 December 1972, p. 1.

"Pentagon Says Bombings Wreck Military Targets . . ." 21 December 1972. p. 1. (Includes pictures of crewmembers.)

"3 B-52s Lost . . ." 20 December 1972, p. 1.

"4 More B-52s Lost in the Hanoi Area . . ." 22 December 1972, p. 1.

"Communists Quit Session in Paris." 22 December 1972, p. 1.

"Hospital Deaths ..." 24 December 1972, p. 1.

"B-52 Vindicates Its Role, Air Force Aides Assert." 24 December 1972, p. 6.

"Hanoi Reported Scarred, but Key Services Continue." 25 December 1972, p. 6.

"U.S. Lists Targets of Heavy Attacks ..." 28 December 1972, p. 1.

"2 More B-52s Downed, Bringing Total to 14." 29 December 1972, p. 1.

"The War Is Suddenly Grim for the B-52 Fliers Based on Guam." 30 December 1972, p. 1.

"Congress Opens: Democrats Plan Anti-War Action." 5 January 1973, p. 1.

"Hanoi Negotiator Arrives in Paris, Takes Rigid Stand." 7 January 1973, p. 1.

"Hanoi under the Bombing: Sirens, Shelters, Rubble and Death." 7 January 1973, p. 6.

"Kissinger Arrives in Paris to Renew Cease Fire Talks." 8 January 1973, p. 1.

"Grumbling and Rumbling over an Unraveling War." 30 April 2000, p. 14.

Books and Monographs

Anderton, David A. *Strategic Air Command: Two-thirds of the Triad.* New York: Scribner, 1971.

Baez, Joan. *And a Voice to Sing With: A Memoir.* New York: Summit Books, 1987.

Boyne, Walter. *Boeing B-52, A Documentary History.* Washington, D.C.: Smithsonian Institute Press, 1981.

Broughton, Jack. *Thud Ridge.* Philadelphia: Lippincott, 1969.

———. *Going Downtown: The War against Hanoi and Washington.* New York: Orion Books, 1988.

Castle, Timothy. *One Day Too Long.* New York: Columbia University Press, 1999.

Clodfelter, Mark. *The Limits of Air Power.* New York: Free Press, 1989.

Dolione, John A., *et al. Air Power and the 1972 Spring Invasion.* USAF Southeast Monograph Series, vol. 2.

Dorr, Robert and Lindsay Peacock. *B-52 Stratofortress: Boeing's Cold Warrior.* London: Osprey Aerospace, 1995.

Drendel, Lou. *B-52 Stratofortress in Action.* Squadron/Signal Publications, no. 23, 1975.

Eschmann, Karl J. *Linebacker: The Untold Story of the Air Raids over North Vietnam.* New York: Ivy Books (Ballantine), 1989.

Ethell, Jeff, and Joe Christy. *B-52 Stratofortress.* Great Britain: Charles Scribner and Son, 1981.

Ethics in the Air Force: 1988. Written by members of the Air War College Class of 1988. Washington, D.C.: U.S. Government Printing Office.

Futrell, R. Frank, *et al. Aces and Aerial Victories: The United States Air Force in Southeast Asia, 1965–1973.* The Albert F. Simpson Historical Research Center, Air University, and the Office of Air Force History, 1976.

Gilster, Herman L. *The Air War in Southeast Asia: Case Studies of Selected Campaigns.* Maxwell AFB: Air University Press, 1993.

Gunston, Bill. *Modern Fighter Aircraft: The F-111.* New York: Arco Publishing, 1983.

Haig, Alexander M., Jr., with Charles McCarthy. *"Inner Circles": How America Changed the World, a Memoir.* New York: Warner Books, 1992.

Halberstam, David. *The Best and the Brightest.* New York: Random House, 1972.

Haldeman, H. R. *The Haldeman Diaries.* New York: Putnams, 1994.

Hall, R. Cargill. *Case Studies in Strategic Bombardment.* Washington, D.C.: Air Force History and Museums Program, 1998.

Hartsook, E. H. *Air Power Helps Stop the Invasion and End the War, 1972.* Washington, D.C.: Office of Air Force History.

Herz, Martin F., and Leslie Rider. *The Prestige Press and the Christmas Bombing, 1972.* Washington, D.C.: Ethics and Public Policy Center, 1980.

Johnson, Gerald, with John and Charlotte McClure. *Called to Command: A World War II Figher Ace's Adventurous Journey.* Paducah, Kentucky, 1996.

Kissinger, Henry. *White House Years.* Boston: Little and Brown, 1979.

LeMay, Curtis, with Mackinlay Kantor. *Mission with LeMay.* Garden City, New York: Doubleday, 1965.

Maxson, William B., former Commander, 340CAM, U-Tapao. *Recollections of Linebacker II.* Unpublished memoir.

McCarthy, James R. and Robert E. Rayfield. *B-52s over Hanoi.* Irvine: Pepperdine University Press, 1994.

——, and George Allison. *Linebacker II: A View from the Rock.* USAF Southeast Monograph Series, vol. 6.

Michel, Marshall L. *Clashes: Air Combat over North Vietnam, 1965–1972.* Annapolis: Naval Institute Press, 1977.

Momeyer, William W., Gen. USAF (retired). *Air Power in Three Wars (WWII, Korea, Vietnam).* Washington, D.C.: U.S. Government Printing Office, 1978.

Nalty, Bernard C. *Air Power and the Fight for Khe Sanh.* Washington, D.C., 1973.

——. *Tactics and Techniques of Electronic Warfare: Electronic Countermeasures in the Air War against North Vietnam, 1965–1973.* Washington, D.C., 1973.

Nixon, Richard M. *In the Arena: A Memoir of Victory, Defeat, and Renewal.* New York: Simon & Schuster, 1990.

——. *RN: The Memoirs of Richard Nixon.* New York: Simon & Schuster, 1990.

Pape, Robert A. *Bombing to Win: Air Power and Coercion in War.* Ithaca, New York: Cornell University Press, 1996.

Regan, Geoffrey. *Great Military Disasters: A Historical Study of Military Campaigns.* New York: Barnes & Noble Books, 1987.

Rochester, Stuart I., and Fredrick Kiley. *Honor Bound: The History of American Prisoners of War in Southeast Asia, 1961–1973.* Annapolis: Naval Institute Press, 1999.

Schlight, John. *A War Too Long: The USAF in Southeast Asia, 1961–1975.* Washington, D.C.: Air Force History and Museums Program, 1996.

Strategic Air Warfare: An Interview with Generals Curtis LeMay, Leon W. Johnson, David Burchinal, and Jack J. Catton. Washington, D.C.: Office of Air Force History, 1988.

Strober, G. S., and D. H. *Nixon: An Oral History of His Presidency.* New York: Harper Collins, 1994.

Thompson, Wayne. *Rebound: The Air War over North Vietnam, 1966–1973.* Air Force History and Museums Program, July 1997 draft.

———. *To Hanoi and Back: The U.S. Air Force and North Vietnam, 1966–1973.* Washington, D.C.: Smithsonian Institute Press, 2000.

Thornborough, Anthony, and Peter Davies. *F-111: Success in Action.* London: Arms and Armour Press Ltd., 1989.

Tilford, Earl. *SETUP: What the Air Force Did in Vietnam and Why.* Maxwell AFB: Air University Press, 1991.

Toperczer, Istvan. *Air War over North Vietnam: The Vietnamese Peoples Air Force, 1949–1977.* Carrollton, Texas: Squadron/Signal Publications, 1998.

Vassiliev, Alexei. *Missiles over the Lotus Blossoms.* Unpublished. (Author is Director of the Institute of African and Arab Studies, Russian Academy Sciences, Moscow).

Warden, John A., III. *The Air Campaign.* Washington, D.C.: 1988.

Warrell, Kenneth P. *Archie, Flak and SAM: A Short Operational History of Ground Based Air Defense.* Maxwell AFB: Air University Press, 1988.

Wells, Mark K. *Courage and Air Warfare: The Allied Aircrew Experience in the Second World War.* Portland, Oregon: Frank Cass, 1995.

Worden, Mike. *The Rise of the Fighter Generals: The Problem of Air Force Leadership, 1945–1982.* Maxwell AFB: Air University Press, 1998.

Zaloga, Steve. *Soviet Air Defense Missiles: Design, Development, Tactics.* London: Jane's, 1988.

Zumwalt, Elmo. *On Watch: A Memoir.* New York: Quadrangle, 1976.

End of Tour Reports/Oral Histories

Johnson, Gerald W. Interview. Andersen AFB, Guam, 3 April 1973.

McCarthy, Joseph R. Interview. USAF Oral History Program. June 1973.

Ryan, John, Chief of Staff, USAF. USAF Oral History Program. 20 May 1972.

Slay, Alton, Director of Operations, Seventh Air Force, Saigon. End of Tour Report 1972. August 1972.

Smith, Col. Scott G., Commander, 432nd Tactical Reconnaissance Wing, Udorn RTAFB, Thailand. End of Tour Report covering April 1972–18 March 1973. 31 May 1973.

Vogt, John W. USAF Oral History Program. August 1978.

Zuckert, Eugene M. USAF Oral History Program. 28 September 1977.

Air Force Official Biographies

Brown, Bill V.

Cordes, Harry N.

Davis, Donald M.

Johnson, Gerald W.

LeMay, Curtis

Martin, Glenn W.

McCarthy, James R.

Meyer, John C.

Sianis, Pete C.

Sullivan, Glenn R.

Vogt, John W.

Author Interviews

Allison, George

Brown, Bill V.

Brown, Steve

Clodfelter, Mark

Cobb, J. B.

Cordes, Harry

Diefenbach, Brent

Haig, Alexander

Maxson, Bill

Rivolo, Dr. A. Rex

Schemmer, Benjamin

Schilling, David

Smith, Bruce

Sowell Jerry, 53rd Wing, Eglin AFB, Florida

Steffen, Bob

Sullivan, Nadine (Mrs. Glenn R.)

E-mail Messages

B-52 CREWMEMBERS

Anich, Mark D.	Hymel, Bob
Beavers, Bill	Kovich, Steve
Brown, Charles A.	Mayall, Bill
Brown, Steve	Mize, John
Buckley, Bill	Mizner, Craig
Burns, Peter D. "Scotty"	Moore, Dwight
Camerota, Peter	Nocito, Ken
Carlton, Jim	Russell, Glenn
Certain, Robert	Scheideman, Jim "Bones"
Cook, Jim	Sherman, John S. "Tanks"
Craig, Don	Shivley, Ron
Daniel, Terry A. "Ted"	Short, Jim
Dunn, Fred	Smith, Bruce
Emerson, Paul	Smith, R. J.
Farmer, Jim	Steffen, Bob
Giroux, Pete	Whipple, George N. "Nick"
Hope, Kenneth	Wildeboor, Ed
Hortuchi, Gerald T.	Wilson, Hal "Red"
Hudson, Bob	Woody, Bruce
Hughes, Harold H. "Bud"	Yuill, John

OTHER AIRCREW

Barry, Dan, F-105G	Hipps, Bob, F-4
Boyd, Al, F-105G	Morrison, John, A-7
Connelly, Bob (B. C.), F-4	Rasimus, Ed, F-4E
Gotner, Norb, F-4 (POW)	Rivolo, Rex, F-4E
Henry, Don, F-105G	Rock, Ed, F-105G

OTHERS

Borden, Andy	Drenkowski, Dana
Clodfelter, Mark	Geloneck, Ms. Jane

Hruby, Ms. Pat	Sheldon, Joe
McDonald, Jack	Sullivan, Glenn R., Jr.
Orgon, E. A.	Thompson, Wayne
Ochs, Ms. Nancy	Walters, Ms. Charleen
Seifert, Bodo	Zlinsky, Anton

SURVEYS RETURNED TO MAJOR JOHN ZENTNER (MADE AVAILABLE TO THE AUTHOR WITH THE PERMISSION OF THE PARTICIPANTS)

Beavers, Bill	McCarthy, James R.
Hope, Kenneth	Moore, Dwight
Hortuchi, Gerald T.	Sherman, John S. "Tank"
Klingbeil, Roger A.	Stocker, William F.
Kovich, Steve	Wildeboor, Ed

North Vietnamese Histories, Books and Articles

"The Aerial Dien Bien Phu." Memoirs of Major General Tran Nhan, former deputy commander of Hanoi air defenses. *Nhan Dan* (official Vietnamese government newspaper), 14–19 December 1987, FBIS EAS 88–006:

"Report on Intelligence Gathered," 14 December.

"Radar Companies Actions Recounted," 15 December.

"Meeting Again Those Who Vanquished 'the Flying Fortresses,' " 15 December.

"Fate of U.S. Pilots Reported," 16 December.

"General Tran Nhan Remembers U.S. Air Raids," Part I, 17 December.

"General Tran Nhan Remembers U.S. Air Raids," Part II, 18 December.

"Final Installment," 19 December.

"B-52 Air Blitz Recalled." Hanoi Radio in English, 21 December 1987.

Dien Bien Phu Tren Khong (Aerial Dien Bien Phu) magazine of personal accounts that contains the following:

"If You Talk about Luck." Interview of Than Nguyen, CO of the 59th Battalion, December 1982.

"A Reliable Person"

"The Last Missile"

"The Battle after Christmas Night"

"Keeping the Promise" (story of the 72nd Missile Battalion)

"General Recalls December 1972 Air War over Hanoi." Hanoi Radio, 26 December 1985.

"Hanoi Air Defense Develops Its Old Fighting Traditions." *Tranh Vien,* Hanoi Radio Domestic Service, 24 December.

"Lessons from the 1972 Air War." FBIS-SEA-88-009, 24 February 1988.

"Rally Marks Victory over U.S. Air Raids." Hanoi Radio in English, 18 December 1987.

"Reviewing a Highlight in the Historic Struggle." *Tap Chi Quan Doi Nhan Dan,* December 1982, pp. 46–51.

"Taking Aim at the B-52s." General Hoang Van Khanh, *Nhan Dan* (official Vietnamese government newspaper), 6–10 December 1982. Translated by Linh Cuu My, *Vietnam Magazine,* April 1996, pp. 26–33.

"Tranh Vinh Writes Article on 1972 Air War." Hanoi Domestic Service, 23 December 1987

"The Twelve-Day Air Defense Campaign in December 1972 (18–29 December 1972)." *Tap Chi Quan Doi Nhan Dan* magazine, pp. 24–31, 41.

"VAN on UB B-52s Downed in 1972 Air Raids." Hanoi Radio in English, 22 December 1987.

Books and Monographs

Ban Roi Tai Cho May Bay B.52 (B-52s Shot Down on the Spot). PAVN Senior Officer Interviews.

Lich Su Su Doan Phong Khong Hanoi (Su Doan 361) (History of Hanoi Air Defense Division, 361st Division).

Chien Thang B.52 (Victory over the B-52s).

Lich Su Nghe Thuat Chien Dich Phong Khong (12–1972) (Historical Notes of the Hanoi Air Defense, December 1972).

Thuyet Minh Phim Ba Man Hinh, English Script for the B-52 Museum, Hanoi.

Index